THE BUSHMEN OF SOUTHERN AFRICA

Slaughter of the innocent

Other books by Sandy Gall

Gold Scoop
Chasing the Dragon
Don't Worry About the Money Now
Behind Russian Lines
Afghanistan: Agony of a Nation
Salang
George Adamson: Lord of the Lions
News From the Front

THE BUSHMEN OF SOUTHERN AFRICA

Slaughter of the Innocent

═══

SANDY GALL

Chatto & Windus
LONDON

Published by Chatto & Windus 2001

2 4 6 8 10 9 7 5 3 1

Copyright © Sandy Gall 2001

Sandy Gall has asserted his right under the
Copyright, Designs and Patents Act 1988 to be identified
as the author of this work

First published in Great Britain in 2001 by Chatto & Windus
Random House, 20 Vauxhall Bridge Road, London SW1V 2SA

Random House Australia (Pty) Limited
20 Alfred Street, Milsons Point, Sydney,
New South Wales 2061, Australia

Random House New Zealand Limited
18 Poland Road, Glenfield,
Auckland 10, New Zealand

Random House (Pty) Limited,
Endulini, 5A Jubilee Road, Parktown 2193, South Africa

The Random House Group Limited Reg. No. 954009
www.randomhouse.co.uk

A CIP catalogue record for this book
is available from the British Library

ISBN 0 701 169060

Papers used by Random House are natural,
recyclable products made from wood grown in sustainable forests;
the manufacturing processes conform to the environmental
regulations of the country of origin

Typeset by Deltatype Ltd, Birkenhead, Merseyside
Printed and bound in Great Britain by
Mackays of Chatham PLC

Contents

List of Illustrations

P. J. Schoeman, Chairman of the Commission for the Preservation of Bushmen (*'The Argus', Cape Town*)

Toma, leader of the Bushmen of Nyae Nyae and friend of the Marshall family (*Photo: Lorna Marshall. From 'The Harmless People' by Elizabeth Marshall Thomas*)

'Beautiful Ungka' (*Photo: Lorna Marshall. From 'The Harmless People'*)

Bushman mother and child, early 1950s (*Photo: Lorna Marshall. From 'The Harmless People'*)

Bushman soldier, during the Angolan war, 1980s (*State Archives, Windhoek*)

Second black and white section

Tom Hardbattle (*Photograph by Michaela Gall*)

Khwa, whose mother was a Nharo Bushman (*From 'Afrikaners of the Kalahari', Cambridge University Press. Photograph by Martin Russell*)

Khwa with her children (*By courtesy of Tom Hardbattle*)

Tom Hardbattle in 1954 (*By courtesy of Tom Hardbattle*)

John and young Tom Hardbattle as schoolboys (*By courtesy of Tom Hardbattle*)

John Hardbattle in the army (*By courtesy of Tom Hardbattle; main photograph by M. B. Leach*)

Woman sprawling on sand (*Photograph © David Stewart-Smith*)

Khomtsa Khomtsa, Nharo Bushman community leader from Botswana, London, July 1993 (*© Survival*)

The 'Magnificent Seven' – campaigners for the rights of Bushmen, 1992 (*By courtesy of Arthur Krasilnikoff*)

Bushman mounted on a horse (*Michaela Gall*)

Ketlhalefang in the Bushman village of Gope (*Michaela Gall*)

Second colour section

Tsodilo and its rock paintings (*all pictures Michaela Gall*)

Tourist attraction: Bushmen at Kagga Kamma (*Michaela Gall*)

Cait Andrews at the Welkom squatter camp (*Michaela Gall*)

Tom Hardbattle with his half sister, Christina (*Michaela Gall*)

Frederic Langman, Chief Designate of Omaheke North (*Michaela Gall*)

Roy Sesana, now chairman of First People (*© F. Watson/Survival*)

Roy's brother, Mathambo Sesana, headman of the village of Molapa (*© F. Watson/Survival*)

Representation of the death of Regopstaan (*Photographed by Michaela Gall*)

Dawid Kruiper talking to Cait Andrews (*Michaela Gall*)

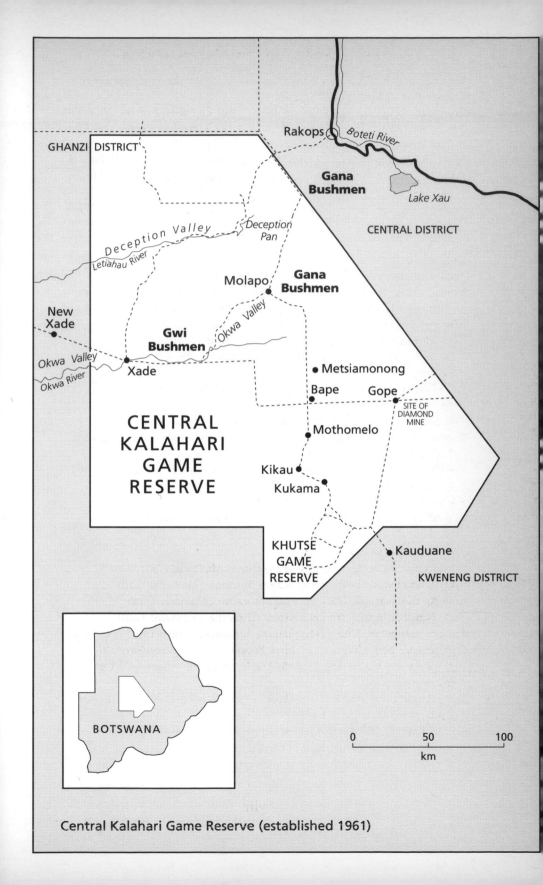

Central Kalahari Game Reserve (established 1961)

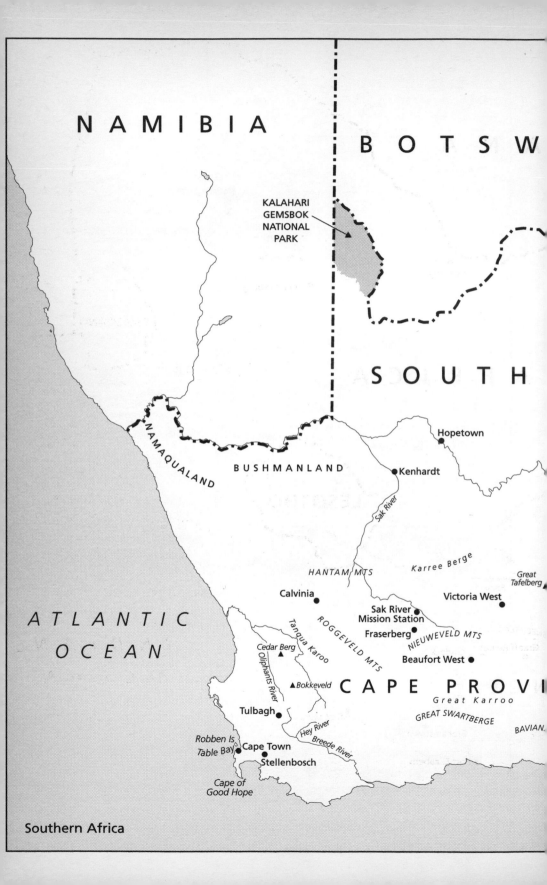

NAMIBIA

BOTSW

KALAHARI
GEMSBOK
NATIONAL
PARK

SOUTH

Hopetown

Kenhardt

NAMAQUALAND

BUSHMANLAND

Sak River

Karree Berge

*Great
Tafelberg*

HANTAM MTS

Calvinia

Sak River
Mission Station

Victoria West

ATLANTIC

OCEAN

ROGGEVELD MTS

Fraserberg

NIEUWEVELD MTS

Tangua Karoo

Beaufort West

Cedar Berg

Oliphants River

▲Bokkeveld

CAPE PROVI

Great Karroo

GREAT SWARTBERGE

BAVIAN.

Tulbagh

Hey River

Breede River

Robben Is
Table Bay
Cape Town

Stellenbosch

*Cape of
Good Hope*

Southern Africa

ANA

AFRICA

Mafeking

Pretoria

Johannesburg

SWAZILAND

St Lucia Bay

Orange River

Seekoei

LESOTHO

Durban

Plettenberg's
Beacon

NEEUBERG

Graaff Reinet

Cradock

NCE

Great Fish River

LOOF MTS

Grahamstown

East London

INDIAN

OCEAN

Port Elizabeth

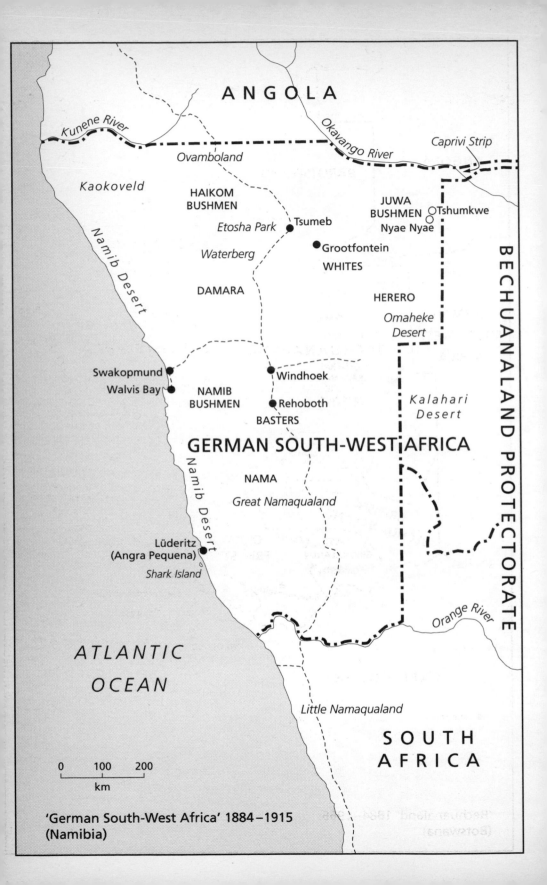

ANGOLA

Kunene River

Okavango River

Caprivi Strip

Ovamboland

Kaokoveld

HAIKOM
BUSHMEN

JUWA
BUSHMEN

○Tshumkwe

Etosha Park

Nyae Nyae

●Tsumeb

Namib Desert

●Grootfontein

WHITES

Waterberg

DAMARA

HERERO

*Omaheke
Desert*

BECHUANALAND PROTECTORATE

Swakopmund●

●Windhoek

*Kalahari
Desert*

Walvis Bay●

NAMIB
BUSHMEN

●Rehoboth

BASTERS

GERMAN SOUTH-WEST AFRICA

Namib Desert

NAMA

Great Namaqualand

Lüderitz●
(Angra Pequena)

Shark Island

Orange River

ATLANTIC

OCEAN

Little Namaqualand

SOUTH
AFRICA

0   100   200

km

'German South-West Africa' 1884–1915
(Namibia)

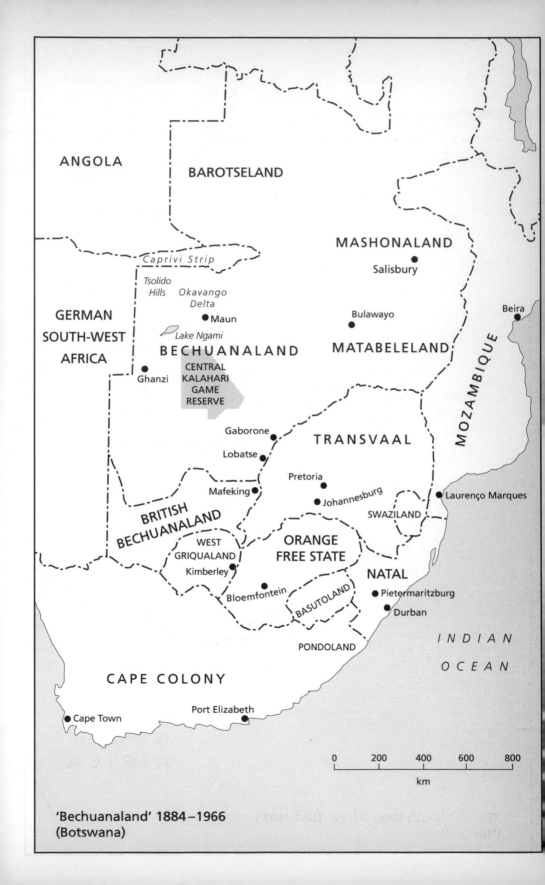

ANGOLA

BAROTSELAND

Caprivi Strip

GERMAN
SOUTH-WEST
AFRICA

*Tsolido
Hills*

*Okavango
Delta*

●Maun

Lake Ngami

BECHUANALAND

●Ghanzi

CENTRAL
KALAHARI
GAME
RESERVE

MASHONALAND

Salisbury●

Bulawayo●

MATABELELAND

●Beira

MOZAMBIQUE

Gaborone●

TRANSVAAL

Lobatse●

Pretoria●

Mafeking●

●Johannesburg

●Laurenço Marques

SWAZILAND

BRITISH
BECHUANALAND

WEST
GRIQUALAND

ORANGE
FREE STATE

Kimberley●

NATAL

●Pietermaritzburg

Bloemfontein●

BASUTOLAND

●Durban

PONDOLAND

INDIAN

OCEAN

CAPE COLONY

●Cape Town

Port Elizabeth●

0   200   400   600   800

km

'Bechuanaland' 1884–1966
(Botswana)

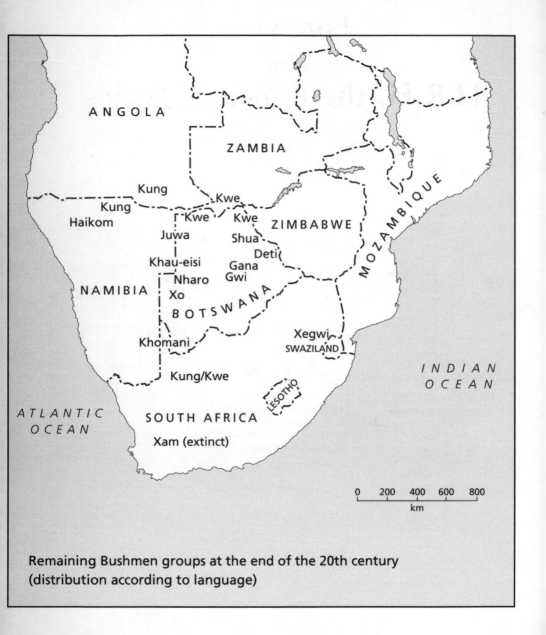

ANGOLA

ZAMBIA

Kung

Kung

Haikom

Kwe

Kwe

Kwe

ZIMBABWE

MOZAMBIQUE

Juwa

Shua

Deti

Khau-eisi

Gana

Nharo

Gwi

NAMIBIA

Xo

BOTSWANA

Khomani

Xegwi

SWAZILAND

INDIAN
OCEAN

Kung/Kwe

LESOTHO

ATLANTIC
OCEAN

SOUTH AFRICA

Xam (extinct)

| 0 | 200 | 400 | 600 | 800 |

km

Remaining Bushmen groups at the end of the 20th century
(distribution according to language)

Foreword
by
H.R.H. the Prince of Wales

It was Laurens van der Post's book, *The Lost World of the Kalahari*, published over forty years ago, that first alerted many of us to an extraordinary civilisation that had survived in its pristine state at the heart of Africa for thousands of years. The secret of the San people, the first people of the Kalahari – those we commonly know as Bushmen – was and still remains their complete immersion in the natural and spiritual rhythms of existence. This understanding of Mother Nature – something we in the developed world have almost entirely lost, as we are only now, to our cost, beginning to realise – lies at the very heart of the Bushman way of life. As Sir Laurens explained, the Bushman hunter 'knew the animal and vegetable life, the rocks and stones of Africa as they have never been known since . . .'. The Bushman is the essence of Africa.

I was fortunate enough to visit the Kalahari with Sir Laurens in 1987, to see and try to learn a little for myself of Bushman life and culture. What I discovered was the profound and intuitive ties that bind the San to their land; their awareness of the workings of the natural world and of the delicate balance between life, physical surroundings and inner spirituality that they had maintained for so long in the harshest of the environments; and the beauty and grandeur of the apparent wilderness in which they survived. I came away with a sense of wonder that the Bushmen, a so-called 'primitive' people, had a wiser understanding at a deeper, mysterious level of how Nature worked, and how to cope with it, than all the batteries of scientists and experts mobilised by more 'modern' civilisations. And although it is easy to sound over-romantic about these things, I was moved by the instincts and techniques for survival of the Bushman in their unforgiving climate that are perhaps rivalled only by the Aboriginal peoples of Australia.

Yet this ancient and instinctive civilisation is under threat as it has never been before. Sandy Gall's history of the treatment of the Bushmen by colonial and indigenous governments alike is, in itself, an appalling tale of greed, cruelty, miscomprehension and mistake. Yet the implications of his argument are even more disturbing – that this gentle civilisation, so in tune with its past, its inner spirituality, and its natural surroundings, may be on the verge of extinction. There is no single cause for this – no single individual or government responsible in this tragic tale – except perhaps the eternal lesson that we meddle with the natural world at our peril. (Who knows, for instance, what ancient, traditional knowledge we may need to turn back to in the future for our very survival in a world sorely damaged by our own carelessness and folly? Will we not then curse the day we let slip the great store of Bushman wisdom and abandoned such a people to their destruction?) What, however, is inescapable, is that the Bushman is an innocent victim of what, far too glibly, too many of us would call 'progress'.

Sandy Gall has performed a crucial service in reminding us that turning a blind eye is no longer an option if the Bushmen are to survive. There are heroes as well as villains in this tale, none more heroic than John Hardbattle, whom I was fortunate enough to meet before his tragic early death. It is now up to all of us to ensure that the legacy of such defenders of this remarkable civilisation does not simply vanish with a shrug of the shoulders and further sacrifices on the shrine of the gods of modernity. We all lose if the Bushman disappears.

Author's Note

Africa has drawn me since I first went to Kenya as Reuters' East Africa correspondent in 1955. With Mau Mau little more than an unpleasant memory, I found Nairobi an exciting, sun-drenched, rather beautiful provincial town, its colonial mansions surrounded by emerald lawns and embowered in dazzling red and purple bougainvillaea. A year later Suez cut short this dalliance, but I was back again in 1960, this time in Johannesburg. From there, I travelled to (as they then were) Mozambique and Angola, Northern and Southern Rhodesia, Nyasaland, and the newly independent ex-Belgian Congo, already plunged in anarchy. In 1964, having recently joined ITN, I went back to the Congo and made a short film about the pygmies of the Ituri Forest – the first time I had encountered one of Africa's original, indigenous peoples. I was struck by their gaiety and intelligence and also by the fact that, although much smaller than their fellow Congolese, they were feared for their skill with bow and arrow, and their knowledge of poisons. Their similarity to those other hunter-gatherers, the Bushmen, is in many respects remarkable, but I did not think very much about it because I believed, like most other people, that the Bushmen were virtually extinct. It was not until many years later, in March 1998, when I visited the Central Kalahari Game Reserve in Botswana for the first time, that I realised how wrong I had been. I also discovered how attractive the Bushmen could be, both physically and in their innate cheerfulness.

My visit coincided with the local Ghanzi Council's eviction of several Bushman families from Molapo. It made a strong impression on me, and it was the spur for what followed. On that same journey I met Tom and Andrea Hardbattle, children of a Yorkshire father and half-Bushman mother, and whose late brother John had become a Bushman hero. John's story fascinated many people including two London film makers, Ilona Benjamin and David Hart, who introduced me to Claire Ritchie, a film maker-cum-anthropologist, who had spent several years with the Bushmen in Namibia. At the end of our first talk she asked me what kind of book I intended to write: mythology or reality? She meant: was this to be a romanticised picture of a hunter-gatherer society which no longer existed, or a factual, warts-and-all account of a desperately downtrodden people? The latter, I said immediately, although I did not realise how difficult it would be not to romanticise the Bushmen.

In January 1999, I flew to Windhoek, the capital of Namibia with my daughter Michaela, whom I persuaded to come with me as expedition photographer, artist and occasional cook, and Tom Hardbattle, who offered his services as guide and expert at driving in deep sand. There we had the good fortune to meet James Suzman, a young South African anthropologist who showered me with documents and advice, and Axel Thoma, the co-ordinator of WIMSA, an organisation which actively supports the Bushman cause all over southern Africa, who sent us to see a number of Bushman communities. Axel also did me the inestimable favour of helping me to find, at extremely short notice, Willem Abuse, the first Bushman I got to know. Willem was not only an excellent interpreter, but looked the part – small, slight, athletic with a smooth, oval face, high cheekbones, small flat nose and ears, and bronze skin, 'apricot-coloured' as Laurens van der Post would have said. Leaving Windhoek, we drove east to Gobabis and then north along the western edge of the Kalahari, meeting on the way two remarkable Bushmen, Frederic Langman, at Skoonheid, and Thadeus Chedau, in the Caprivi Strip, the long lizard's tongue of territory which survives as a reminder of the days of the colonial scramble for Africa. Crossing the border into Botswana, we headed south for Tsodilo, a mysterious group of sacred hills filled with Bushman rock art. From there, we pushed on to Ghanzi, staying at one of the Hardbattle farms where Tom recruited a Bushman guide, Karnels Morris. A few miles north of Ghanzi we visited the Dutch Reformed Church settlement at D'kar and, Willem having departed because as a Juwa speaker he would be out of his linguistic depth, engaged a second Bushman interpreter, another member of the large Morris clan also called Karnels. To avoid confusion, Tom christened them Number One and Number Two. From Ghanzi we drove east towards the Central Kalahari Game Reserve, our ultimate goal. There we visited all six Bushman villages, starting in Molapo, and continuing to Metsia-monong, Mothomelo, Gope, Kukama and Kikau. Since there were then few facilities in the Reserve we had to carry food for a week – we were able to get water – and enough fuel to drive nearly 600 miles through the Kalahari.

Sitting in the shade of a grass hut or tree, with the temperature well above 100 degrees fahrenheit, I interviewed a cross-section of the inhabitants of each village – male and female, young and old, innocent and wise. Virtually everyone I spoke to declared that despite pressure and even threats from government officials they were determined not to leave the Reserve. It was where they had been born, where their ancestors were buried, and where their hearts were. They all believed that the government was intent on pushing them out for one reason only: to make money out of the diamonds which lay under the Kalahari, and from the tourists who would be encouraged to flock there.

Farther south, in Gaborone, we stayed with Clare Flattery, a family friend of the Hardbattles, and more particularly of John, who by the time he died in 1996 had become internationally known as a campaigner for Bushman rights. We also met a number of well-informed individuals, some in positions so delicate they did not wish to be named. Still heading south we left Botswana, and drove the length of South Africa to Cape Town, where we stayed with Peter Hawthorne, bureau chief for *Time* magazine, and his delightful Scots wife, Jessie. We also had the good fortune to meet Pippa Skotnes, an artist responsible for staging the spectacular Bushman exhibition, *Miscast*, the cata-logue of which has proved to be an Aladdin's Cave. It was Pippa who told me about Nigel Penn, a Cape Town University historian who very generously allowed me to borrow liberally from his remarkable unpublished thesis on Bushman resistance to the Dutch in the Cape, *The Northern Cape Frontier Zone, 1700–c. 1815*. Through Tom Hardbattle we met Cait Andrews, a Cape Town musicologist who opened the door to the near-extinct Khomani Bushman community. The Khomani of South

Africa, sensationally, were about to win a land claim which one hopes will have revolutionary repercussions throughout Africa, and even farther afield.

In the autumn of 1999 I made another visit to Botswana and Namibia, travelling first to Ghanzi to see Tom Hardbattle's sister, Andrea, bounding over the desert roads in the indestructible Land Rover of Bernard Horton, the safari guide and hunter who will always be the 'White Bushman' to me, and then on to Windhoek to examine the state archives. Soon afterwards, the final stages of my research took me to New England where I met the famous Marshall family: in Boston, John Marshall, the distinguished Bushman film maker; and in New Hampshire, his remarkable mother, Lorna, then 100, the author of *The !Kung of Nyae Nyae*, and his sister, Elizabeth, who wrote *The Harmless People*, one of the most engaging books ever produced about the Bushmen. From there the great American highway took me to Vermont, where I met and stayed with Professor Rob Gordon and his hospitable wife Rindy. Rob, the author of *The Bushman Myth*, generously allowed me to borrow freely from his magisterial work. My only regret is that I did not have time to extend my journey to Lincoln, Nebraska, to meet in person Professor Bob Hitchcock, a world authority on Botswana and the Bushmen, whose immense scholarship and expert guidance have placed me deeply in his debt.

He and two other noble souls have done me the honour of reading the MS. Douglas Williamson, an expert on Botswana's wildlife, has given me some excellent advice as has the matchless George Silberbauer, who established the Central Kalahari Game Reserve on behalf of the government of the British Protectorate of Bechuanaland in 1961. George has given me great assistance, both in his comments and through his books, notably his *Report to the Government of Bechuanaland on the Bushman Survey* and the classic *Hunter and habitat in the central Kalahari Desert*. He has also provided a fascinating Preface. The help of all these friends has been unstinting and invaluable; any errors and omissions are all mine.

Finally, I am greatly indebted to HRH The Prince of Wales, who has done me the honour of writing the Foreword. As a close friend of the late Laurens van der Post, who probably did more than anyone else to make the world aware of the Bushman's unique qualities, and whose words I have quoted with admiration, no one is better qualified than Prince Charles. He has personally given the Bushmen of the Kalahari generous material support, and the knowledge that someone of his eminence is prepared to give them moral support as well will, I hope, have far-ranging consequences. I am doubly grateful that he has been able to find time to make such an eloquent contribution.

Much has been written about the Bushmen – perhaps too much – but this is the first time, as far as I know, that anyone has attempted to trace their tragic history from the start to the present day, and to bring it, however inadequately, under one cover. It is the most terrible of all stories, worse in many ways than that of the Jews, but almost unknown to the world at large. It is a story of a genocide which started centuries ago, and reached a climax in the 18th, 19th and early 20th centuries. While man's inhumanity to man came as no surprise, what did amaze me, and continues deeply to impress me, is the unbelievable and often suicidal courage of the Bushmen as they fought for their land. Sadly, the persecution continues among the 100,000 or so who are left today – some of the most dispossessed, downtrodden and impoverished people on the planet.

They say the British are always moved by the plight of the underdog and Bushmen are the archetypal underdog, hounded to near-oblivion by both black and white. If I can illuminate, however fitfully, the dark corners of the Bushman agony, it will have been worth the effort – a thousand times.

Anyone embarking on a book about the Bushmen is faced by a host of difficult decisions. One is the name itself. 'Bosjesmans', or 'people who live in the bush', was the word the early Dutch settlers gave to the semi-nomadic hunter-gatherers they met when they first started moving into the Cape interior. It was derogatory but it stuck, and in English became 'Bushmen'. Thanks, however, to Laurens van der Post, who wrote so magically about the Bushmen of the Kalahari, and to debate among historians and scholars, the word 'Bushman' is today widely known and accepted. The alternative, 'San', is used mostly by anthropologists. Similarly – although some non-African readers may be mystified – I have chosen in my historical chapters to use the term 'Khoikhoi' (or 'Khoekhoe' or 'Khoi') instead of 'Hottentot', because nowadays 'Hottentot' is considered objectionable to some.

The next problem is spelling: what to do about 'the clicks' which pepper all Bushman languages? Only Bushman languages – and there are many, divided into four main groups – use a full range of clicks, although two East African languages, Hadza and Sandawe, and the Southern Bantu Nguni languages – Zulu, Xhosa and Swazi – also have clicks, inherited from the Bushmen. There are five main Bushman clicks, described by Alan Barnard of Edinburgh University as 'consonant sounds produced by allowing air to pass into [rather than out of] the mouth.' He lists them as follows:

⊙ Bilabial . . . produced by releasing air between the lips, often as in a kiss, hence 'kiss click'. Found only in Southern Bushman languages.

/ Dental . . . produced by a sucking motion with the tip of the tongue on the teeth, as in the English expression of annoyance written, 'Tisk, tisk'.

≠ Alveolar . . . produced by pulling the blade of the tongue sharply away from the alveolar ridge, immediately behind the teeth.

// Lateral . . . produced by placing the tip of the tongue on the roof of the mouth and releasing air on one side of the mouth . . . the clicking sound film cowboys use [according to Barnard] to make their horses go.

! Palatal . . . produced by pulling the tip of the tongue sharply away from the front of the hard palate. When made with lips rounded, it sounds rather like a cork popping from a wine bottle.

Put like that, it sounds quite jolly, but when, for example, the average reader comes across a legendary Bushman hero written as 'the ≠Au//gei man ≠Dukuri . . .' he can be forgiven if his eyes glaze over. We have decided therefore, for the sake of legibility, even at the risk of losing credibility, to drop all click signs. George Silberbauer, although he says his 'delicate sensitivities are bruised by the omission of clicks', which he thinks 'smacks of condescension', believes there is an acceptable compromise; namely to make *amende honorable* by stating unequivocally, as I now do, that the lack of clicks in no way diminishes my 'respect and affection' for the Bushmen. Indeed, I hope that by making the text more accessible, it will help to increase respect and affection for them generally.

Apart from the benefactors listed above, I have had help and kindness from many other people, to whom I am extremely grateful: Rebecca Adamson, Douglas Alexander, Christine Anderson, Fiona Archer, Ivan Baehr, Prof. Alan Barnard, Liz and Boy Barrell, Megan Biesele, Kristyna Bishop, Christopher Booker, Alec Campbell, Roger Chennells, Stephen Corry, David Coulson, Caitlin Davies, Hilary and Janette Deacon, Rein Dekker, Andrew Dooley, Jane Durham, Dick Eaton, Clare Flattery, Ted Flattery, Birthe Gjern, Fran Griffith, Mathias Guenther, Khwa and Polly Hardbattle, Carl Hartman, the late Doc Heinz, Janet Hermans, Anne-Mette Hybertsen, Stephen Johnson, John Kalmanson, Rahim Khan, Emy Koen, Arthur Krasilnikoff, Dawid Kruiper, Roger Laker, Andrew Lamont, Louis Liebenberg, Virginia Luling, Mario Mahongo, Philip Marshall, Andy and Gay McGregor, Lord Pearson of Rannoch, Douglas van der Horst, Lucia van der Post, Herman van Wyk, Geoffrey and Ro Rainbird, Tim Reiser, Mandy and Peter Sandenbergh, Sidsel Saugestad, Roy Sesana, Paul Sheller, Sheila Southey, Allister Sparks, Renee Sylvain, Julian and Tessa Ogilvie Thompson, Meregan Turner, Reg Vize, Christine Walker, Fiona Watson, Polly Wiessner, and Glyn Williams.

My thanks also to Survival International, London. I refer readers to their website: www.survival-international.org.

Last but not least, I must make special mention of my tireless editor, Penelope Hoare, my encouraging agent, Michael Sissons, my wife, Eleanor, for typing my emails and putting up with all the stresses and strains, and my daughter, Michaela, who was not only a wonderful travelling companion, but kept me on course and sane through many a tricky patch. Michaela took the cover photograph as well as a number of photographs reproduced within this book, and she sketched the illustrations on the part title pages.

Sandy Gall
April, 2001

The Common Circumstances of Oppression

As District Commissioner of Ngamiland, later of Ghanzi, and as Bushman Survey Officer in the 1950s and 1960s, I travelled among the Bushmen of Botswana and spent long periods living with some of them. I was the ignorant, inept, bothersome intruder whom they initially tolerated with anxious, but ever-kindly puzzlement. As we gradually came to understand one another, we formed the variety of relationships that one does in any small, isolated community. Open enmity is an unaffordable luxury at such close quarters. With those with whom amity did not develop, we talked and walked and worked together, but kept our reserve. With others grew close and warm companionship and, with a few, came lasting and happy friendship. I even had two wives; one was a prickly, cross-grained old harridan and the other the charming, very intelligent, beautiful daughter of my closest friends. It was all a pleasant, complicated practical joke (on me, not on the wives), the punch line of which had no consummation. All, in their different styles, were my patient teachers.

In *Hunter and habitat in the central Kalahari Desert* I wrote of the Gwi, with whom I stayed longest. At that time, their subsistence was based entirely on gathering and hunting and they lived in one of the most remote regions. I needed to understand that way of life as a sort of baseline from which to comprehend the changes that other Bushmen groups had experienced in their contacts with black and white cattlemen. In scientific terms, it was a sound choice. In personal terms, it was immensely rewarding.

The Bushman Survey was not always enjoyable. Its relatively high cost, in a slender-budgeted Protectorate, and its obvious pro-Bushman orientation aroused hostility. There were times of exhaustion, moments – some protracted – of high anxiety, an awful lot of despair and frustration (I learn slowly . . .) and long stretches of loneliness: all the normal lot of an anthropologist in the field. But this was against a background of warm and close affection and – as I (so slowly!) learned so much from my mentors – a growing admiration and respect for their ways. It is remarkable that Africa was the cradle of our species for, in its ecology, it is the most violent and unforgiving of the inhabited continents. The central Kalahari is one of the least hospitable parts of Africa. Yet the Gwi, like other Bushmen in other parts of southern Africa, contrived social and cultural solutions to the problems of survival that were economical of time and effort, and highly effective. Their ingenuity and practised, elegant simplicity were, when I eventually came to understand each polished facet and its many layers of implications, my constant, surprised delight. It was like coming, at last, to comprehension of a great work of art or an equation, each beautiful in its truth and rightness. But with the added dimension of dynamism as people adjusted and shuffled their knowledge, skills and aspirations to the unending changes about them and within themselves.

Many changes, when they came, were too great and too sudden for most Bushmen people, and they were overwhelmed. Think of what is lost.

Sandy Gall's book is about human beings and the human spirit. The dispossessed and their descendants still have that spirit and, given their just recognition, they can turn it to different social and cultural creations of equal efficacy and beauty.

The Bushmen are not one people. They have somewhat the same distinctive physical appearance, are hunters and gatherers (or the descendants of hunters and gatherers) and their many languages all have a high proportion of click consonants. Within these similarities are many differences of ethos, beliefs, adaptations to the particular part of southern Africa in which each group lives (or once lived), forms of social organisation and language.

Tony Traill, the leading scholar of Bushman languages, has identified four families of Bushman languages which, apart from the phenomenon of click consonants, appear to resemble one another no more than English does Arabic. The Bushmen are many peoples and the social, cultural and historical variety among them is important to those who want to understand them. It invalidates the claims of their detractors that 'they are all thieves, murderers, little better than animals ...' When 'at home' and leading their normal lives they can be clearly seen, and fairly judged. Each people has its own style of self-expression; some are reserved and gentle, others have a more bruising way. Like any society, each inevitably includes some who steal, fewer who kill and fewer still – if any – 'little better than animals'. Rich humour and imaginative creativity are enjoyed by all and practised most rewardingly by many. Most are decent, lively, sensitive and socially adept; it is very difficult to get by as a hunter or gatherer living in a small group if you are not.

That we label all of them with the same epithet, and seldom distinguish among them, is a mark of our lack of knowledge and general indifference. It is an inaccurate discourtesy of the same order as calling a Canadian an American, or a New Zealander an Australian – but is more politely tolerated.

Despite their variety, Bushman peoples share another characteristic: they have been oppressed, despised, hated and hunted by almost everybody else in southern Africa. This is the burden of Sandy Gall's book. Their common fate and hunter-gatherer heritage and, paradoxically, the gross singularity we have thrust on them have given them a measure of moral unity and shared identity. As Sandy shows, there are today the beginnings of a movement of mutual support and concerted legal and political action.

First Nations (in Canada and the United States) and Aborigines (in Australia) have been successful in transcending their social and cultural diversity and in forging a unity that has been effective in regaining some of their lost status as owners and occupiers of the land that – and 'the memory of man runneth not to the contrary' – was theirs. Southern Africa is a more difficult setting in which to prevail; black and white are already struggling among themselves with the problem of rights to land.

Assuming their unity of action in this context, Bushmen have enormous handicaps to overcome before they are heard, and yet greater ones to conquer before justice is done. They will draw support and strength from the impact of Sandy's book on every fair-minded reader.

The past two hundred years of the history of the Bushman people is an unhappy tale of brutal cruelty. Even more unhappily, it is not unique. In fact, to a black-mooded reader of yesterday's history or today's news, it is hardly even unusual. *The Bushmen of Southern Africa* is not only the faithful history of the persecution of southern Africa's oldest lineages of men, women and children; it is also a case-study of the systematic inhumanity so frequently dealt to fellow humans, not only by 'ordinary' men but also by their governments and leaders who pride(d) themselves on their guardianship of freedom, liberality and, yes, humaneness.

Some sociobiologists claim that mankind is inherently aggressively violent – that, beneath the pinstripe suit or spotted bikini of even the most outwardly 'civilised' members of our species, there beats a savage, cruel heart, bent on frightful murder and mayhem. Were they and, for that matter, Hobbes correct, our natural condition would be war, and our lives solitary, poor, nasty, brustish, and short. There is, of course, almost always war being waged somewhere; there are many millions who are miserably poor; and there are lives that are tragically solitary, or nasty, or brutish, or short.

Obviously mankind is *capable* of aggressiveness and frightful violence. The question is whether this is an inherent, natural condition, or a latent response to certain circumstances? I believe the evidence favours the latter view. After all, a canary is not usually seen as threatening. But, sufficiently irked, it becomes a little yellow demon, bent on as much aggressiveness and violence as lie within its feeble capabilities. Canaries are said to be descended from dinosaurs (not, perhaps, directly from *Tyrannosaurus rex*), but such is not their normal behaviour. This tiny explosion of fury is sparked by the dire situation in which the bird perceives itself to be. What moved the majority of those who encountered Bushmen to such brutality? Why was the tiny minority who tried to accommodate them not moved to be cruel also?

One of the tasks of social anthropology is the explanation of human behaviour. In all candour, we in the discipline still have a long way to travel, but we have made some progress. To start to understand another's behaviour entails wearing that person's shoes and standing where she or he does, in the same social and cultural universe in which that person lives. Anthropologists study each such universe simultaneously, as observers and as learning participants, and, from an holistic perspective, in as much of its entirety as is feasible. Domestic manners, basket-weaving and political plotting are all grist to our slow, but not always fine-grinding mills. Having learned as much of a society and its culture as our individual circumstances and skills allow, we translate the experience, with its vernacular colours, nuances and accents, into the discipline's own stock of shared concepts, values and meanings. Then we can report our individual findings about those people(s) among whom we have done our fieldwork and other research and compare them with colleagues' results towards a wider and clearer understanding.

Cross-cultural comparison of ethical systems indicates that all societies have three principles in common: respect for the integrity of social order, reciprocity, and – having taken into account all known and relevant factors – seeking to prolong the lives of those within a recognised social circle. The 'natural condition of mankind' is, in fact, that of living in tolerably orderly society and treating one another with a modicum of decency. We cannot survive otherwise. Mercifully few people can be bothered gratuitously to harm others.

Why, then, are history and the daily news replete with examples seemingly to the contrary? What circumstances prompted the cruel oppression practised by almost everyone against every Bushman they encountered? Perhaps, once conflict had become habitual, there could be found (in their eyes) some rationality in reprisal and pre-emptive strikes. But Europeans settling on the southern tip of Africa did not initially see

Bushman peoples as enemies. The systematic excesses of Apartheid did not spring forth in full frightfulness with the declaration of the polls in 1948. When the First Fleeters disembarked at Sydney Cove, they did not immediately set upon the local Aborigines. The people of the Balkans, through all their vicissitudes and changes of nationality, did not always murder, pillage and seek to exterminate one another. Jews were respected in Germany, gypsies were tolerated and discreet homosexuals allowed to be invisible, until Hitler, by his legerdemain of fact and history, deceived their fellow-citizens into the perversions of the Nazi years. In all of these, and in scores of similar shameful tragedies, propinquity was a common factor. Oppressors and oppressed shared the same turf. Why was the commonality of social significance denied the latter?

Competition for scarce resources is a tempting explanation. Gause's Principle of Competitive Exclusion states that two species with identical ecological requirements cannot exist in the same habitat. Unless there is a superabundance of resources one, or both, will be unable to survive. That has a dismal knell of finality to it.

How, then, do all four filling-stations that we seem to find on every major intersection continue to sell their overpriced petrol? How do the clerks of all those barristers stacked in high-rise Chambers continue to field lucrative briefs? Like many of the laws that bring forth those briefs, that of Gause has a loophole; in this case, speciation. Plants and animals, finding themselves in danger of being edged out by competitors, diversify and develop new niches on the old patch. Thus, barristers do not all appear for the same type of client with the same kind of cause. Horace Rumpole did for your petty crims down at the Old Bailey but, I believe, was never heard before the Queen's Bench. His more august and learned friends rose to present their divers pleas in Chancery, or Probate, Divorce and Admirality, or Common Pleas and Exchequer. With no disrespect to lawyers (my middle daughter is the fifth generation of us in its practice), average human ingenuity is equal to that of barristers' clerks. Finding one another in the same paddock, we usually contrive some means of sharing its riches; perhaps not always very equitably, but sufficiently so as to leave something for the other. We seldom squeeze, or allow ourselves to be squeezed, to extinction. In the generality of instances it requires some additional motivation for anybody to invoke competition as the excuse for placing the Other beyond the pale. But, when that additional motivation is present, it can become the very powerful rationalisation of murderous hostility.

Superior power, whether military, political or economic, is the necessary means of subjugation. Its use for this purpose, however, requires a motive.

In a situation devoid of overt threat, human beings tend to adopt an initial stance of cautious, reserved neutrality towards strangers. If they are in continuing proximity, they will each be seen. But, if they do not communicate effectively, they will not be heard, and will not get to know one another. Having insufficient information on which to build valid expectations of one another's observed behaviour, the common tendency is to fabricate negative ones. However, this will seldom flower unless the Other's otherness is accentuated, nudging her or him towards, or beyond, the pale. Perceived differences in habits and customs can be interpreted as deviance, and can become affronts to decency. Insular self-righteousness can become spurious licence for defence of one's idealised way of life. Natural and inevitable use of the same resources can be construed as competition, which information-starved imagination can easily escalate to competitive exclusion. At this stage the situation is easily retrieved; no real wrongs have been done. (When my new rural neighbour's university-student children began to hold regular parties in their barn, I morosely feared for my sleep on Friday and Saturday nights. It was only after meeting the youngsters and finding them likeable that I noticed that the music always stopped before midnight.) But, if unfavourable interpretation turns to hostile action, recrimination leads to retribution and the fat's in a fire from which it is difficult to retrieve in anything like usable condition.

Neighbourliness can be problematic in comfortable, stable society in which its members can expect a measure of civility. It is immensely more uncertain when strangely-dressed men appear on horseback ahead of creaking wagons, or come ashore from towering caravels, cogs or brigs, making themselves large in the hitherto undisputed ancestral chases, pastures or gardens of hunter-gatherers, tribal pastoralists or horticulturists. Nor is neighbourliness readily extended by ill-educated sailors, soldiers and settlers who, having faced mortal dangers in every day's travel to the remote yonder, are confronted by what they have been taught to see as savages. In the narrow world of each, the otherness of the Other would, indeed, be striking and the opportunities many for inadvertent affront.

Samuel Wallis's 1767 visit to Tahiti started off badly. His ship, *Dolphin*, hove-to one night when fog enveloped her. The next morning the sailors were astonished to find their ship surrounded by about a hundred canoes. Some islanders were invited aboard. Unfortunately one was butted in the backside by a goat that was wandering about on deck. Never having seen such a creature, the man and his companions prudently fled. A few days later, as *Dolphin* was coming up to her anchorage, men in more than 300 canoes besieged and stoned her. Several of the Europeans were wounded and *Dolphin*'s crew replied with muskets, killing one islander and wounding another.

Captain Wallis managed to strike a truce and eventually win the islanders' confidence. The sailors and Tahitians made peace so successfully that, when *Dolphin* left five weeks later, Queen Obera wept openly – nor was she the only one. Perhaps because the Polynesians were also seafarers or perhaps because European sailors were entranced by the beauty of the women, many Pacific encounters were not initially fatal. Nor were many on the shores of Asia where Portuguese, Dutch, French and English sailors treated with established rulers of large and small states, and there was some shared understanding of the mixture of horse-trading and diplomacy that was the idiom of their interaction. The social significance of the Other was unequivocally acknowledged.

Diplomacy also smoothed the way for many European explorers and hunters in southern Africa. Their encounters and sojourns with Bushmen, Khoi and Bantu-speaking peoples are marked by their recognition of the sovereignty of their hosts; they 'begged the road and asked (for) the water'. Ownership of the land and its resources were acknowledged, and the principle of reciprocity honoured. The newcomers were driven by curiosity and adventure. Their search was for knowledge about the country and its people, which could only be gained from friendly relationships. (The Frenchman, François le Vaillant seems to have been become especially friendly with the comely Gonaqua girl, Narina.) The resources that hunters tapped – ivory and other proceeds of the chase – were renewable and were paid for in various ways. Perhaps, also, the explorers and hunters and their hosts could tolerate one another's Otherness the more easily because they knew that it would not be for long.

Then the permanent settlers arrived. They found themselves among small-scale societies with no great number of members. These inhabitants had small inventories of material artefacts of relatively simple manufacture. There was little to *show* for their intellectual wealth in knowledge of their environment, their arts and the ingenuity of their social arrangements. They were judged to be primitive and, hence, inferior in ways that were reckoned to matter.

In Australia early British explorers' and settlers' disdain of Aborigines was such that they starved, rather than unbend and learn from the inhabitants anything of the wealth of foods that surrounded them. We should not hasten to judge such folly. Although many settlers were convicts, few had been transported for crimes that were gravely reprehensible. These poor souls were the ordinary folk of their times and their values and attitudes those of the prevailing ethos. Their traumatic, demoralising experiences, before and during the hazardous voyage halfway round the world, and their feelings of insecurity in this strange and, to them, forbidding land, left them with little confidence in their expectations of the place or one another. However, curiosity quickly stirred and the spirit of adventure asserted itself. Convict and keeper alike squeezed their perceptions of what they found in Australia's interior into the narrow, sometimes irrelevant confines of what was known and familiar. For nearly two hundred years the constricting mould was scarcely cracked and experience of the continent was either construed in European terms or, if it would not yield to such rough treatment, ignored. The flora and fauna and the land obstinately refused to be British. Tragically, exploration barely extended to the peoples encountered on the land. Their ways and thoughts, although known to a handful of gifted, sensitive amateurs, continued to be obscured by unmovable public indifference. The developing discipline of anthropology, alas, performed no better. The need for sustained fieldwork was not yet appreciated. So anthropology was without the experience that might enable it to develop concepts and valid metaphors to accommodate the ways in which hunter-gatherer groups differed from pastoralists or gardeners. Until the middle of the twentieth century, hunters and gatherers were, in essence, below the anthropological bottom line. They were either the subjects of Ripleyesque *Believe It or Not* snippets or, comparably, depicted as cardboard characters with this or that remarkable cultural feature. But these features were never related to how hunter-gatherers led their full, purposeful, rational lives which represented effective and elegant social and cultural adaptations to the same problems of survival as were faced by all other human beings.

Elsewhere, as in Australia, settlers, sailors, soldiers and administrators and, later, citizens, having been left in darkness and silence as to what hunters and gatherers *were*, only saw them for what they were *not*. It was seen only that they did *not* till the soil or tend herds and flocks. It was not seen that they disposed themselves in well-ordered social groups, and built structures of relationships within them, to facilitate the use of their simple, efficient material technology and deep knowledge of the seasons and the flora and fauna of their habitats. It was seen only that they did *not* have kings and towns. The ingenuity of their polities' regulation of the exertions of groups and individuals, the resolution of disputes and conflicts and the facilitation of interaction between people remained unquestioned and unknown. The conclusion was drawn that what they were *not*, and did *not* have, or did *not* do, was because they did not even think to exert themselves to be, acquire, or do those things. Judged by these rules, no wonder they came out as irredeemably inferior in every way.

Different, other and inferior beyond redemption in their perceived slothfulness and stupidity, they were undeserving of what they had: notably, their land and its resources. Richard Hakluyt described North Americans as 'more brutish than the beasts they hunt, more wild and unmanly than that unmanned wild countrey, *which they range rather than inhabite*' (my emphasis). Europeans were concerned only to justify to one another their colonising of the Americas, Africa, Australia and parts of Asia. Without any reference to the autochthonous inhabitants, they fastened their claims to suzerainty to manufactured myths. The legend of Prince Madoc persuaded Englishmen (and, presumably, Welshmen) that 'that country was by Britons discovered, long before Columbus led any Spanish thither'. Then, through no fault of his, they credited Captain Cook with the discovery of Australia, conveniently overlooking the charts of Portuguese, Spanish and Dutch visitors of centuries earlier. Britain also ignored the Aborigines' occupancy of their land; *terra manens vacua occupanti conceditur* (land lying unoccupied is given to the first occupant) says the legal doctrine, and the Crown deemed Australia *terra nullius* and assumed ownership and rights of its allocation. At least John Batman gave the local elders presents of knives, mirrors, scissors and blankets as his part of the treaty that ceded to him the area that is now Melbourne, while the Dutch gave the Iroquois £8 worth of trinkets for Manhattan.

Hunters and gatherers commit the deadly economic 'sin' of not exploiting their resources to maximise their productivity. Pastoralists, farmers, miners and timber millers were (and are) outraged by their neglect of their opportunities. Oblivious to, or unmoved by, the fact that hunting and gathering depended on ecological integrity, they seized those opportunities for themselves, offering no accommodation of the needs of the inhabitants, or their rights to meet them. Bushmen, Aborigines and First Nations found themselves displaced by alien settlers whose activities dispossessed them of their living. Desperate, and without grounds for hope, they tried, like the canary, to defend themselves. Now the newcomers' negative catalogue of what the natives were *not* was replaced by an entry in the positive – the natives were mad, bad and dangerous to know.

Whatever slender thread of logic remained turned in on itself. Fear, having compounded ignorance, closed it off from reality to free perceptions to invent demonising mythology. The inhabitants' social status as rightful occupiers of their land had already been denied; now even the fellowship of humanity was refused them. They became the enemy, Unpersons. Now it would be culpably contrary to seek solutions or to reach out with the hand of charity. It would become one's rightful duty to use superior force of arms, the economy and the ballot-box ruthlessly to subjugate them.

Closure was the last link in the tragic chain of the circumstances of oppression. In earlier history, the factors were fortuitous, and their linking together largely happenstance. While no excuse, the plea of ignorance may soften judgment. However, where ignorance is deliberately inculcated through sly disinformation, deliberate demonising, false representation of rivalry and malicious provocation – such as have been seen in the conflicts of the last hundred years – there are no grounds for mitigation.

The chain must be unlinked if Bushmen and other oppressed peoples are to succeed in regaining their birthright. Each of the links has contaminated the others and the chain must be taken apart systematically. It is necessary to replace ignorance with knowledge and to counter false myths with logic. Perceptions of rivalry are not erased by facts alone; trust is also needed. And trust can only be painstakingly earned by each of the participants, while some measure of trust is a precondition to withholding force.

To unlink the chain, each of the protagonists must contribute to its undoing with – as Nelson Mandela pleaded in a comparable context – good will, courage and readiness to extend and to accept forgiveness.

Sandy Gall's book will inspire sympathy for the dispossessed. I hope that from this sympathy will grow respect. Without respect, hunter-gatherers will not be perceived as deserving of the right to choose their way of life. Without respect for that choice, they will gain nothing more than ritualistic tokens of sorrow and repentance. Without respect, drowning people in dollars ultimately kills them dead.

George Silberbauer
May, 2001

Part One

Ganema, wife of the shaman

CHAPTER ONE

The Right to Choose a Life of One's Own

The destruction of the Bushman is the destruction of the best in all mankind.

Laurens van der Post, *Testament to the Bushman*, 1984

They came early in the morning, four of them, stepping lightly through the bush, as insubstantial as shadows against the sun. One carried a bow and a quiverful of arrows, each of the others had a spear. They sat down just beyond the camp, lounging in the pale golden grass, talking and laughing quietly. One of them rolled a cigarette out of a scrap of paper and coarse tobacco, lit it and took a long pull, swallowing the smoke so completely that hardly a wisp remained in the air. As he held it in his lungs, he passed the glowing paper to the next man, who also drew the smoke deep into the inmost recesses of his being, before passing it to the third man who did likewise, and then gave it to the fourth, all of them inhaling with the same absorption, until only the butt of the cigarette remained. As the price of survival, Bushmen learned a long time ago to share practically everything.

Of the four hunters, two were young, in their early twenties, I guessed, and the other two a little older, probably in their late twenties or early thirties. They were dressed only in 'skins', a loincloth made of antelope hide, probably springbok or gemsbok, and their torsos, legs and even their feet were bare. Each man carried a little pouch, made from the skin of one of the smaller antelopes, a steenbok or duiker, in which he kept his tobacco if he had any, and perhaps a small pipe. Bushmen have, and need, the minimum. Small and lightly muscled, they move 'with an oiled activity altogether delightful to watch', as Lawrence of Arabia said of the Beduin in *Seven Pillars of*

3

Wisdom. When they smile, the skin crinkles in hair-fine lines at the corners of their eyes.

The four Bushmen got to their feet and, led by the bowman, walked down the gentle slope towards the bare, dry valley of the Okwa, an ancient fossil river which runs across the middle of the Kalahari Desert, from Namibia in the west to the Makgadikgadi Pans of Botswana in the east. The knowledge that since time immemorial Bushmen had travelled this route in their perennial quest for game and water lent the scene a sense of mystery and excitement. On the far side of the valley, 400 yards away, about 200 springbok were grazing peacefully. I had been watching them from camp while I ate my breakfast. At one point, the males had started chasing one another at top speed, racing across the sandy plain, kicking up clouds of dust, and then bounding seven or eight feet into the air with tremendous, stiff-legged jumps – hence their name. This display is known as pronking. 'Showing off to the females,' said Harry, my guide, 'and telling any predator, look how fit I am, you needn't bother trying to catch me.'

Our little party stopped at the foot of the slope, letting the hunters, who were by now about 100 yards ahead of us, continue on their own. They were going to show us how Bushmen hunted springbok in the traditional manner – with no dogs, no guns, only bow and poisoned arrow, and spears. They walked close together in single file, in step, holding their upper bodies still, their slim brown legs floating over the ground. This was how they must have hunted 30,000 years ago, when the Bushmen were the inhabitants of the southern two-thirds of Africa. A springbok herd always has sentries on the flanks, keeping a wary eye open for predators, and because the animals knew their sentries were watching, the rest of the herd grazed unconcernedly as they drifted slowly along the side of the valley.

When they were about 300 yards from the herd, still in single file, the Bushmen slowed and dropped into a half crouch to begin the stalk proper. They moved more slowly now, carefully and unobtrusively, dark shapes against the pale glare of the sand – although to stalk at all seemed a near impossibility in the bone-bare surroundings of the Okwa valley. I wondered how the

4

hunters would deal with the absence of cover: would they drop flat and crawl as close as possible, and then rush the herd in the hope of wounding a straggler, leaving the poisoned arrow to do its deadly work? Almost imperceptibly, on some hidden signal, the herd began to divide in front of the hunters, one group, the larger, moving to the right, and the other to the left. In response, the Bushmen, all four moving as one, began to swing right, and as they did so the springbok directly in front of them, like a chess player threatened by an opponent's queen, backed off and started to drift away, a little faster now. Again, I wondered how the Bushmen would react: they must make their move soon, or the herd would be out of range.

Suddenly, the drama of the hunt and the stillness of the morning were shattered by a distant roar. Two big lorries appeared over the skyline, and came bumping noisily down the sandy track towards us. The four hunters halted in mid-stride, as Mathambo, the Molapo village headman who was with us, ran forward to intercept the intruders. He reached the road just in time to flag down the first lorry, shouting up at the driver in his high cab, and waving his arms to make him wait. They parleyed for a few seconds until the driver, revving his engine impatiently, noisily engaged first gear and roared off down the road between the hunters and the springbok. After a few seconds' hesitation, the second lorry followed. As the clouds of dust billowing behind them cleared, I could see the hunters staring non-plussed after the springbok which had scattered in every direction and were now a mile away, stampeding across the plain.

In the brief moments of confrontation, I noticed two things. The first was that the two lorries belonged to the District Council of Ghanzi, in western Botswana, which is responsible for the northern portion of the Central Kalahari Game Reserve. I clearly saw the coat of arms painted on the cab doors which, irony of ironies, depicted a Bushman hunter with drawn bow, flanked on his right by a magnificent eland, and on his left by an equally fine gemsbok. The other thing I could not fail to see was that both lorries were piled high with long wooden poles, such as might be used to build a substantial hut, sheaves of thatching grass, some pots and pans, and three or four bemused-looking Bushmen. Although the full implications did not become clear until later, I had just witnessed the eviction of some of the few remaining Bushmen from the Reserve. It was the latest move in the long, bully-boy campaign to push out the Bushmen, a campaign which has besmirched Botswana's human rights record since 1986.

When we reached the hunting party a few minutes later the four Bushmen, philosophical as ever, were sitting down to make fire by twirling between their palms a thin stick in a hard piece of wood with a hole bored in it. As the thin stick rotated faster than the eye could follow, a few strands of dead grass were dropped in the hole and seconds later there rose a puff of smoke, quickly followed by a small flame.

Bushmen have many different myths and legends to explain the functioning of the universe, and man's place in it; each language group, for example, has its own myth of how man first discovered fire. The Gwi, to whom our hunters belonged, tell the story of Pisamboro, one of their lesser gods, who spotted a red-hot coal under the wing of the Ostrich, a legendary being. Intrigued, he stole the coal and from it gave fire to men. He then threw the red-hot coal high in the air. Twice it fell back to earth, but the third time it stayed in the sky and became the sun. Many early travellers and missionaries, including David Livingstone, made the mistake of thinking the Bushmen were godless – although Livingstone, to his credit, later admitted that the fault was due to his own ignorance, confessing, 'If I had known the name of God in the Bushman tongue the mistake could scarcely have occurred.' Bushmen believe in a Great God, or Supreme Being, although different language groups have different names for such a God. The extinct southern Xam, for example, called him Kaggen, while the Gwi of the Central Kalahari call him Nadima. Many of the lesser gods are tricksters, about whom the Bushmen love to tell bawdy stories.

Our hunters, whether or not they knew the myth of Pisamboro, were adept at fire-making and moments later were happily smoking while they discussed what we should do next, the springbok hunt having been irrevocably disrupted. It was finally decided that they would take us on a hunt for spring hare, a nocturnal rodent with exceptionally long back legs which lives in deep burrows in the sand, and is known jokingly as a Kalahari kangaroo. A little larger than the European hare, it provides a tasty couple of pounds of rich protein, and although small makes a welcome addition to the Bushman diet.

A delay ensued until another hunter could be found with the requisite 20-foot hunting pole, consisting of several flexible rods, joined together, and with a hook made from a steenbok horn fastened to the end. This is thrust down a hole which seems to be occupied and twisted about in the hope that the needle-sharp hook will strike lucky and pull up a plump victim. But the spring hare tunnels deep, and although the five hunters scoured the side of the valley for an hour or more, pushing their long, hooked pole down dozens of holes, they failed to find a single animal. 'Sometimes we catch as many as fourteen,' one of the men boasted; but hunting, as we were beginning to realise, is a demanding, and often frustrating business.

Having glimpsed, even if extremely briefly, something of the magic of the hunt, I was eager to witness the other half of the equation, the food-gathering. Next morning, there arrived the mothers and grandmothers of Molapo, cheerful and smiling despite having walked three miles to our camp, ready to show off their bushcraft skills. Armed with pointed digging sticks and capacious skin shoulder bags, they headed into the bush, foraging in line abreast, shouting to one another and making jokes, no doubt about us. 'They discuss everything,' explained Harry, 'that's why their culture is so strong.' They talked and sang as they descended on the raisin, or *grewia*, bushes which at this time of year were thickly covered with a firm, sweetish golden-brown berry with a large seed in the middle. When they came on an especially plentiful bush, one of the more senior ladies did a joyful jig around it with a suppleness and sense of rhythm that defied her years.

The Bushman women had an unerring eye for what lay beneath the sand, being able to tell from an insignificant cluster of dry leaves on the surface that deep below would be a succulent bulb or root. Squatting down on the ground, legs straddled in a business-like position, they dug with great energy, driving their pointed, hardwood sticks deep into the sand, and then scooping it out with their hands. One younger, powerfully-built lady, accompanied by her small daughter, took 15 or 20 minutes digging a hole three or four feet deep in pursuit of an outsize tuber. But being still short of her objective, she was forced to lie flat on the ground, on her side, wriggling her whole shoulder into the hole and reaching to the limit of her outstretched arm, before she was able to grasp the prize, a thick white root a foot long. She emerged triumphant, brandishing it aloft, and shaking the sand from her head and body.

In the space of an hour, she and her friends had harvested more than a dozen edible plants – Bushman women are said to know and make use of as many as 150 different varieties; one, clearly a favourite, resembled a leek, others looked like parsnips and beetroots. Then, with a cry of triumph, the dancing lady held up a big black and yellow jewel beetle, known in Nharo as *Xoroghum*. Removing its legs and antennae so it could not escape, she popped it into her skin shoulder bag to join half a dozen others. Roasted, she assured us, they would make a delicious mouthful, full of protein.* Later, accompanied by the medicine man and another healer, the women visited a different area, rich in medicinal plants. Ganema, wife of the shaman, the medicine man, held up one root for us to see. 'This,' she said 'is called *Xdaro guian*, ostrich foot, and is good for aches and pains. And this one, *Xnave tsao*, or giraffe's tail, is used for miscarriages, and also' – she smiled coquettishly – 'as a love potion.'

Next day, the hunters were jubilant, having run down and finally despatched a kudu, a superb, spiral-horned antelope, second only to the eland in the Bushman pantheon. I saw the end of the hunt, when the proud animal was stretched out on the grass, and the Bushmen were preparing to skin and butcher it, which they do expertly, wasting nothing. Even the rumen, the stomach contents, is squeezed out, and the juices drunk. There would be jubilation in Molapo that night, because everyone, young and old, would be given a share of the fresh meat.

---

* George Silberbauer says they have a nutty, slightly sweet taste, 'like a very superior Nutella'.

Believing, as they do, that animals are as important in the scheme of things as man, Bushmen revere all the animals they hunt and kill, above all the eland. This mystical bond with wild animals is reflected in their dances, many of which revolve around the hunt. Among them are the eland dance and the gemsbok dance, but most important of all is the trance dance, because it is central to all the Bushmen believe in, including healing and rain-making. Many Bushman rock paintings depict people in trance, bleeding from the nose; these were probably the shamans, many of whom were also the artists.

One night, as the sun dropped fiery red beneath the rim of the Kalahari, and the pale moon rose in perfect counterpoint, the villagers gathered at our camp. The sand had been smoothed, the fire heaped high, men and women ranged in separate groups in an expectant circle. Suddenly the women began to clap and sing, a wild, high-pitched, haunting sound which drew the men to their feet and into the dance, the old men shuffling, the young men stamping the ground, their steps fast and intricate, round and round, the clapping as rhythmic as a drum beat. After a time, one or two women joined in, led by Ganema, who danced closer and closer to the flames, at one point picking up a live coal, and then, in a state of trance, falling headlong into the fire. She was quickly pulled out, and lay moaning in the darkness while the dance went on, hour after hour. From time to time, their bare chests heaving and running with sweat, the men dropped out of the circle, exhausted, and the women fell silent. But after only a short pause the singing would start again, a woman's voice piercing the darkness, the dancers moving back into the circle, and the insistent beat of the clapping throbbing across the flames. When I saw Ganema next day, she smiled and pointed to her face and hands. Amazingly, there was no sign of any burns.

The establishment of the Central Kalahari Game Reserve by the British colonial administration of what was then Bechuanaland in 1961 was one of the more enlightened pieces of legislation which distinguished the final years of Empire. The brainchild of George Silberbauer, a South-African born district commissioner in the British colonial service, who studied linguistics and social anthropology at Witwatersrand University, in Johannesburg, before undertaking his famous Bushman survey in 1958, it was designed to protect both the wildlife and the Bushmen of the Kalahari. It was not intended, as he states in his official report, 'to preserve the Bushmen of the Reserve as museum curiosities and pristine primitives, but to allow them the right of choice of the life they wish to follow' – a liberal, civilised and above all humanitarian objective which I had just seen being ground into the dust before my eyes.

All the Bushmen we had met came from Molapo, a big village in terms of acreage, with a lot of space between the huts – Bushmen do not like to be crowded together – but with only about 120 residents, divided among 20 to 25 families. Over the past few days, I discovered, five or six Bushman *scherms* – round huts made of poles thatched with grass – had been pulled down, loaded on to council lorries along with the families who owned them, and driven off to New Xade, a bleak settlement just outside the Reserve. One Bushman named Sesi, his wife, Xmodau, and five children, had changed their minds when they got to New Xade. They did not like living there because there was no bush food and no work. It was, they said, 'a place of death'. So they decided to come back to their home village of Molapo. When the council officials discovered what had happened, they remonstrated with Sesi and his family, telling them they had broken the rules, since Sesi had accepted a small amount of money as compensation for moving. Now, he was being made to leave a second time, despite the fact that his father was dying. It was Sesi and his family, looking dejected and bemused, whom I had seen being driven away in the Ghanzi District Council lorries. I met another, older Bushman, Stadeli, who said he had agreed to move because council officials had told him that 'everyone else has agreed to leave'. When he found out that this was untrue, he had come back, but he too was living on borrowed time and would, it seemed, also be forcibly evicted.

The Botswana government has always claimed, and still claims, that it is 'persuading' not forcing the Bushmen to leave, 'for their own good'. But this seems, frankly, sheer sophistry.

Roy Sesana, chairman of First People of the Kalahari, a Bushman liberation movement with an office in Ghanzi, and Mathambo's younger brother, told me that the Botswana government was using a mixture of 'bribery and threats' to make people move. They had falsely promised Bushmen enough money 'to buy two cars', he said, and at the same time cut off amenities by closing down boreholes in the Reserve, and stopped visits by a mobile clinic. The last charge is undeniably true and, many would argue, clearly constitutes coercion. The council officials, however, had experienced some difficulty in 'persuading' the residents of Molapo to up sticks and leave; only a handful could be tricked into doing so by a combination of money, lies and, if all else failed, threats of violence. Some Bushman families had taken the bribes and had then come back to Molapo. Thus the officials, the tricksters, had themselves been tricked in turn – an irony which appealed to the Bushman sense of humour.

Sitting in the shade of a big acacia tree, and with Andrea Hardbattle, part Bushman herself, as interpreter, Mathambo tried to explain to me, stranger that I was, how attached the Bushmen of the Central Kalahari are to their ancestral land. 'We all want to stay,' he said, speaking quietly in Nharo, one of the many Bushman click languages, which are among the most complex as well as the most ancient on earth, rich in imagery and phonetic artistry. To make his point, Mathambo scooped up a handful of Kalahari sand, letting it trickle slowly through his fingers. 'Xnee ghom's e a Kurue, Kama ta se ta e, Kama se ta Xhong o.'*

Everyone I talked to in Molapo was determined to resist pressure to leave the Reserve. Ganema, the wife of the medicine man, gave me the most articulate account of how local government officials set about 'persuading' the residents to move. 'They say we have come to pour money over you. We will take down your houses and help you to move towards the sunset – but I don't want to move towards the sunset, because that is where you die' – a familiar Bushman belief. 'They say to us you

* 'We are made the same as the sand. So this is our land, because we were born here.'

must discourage any visitors from staying and camping here. No one can camp here.* You just want visitors' tea' – meaning money, or handouts. 'This is not your land, you stole this land. You are finishing the game, you have stolen the land and killed the game.'

I asked her if, as was reported in *The Times* of 10 September 1997, people who refused to leave had been threatened with the army. She replied: 'For a long time they have said if you don't move then the army will come in to move you. But we haven't seen the army.' She went on in a matter-of-fact voice, 'They also say they will drop a bomb on us if we don't move. I was born here, my mother suckled me here, so I will not move. Men, women and children do not want to move. I want to die here.'

Ganema said three of her children had left for New Xade, but they were not happy there. 'They look for bush foods but can't find very much.' Ganema was half Nharo and lighter-skinned than her husband, Ngwagaosele Ketheetswele, the medicine man, who, like many of the Central Kalahari Bushmen, was a Gana and dark-skinned. Although middle-aged, Ganema was still good-looking, with fine features, a slim figure, and a flirtatious manner. I watched her running 50 yards through the heavy Kalahari sand one day, and she still had the stride and suppleness of a young woman. Her husband was the first man we met in Molapo, and he welcomed us warmly with a broad smile. His favourite utterance was a loud 'Hey!' which seemed to be part greeting and part an exclamation of approval. Sometimes he would run together two or three 'heys!' in what appeared to be a special mark of pleasure and approbation. He was much sought after as a fortune-teller, and was considered an expert at 'throwing the bones', something the Bushmen take as seriously as the Greeks and Romans took their oracles, the Ancient Egyptians their soothsayers, and some modern Western men and women their horoscopes printed every day in the newspapers.

'Bones', as my daughter Michaela subsequently nicknamed him, surprised us all one evening when, throwing the bones for a fellow guest, a middle-aged Englishwoman, he asked her some

---

* There is in fact a designated tourist camp site near the village.

intimate medical questions, and either guessed or through some sixth sense knew that she had had a major operation. He went on to specify the type of operation, correctly but rather embarrassingly since the seance was conducted in public round the camp fire. He then informed her that she had made a complete recovery. Almost as astonishing was his success with Harry's Zimbabwean camp manager, a strapping Ndebele, the colour of whose car – white – he correctly named, as well as alluding to the fact – also correct – that the camp manager had a wife in Zimbabwe and a girlfriend in Botswana. This made me wonder if Harry, an astute safari operator, had briefed the medicine man privately in advance; it would have been easy, for example, to provide him with colourful details of the camp manager's love life. But it seemed doubtful in the case of the Englishwoman, whose private medical history Harry could hardly have been aware of. Whatever one thought of Ngwagao-sele's skill as a clairvoyant, I was impressed by his robust attitude. He said he had no intention of leaving Molapo, and when I asked him why he thought the Botswana government seemed so determined to expel him and his wife, and the rest of the Bushmen from the Reserve, he replied with devastating directness, '[President] Masire is trying to kill us.'

But these were all older people, and I was curious to know the feelings of the young. The same evening, we attended a meeting arranged by Harry to confirm that the villagers were happy to act as our guides. Afterwards, I talked to a young teacher named Custom. When I asked him for his views about leaving the Reserve, he said, 'I don't want to leave, nor do the other young people.' He explained that he taught the young children of the village at primary level, in their own language, while the older ones went to school in New Xade, where they were taught by Tswana teachers in Setswana. 'But they don't like it there, they want to come back,' he said.

Before we returned to our camp that night, the Englishwoman whose fortune had been told by 'Bones' gave the children a present of sweets. There was no jostling nor fighting as the oldest girl handed them out, one at time, and only when she had given every child a sweet did she take one for herself. As we left in the warm darkness, I looked up into the velvety black of the night sky and was rewarded, appropriately, by the sight of Orion, the Hunter, every star in his Sword and Belt shining with an uncanny brilliance that I have only seen once before, in the wilds of Afghanistan. Here in the desert, there is no light pollution, no extraneous, man-made sound, only the music of the spheres. In the silence of the Kalahari, the Bushmen say, you can hear the stars talking.

We were all hunter-gatherers once, but today very few remnants of these original societies still exist. Among the last of the hunter-gatherers are the Bushmen of the Central Kalahari. Their way of life provides the perfect balanced diet – protein from the fresh meat gained by hunting, which is done by the men; and vitamins and minerals from the bush foods gathered by the women. The Kalahari is rich in hundreds of plants and bushes, many of them edible, many with proven medicinal qualities, and only a few of which are poisonous. The older people know them all, handing down this centuries-old – and indeed millennia-old – knowledge to their children and grand-children. Banishment from the Reserve would extinguish this vast store of inherited knowledge, impoverishing not only Bushman culture, but world culture as well. One of our party put it well: 'To force these people to leave their homeland is worse than cutting down the rain forest.' The wild fruits and roots of the Kalahari are highly nutritious, and an important part of the Bushman diet. One in particular, a wild melon rich in juice, called a *tsamma*, has kept the Bushmen alive in times of drought for thousands of years. It is only when you are aware of the importance to them of this cornucopia, this great horn of plenty of wildlife and the fruits of the earth, that you realise why the Bushmen are determined to stay in the Kalahari, and why they resist so doggedly being moved to overcrowded settlements like New Xade, where there are few if any bush foods left, and where they are forbidden to hunt the little game that remains.

This was my first visit to the Central Kalahari Game Reserve, one of the remotest, emptiest and most unspoilt wildernesses left on earth. At 20,309 square miles (52,600 square kilometres) it is bigger than Belgium, Holland, Denmark or Switzerland, bigger than the states of New Hampshire and Vermont put together, and is one of the two or three biggest reserves in the world. It lies in the middle of Botswana, in the centre of the Kalahari Desert, which is spread across seven countries – from the Congo, Angola, and Zambia in the north, to Zimbabwe, Botswana and Namibia in the centre, and South Africa in the South – covering in all some 463,338 square miles (1.2 million square kilometres). Unlike the Sahara and the Empty Quarter, the Kalahari does not meet the popular conception of a desert, much of it being covered by thick bush and trees, and criss-crossed by under-ground rivers. As a result, it supports a surprisingly wide variety of wildlife, including giraffe and the great antelopes, eland – revered above all others animals by the Bushmen – kudu and wildebeest; the handsome, curly-horned red hartebeest, the pronking springbok and stately gemsbok (oryx), which can survive without drinking, obtaining all the water they need from certain plants; and smaller antelope like the strongly territorial steenbok, which the Bushmen say has magical properties, a belief shared by Laurens van der Post; and the elusive duiker, always diving for cover – the name means diver, in Afrikaans. Inevitably, where there are antelope there are also predators – lion, leopard, cheetah and hyena – which are found all over the Kalahari, but not in every part of it.

The thick bush of the Kalahari also supports myriad birds, from the tiny wren-like cisticola and, most graceful of all, the Namaqua dove, with its rich chestnut and black markings and swerving speed, to the mighty Bateleur eagle and giant Kori bustard, the heaviest bird that flies, and which has to run to take off, lumbering across the sand like a jumbo jet. Being a desert, the Kalahari has its share of snakes and scorpions, one of the commonest and most poisonous being the puff adder, which lies in wait for its prey, well-camouflaged and motionless, unless you have the misfortune to tread on it, when its reaction is lightning swift, and potentially lethal. Menacing-looking but harmless are the big black dung beetles, Africa's compost-makers, which drone overhead like so many Chinook helicop-ters, scenting out their prey, which is dung, which they roll into balls and bury underground. Strangest of all is the praying mantis, usually small – although one species grows to 8 inches – stick-like and apparently insignificant, yet sacred to the Bushmen and the subject of innumerable myths.

However thick and luxuriant the bush, underneath it lies a great ocean of sand. The Kalahari is a vast saucer, into which over the aeons has blown sand formed by erosion until here, in the Central Kalahari Game Reserve, you are in the heart of what Bushmen call the Sandface, where the sun burns with devastating power, there is no surface water, and the unwary or the unfortunate can easily die of thirst. Because of the heat and lack of water, much of the Kalahari's wildlife is nocturnal. Among its most mysterious predators are the brown hyenas, although less so since their secrets were laid bare by the American zoologists, Mark and Delia Owens, in their fascinating study of the northern part of the Reserve, *Cry of the Kalahari*. Among the smaller predators are the pretty bat-eared and Cape foxes, with their beautiful thick brushes; black-backed jackals, trotting purposefully through the grass; yellow and slender mongooses; meerkats, another type of mongoose; ground squirrels, zorillas (striped polecats), black and white porcupines, ubiquitous spring hares, and, fiercest of all, the honey badgers which I glimpsed scuttling through the grass, eyes glowing like coals. Nearly all live underground where the temperature is lower and more constant.

Our last night in camp, I went to the village, and, sitting on the warm sand in the darkness, listened to a storyteller. He came from another village, and spoke Gana, which had to be translated into Nharo for our interpreter, Andrea, and then into English. He told a long and complicated story about a group of Bushmen who, out hunting gemsbok, come upon a strange animal, which keeps changing its shape; turning first into a stone, then a skin, then a human penis, and finally into water in a pot, which vanishes when the pot is broken. It was, said Andrea, a parable of greed.

I wondered if it was a commentary on the present plight of the Bushmen. Despair is driving them either towards the healing power of the trance dance, or, tragically, towards oblivion, and often death, brought about by alcoholism. Already, dispossession and serfdom on white- and black-owned farms in Botswana and Namibia have made them forget many of their myths and legends, some of the oldest known to man, as well as their ancient hunting and gathering skills. If Bushmen are not allowed to hunt, they cannot teach their children how to track game; and if there is no bush food in the new settlements, they cannot learn how to gather. Quite apart from the metabolic need for food, however, as George Silberbauer points out, the spoils of the hunt provide a means of expressing social relationships. 'To give or receive a gift of meat is to affirm not only the existence of a relationship, but to proclaim the state of its health – its emotional flavour. If denied these earnests of structure and sentiment, people are without the means to maintain their relationships, and confusion – eventually puzzled, frustrated hostility – takes the place of order and harmony, or order and balanced, comprehended animosity.'

For all these reasons, it seemed to me vitally important that the last free Bushmen of the Kalahari should not be driven out of the Reserve, but allowed to remain and to continue to exercise, as George Silberbauer recommended forty years ago, 'the right of choice of the life they wish to follow'. This book will attempt to show how the Bushmen, among the first inhabitants of Africa, the original 'noble savages,' as Jean-Jacques Rousseau might have conceived them, have been hounded and harried, decimated and destroyed, and finally exterminated, or consigned – the few who have miraculously survived – to the underworld we now find them in, surely one of the most terrible stories of the past millennium. But let us also hope, in the words of Laurens van der Post, that 'their story may yet help the redeeming moon in us all on the way to a renewal of life that will make now forever.'

CHAPTER TWO

A Louvre of the Desert

'Then, I really believed in the spirits of Tsodilo, Nom and Chokxam, but we don't worship anymore. . . . We think the spirits are dead.'

Kunta, Tsodilo, 1999

Tsodilo is the great rocky outcrop in north-west Botswana, once as sacred to the Bushmen as Ayers Rock, or Uluru, is to the Australian aborigines and one of the most spectacular galleries of rock art in Africa.

As we laboured through the heavy sand in our Land Rover, I caught sight in the distance of a great blue shape rising like some prehistoric monster from the flat expanse of the Kalahari Desert. I guessed this must be the largest of the four Tsodilo Hills named, in descending order of size, Male, Female, Child and North Hill.

Like many visitors to Tsodilo before me, I had read and been fascinated by *The Lost World of the Kalahari*, Laurens van der Post's account of his expedition to find and film the last of the Kalahari Bushmen. Although often accused of over-romanticising his search for the last 'true' Bushmen, van der Post writes so movingly and mystically that any criticism seems petty and misplaced. Born on a South African farm near the Great (Orange) River, and descended from a long line of Dutch and Huguenot settlers, van der Post grew up listening to stories about Bushmen from his grandfather, his aunt and other members of the large van der Post family. His fascination with Bushmen – the 'unique and almost vanished First People of my native land' – was to dominate much of his life, and so it comes as no surprise that he dedicated *The Lost World of the Kalahari* to the memory of his nanny Klara, 'who had a Bushman mother and nursed me from birth'.

When his guide, Samutchoso – not a Bushman incidentally, but probably an Mbukushu* – agreed to take van der Post to Tsodilo, he made a condition: there must be no shooting, no killing of game or anything else; that was the law of the Bushman gods, or the Spirits of the Slippery Hills, as van der Post calls them.

Van der Post gave his word willingly, but in the turmoil of organising the expedition, he forgot to tell his two companions, Vyan and Ben, who when on safari would often shoot for the pot. As they neared Tsodilo, with van der Post and his cameraman, Duncan, at the rear trying to film some zebra, two shots rang out ahead. Immediately, van der Post guessed what had happened. Ben and Vyan, unaware of Samutchoso's condition, had been making sure there was something to eat for supper.

Realising his mistake, van der Post immediately began to apologise, explaining it was his fault – he had forgotten to pass on the warning. Samutchoso said he sympathised but, as van der Post puts it, the implication was that it was not for Samutchoso 'either to understand or absolve'. There was nothing for it but to push on to Tsodilo as fast as possible and soon the hills came in sight, van der Post recalling the psalmist's words 'I will lift up mine eyes unto the hills from whence cometh my help.' In fact no help was forthcoming. They spent an uneasy night, and next morning, without warning, the camp was attacked by hordes of killer bees, every member of the party being painfully stung except for van der Post himself.

Later, as they made their first inspection of the hills, Samutchoso led van der Post to the foot of Female Hill, where his eye was caught by a magnificent, red eland bull high up on the rock face, gazing out across the Kalahari, 'painted as only a Bushman, who had a deep identification with the eland, could have painted him'. Below, and facing the other way, stood a female giraffe, motionless, as if alarmed by some predator. The rock face included several other animals and two blood-red

* Mbukushu are a Bantu-speaking pastoralist tribe. They arrived at Tsodilo two to three hundred years ago.

handprints, still vivid and fresh – the signature, van der Post presumed, of the unknown artist.

Soon afterwards, Duncan arrived, set up his tripod and began to film, only to find after a few seconds that the film magazine had jammed. He replaced it with another, restarted the camera, and, almost immediately, it too jammed. The same fate befell the third and last magazine he had with him. Protesting that he had never before experienced such a thing, Duncan went off thoroughly perplexed to reload his jammed magazines.

Van der Post continued to explore, finally coming to what he describes as 'the master of masterpieces among the Slippery Hills', a large rock face crowded with numerous paintings of animals. It was impossible to tell the age of the paintings, he says, but it was clear to him that he was in 'a great fortress of once living Bushman culture, a Louvre of the desert filled with treasure'.

Not long afterwards, he came to a recently-abandoned Bushman encampment, containing a few flimsy *scherms* and the usual detritus of animal bones, dried melon skins and other signs of hunter-gatherer occupation. The Bushmen had left only about a week before, according to Samutchoso, and would not return until the following winter. A little later Duncan reappeared, anxious to get down to work, only to be frustrated by yet another camera jam. That night the now thoroughly mystified cameraman stripped down all the magazines, cleaning and oiling them until he was certain that there would be no more problems. He was wrong. On the following two mornings not only was the camp again attacked by bees, but during filming one breakdown followed another, until eventually the camera itself gave up the ghost. At that point, van der Post writes, it seemed that 'the grim faces of the hills came near to laughter.' He decided to leave Tsodilo as soon as possible, before something else went wrong – he was worried in case the expedition's two Land Rovers also broke down, leaving them stranded.

Before he could leave, however, Samutchoso alarmed him further by announcing that 'the spirits of the hills are very angry with you', so angry that if they had not known his intentions were 'pure' they would have killed him. Van der Post, the old man said, had offended in a number of ways; he had not asked the spirits' permission to visit Tsodilo, neither had he made a sacrifice of food, nor prayed before drinking the waters. Impressed by the manner in which all this was said, as were his companions, black and white, van der Post asked what he could do to put things right, but for once Samutchoso could offer no advice.

That evening, their last at Tsodilo, van der Post sought inspiration on a solitary walk, and came face to face with a superb kudu bull carrying a great spread of 'curved Viking horn'. For several moments man and animal stared at one another in silence, before the kudu turned and disappeared into the bush. It reminded van der Post so vividly of the painting of the eland on the rock that an idea came into his mind and he hurried back to camp to consult Samutchoso. With his approval, van der Post immediately sat down and wrote a letter addressed 'To the Spirits, The Tsodilo Hills', beginning 'We beg most humbly the pardon of the great spirits of these Slippery Hills for any disrespect we may have shown them unintentionally . . .' and went on to ask their forgiveness. He had everyone in camp sign the letter – although some he admits were sceptical – put it in an empty lime juice bottle, and early next morning buried the bottle in a crack of the rock at the foot of the eland and giraffe painting which had made so great an impression on him. When he asked Samutchoso if he thought all would be well now, the old man consulted the spirits and then, as dawn broke over the Kalahari, announced, 'All is well, Master.' The spirits had relented.*

------

* There is an intriguing footnote to the story about the famous letter. Alec Campbell, an authority on Tsodilo, found it in its bottle, but some six yards to the left of where van der Post described leaving it. The message, written on the notepaper of the Victoria Falls Hotel, was similar but not identical to the wording in *Lost World*, which van der Post admits to quoting from memory. In addition, it bore only van der Post's signature, although van der Post says he made every member of the party sign it – leading Campbell to speculate that the others might have signed a separate piece of paper and later removed it. So many visitors had found the bottle and had been able to extract the letter that the paper had begun to fall to pieces, so Campbell decided to rescue it and place it in the museum. He went to the trouble of leaving a copy of the original in a bottle at the site, but later, he says, someone removed both the new message and the bottle.

On my first night at Tsodilo, I stayed at the foot of Female Hill in a small camp run by a young Scot, Andy McGregor, who for the next two or three days acted as my guide. On that first evening I paid my first visit to the Laurens van der Post panel. It was one of the most memorable occasions of my life to stand on that dusty road, in the hush of early evening, looking up at the slightly overhanging, honey-coloured rock face on which, although a good 30 or 40 yards away, the red eland bull stood out clearly and proudly, lord of all he surveyed, as he had done for hundreds, possibly thousands of years. In the days that followed, I saw many exciting paintings – the brilliantly realistic solitary lion, for example, and an equally unusual painting of a giraffe lying down. On one walk Andy led me along the base of Female Hill, where the acacia forest presses thickly against the mountain, and there half-hidden behind a huge chunk of rock, on another smooth, honey-coloured slab, stained pale mauve by age and weather, two magnificent rhinoceros with enormously long horns, a male above and a female with small calf below, caught and held my gaze. 'Look how they are painted with their heads right next to the crack in the rock,' Andy said. 'As if they are talking to the spirits of the hills.' The Bushmen believe in a mystical bond between humans and the animals, exemplified in their many animal dances, as well as in the all-important trance dance. 'You will see in the paintings how the shamans are often portrayed as having the head and the hooves of an antelope,' said Andy. To the left of the two rhinos, incidentally, is a much less interesting, and less well executed domestic cow, dating back a mere 200 years or so, and probably reflecting the arrival of pastoralists such as the Mbukushu, who settled in Tsodilo comparatively recently. There were still rhino at Tsodilo within living memory, I was told, but none, alas, are left today.

The realisation that a vibrant Bushman culture, capable of producing great art, existed at Tsodilo 2000 or 3000 years ago, was to me hugely exciting, and indeed Alec Campbell's* excavations at White Paintings Shelter show that Bushman ancestors lived there more than 30,000 years ago. That the first

---

* Alex Campbell is a former Director of the Botswana National Museum, Monuments and Art Gallery.

people of southern Africa should have been artists as well as hunter-gatherers belies the popular image that the Bushmen were ignorant savages. The Tsodilo paintings show them, on the contrary, to have been not only highly observant and exceptionally gifted; but also the possessors of a wonderfully earthy view of the world. At Tsodilo there is one painting which exemplifies this Rabelaisian streak, and its dramatic verve, after all these centuries, is astonishing. Known as the Dancing Penises, from the Bushman *Ta-shra*, and painted on a smooth rock face 8–10 feet above the ground, it has a great sense of movement and excitement, as well as being highly erotic. The scene depicts a score or so of nubile men, all with outsized, rampant penises, and a smaller number of women, displaying large breasts, as well as a domestic cow, engaged, according to Campbell, in some kind of ceremony, possibly a fertility ceremony. While I stood admiring the painting, which van der Post might well have called 'the master of masterpieces', Andy told me a disturbing story.

One day in 1998 he was in the vicinity of the Dancing Penises when he heard the sound of someone hammering on rock. Surprised and somewhat alarmed, he hurried towards the sound which led him along the path to the painting where, to his horror, he found a young Motswana with a geologist's hammer in his hand. He had just chipped away a piece of rock, measuring about 12 inches by 6, from the left-hand side of the panel. The chipping had left an ugly scar on the smooth surface of the rock, and was only about 10 feet from the nearest figures in the painting, which by any standards must rank as a national treasure. Andy remonstrated with the young man, saying he was endangering the paintings. This he strenuously denied, saying he was a geology student from Botswana University in Gaborone, and was merely collecting rock samples for his PhD. Andy, of course, had no way of knowing where else the young man had been 'taking samples', but he felt extreme concern that this individual was 'chipping off lots of stone without supervision'. He was accompanied by a local Mbukushu villager, who was carrying his bag, but not by any member of the museum staff. Andy was so incensed that he reported the incident to officials at the museum in Gaborone who, although they claimed to have warned the student not to touch rocks with paintings on them, merely said that the young man 'shouldn't have been doing that', and apparently took no further action. Even if they had, according to Campbell, the university would have told the museum that their students had the right to take samples. Campbell also points out that although the paintings are protected, Tsodilo itself is not a declared national monument, which makes it difficult to prosecute vandals.

One of the most blatant examples of vandalism concerned a local schoolteacher who scrawled his name in paint right across the eland in the van der Post panel. Because the museum was able to clean it successfully, however, the police refused to prosecute, on the grounds that no lasting damage had been caused. The worst case of all, according to Alec Campbell, occurred at the rhino panel when a tourist, believing the white, geometric paintings were graffiti, managed to destroy them with a wire brush. The freedom to wander at will, examining the wealth of rock art which lies round virtually every turn and twist in the path, allows the visitor to see Tsodilo undisturbed, in all its mysterious beauty. It seems to me, however, that such liberty – so rare in an age of mass tourism – has become a liability, and I came away feeling that more needed to be done to protect and conserve one of the greatest Bushman rock art sites in Africa. The museum has done some good work, for example by persuading the Botswana Defence Force to remove themselves from the area, but more needs to be achieved.

The Dancing Penises panel is only one of many outstanding paintings which could easily be damaged. In 1998 or 1999 the beautifully realised giraffe below the central eland figure in the Laurens van der Post panel had its neck and thigh scratched with some sharp instrument. This might have been done by a non-Bushman to obtain some of the red ochre paint for *muti*, African tribal medicine, or it might simply have been vandalism. Andy reported it to the local police who came to investigate, examined the visitors' book and told him that the two suspects came from Gumare, a Bantu-speaking, basket-weaving village to the south. Andy did not know if the police had taken any action. He also showed me a number of other disturbing examples of what

Hunting and gathering used to be the age-old way of life of the Bushmen. The men hunted and the women gathered.

'They came early in the morning stepping lightly through the bush. One carried a bow and a quiverful of arrows, each of the others had a spear. They sat down just beyond the camp, lounging in the pale golden grass, talking and laughing quietly.'

'Legs straddled in a business-like position, they dug with great energy, driving their pointed hard-wood sticks deep into the sand.'

'The sand had been smoothed, the fire heaped high, men and women ranged in separate groups in an expectant circle. Suddenly the women began to clap and sing, a wild, high-pitched, haunting sound which drew the men to their feet and into the dance, the old men shuffling, the young men stamping the ground, their steps fast and intricate.'

The trance dance is at the very heart of Bushman culture. In times of trouble it becomes especially significant, because of its quality of healing and the belief that it brings rain.

(*Above*) 'After a time, one or two women joined in, led by Ganema, who danced closer and closer to the flames, at one point picking up a live coal, and then, in a state of trance, falling headlong into the fire.'

(*Below*) 'When I saw Ganema next day, she smiled and pointed to her face and hands. Amazingly, there was no sign of any burns.'

Bushmen love dancing – and the women have their own dances.
(*Above*) Part of an initiation ceremony.
(*Below*) The Melon Dance. The trick is not to drop the melon.

(*Above left*) Young girl from Molapo: although poor and often in tatters, they all value their independence. (*Above right*) Bushmen women take their babies with them when they go gathering – looking for roots, tubers, berries and insects.(*Below*) Smoking early-morning pipes in the village of Skoonheid: Engau, the storyteller, and his wife Uia.

The junk and litter (*left*) of the modern world has sullied what was once a pristine environment.

(*Right*) Isaac, a Khomani Bushman from Welkom, South Africa, teaching his sons how to hunt. (*Below left*) After a busy morning foraging, this matron refreshes herself by squeezing a watery root, drinking some of the liquid and cooling herself with the overflow. (*Below right*) Mother and child, Molapo, Central Kalahari Game Reserve, Botswana.

(*Above*) About 800 Bushmen were evicted from Xade in 1997. Now it is a ghost village with the old huts gradually collapsing into the bush.

(*Below*) New Xade is outside the Central Kalahari Game Reserve. The Bushmen call it 'a place of death', because there is no bush food and no hunting.

seemed deliberate damage to some of the best-known paintings. Most had been given extra 'eyes'. That is to say some sharp instrument, like a knife or spike, has been used to chisel a small hole in the place where the animal's eye would have been – as a rule Bushman artists did not paint eyes. This did not appear to be mindless vandalism, because it had been done quite deliberately and carefully. It might have been the work of religious zealots trying to harness the spiritual power of the old Bushman gods – Andy found a ZCC (Zionist Christian Church) lapel button on Female Hill one day. Campbell, however, is sceptical, explaining that the museum had remonstrated with the ZCC for using one of the caves at Tsodilo and putting a noticeboard up outside it. Alec himself had had a two-hour meeting with members of the ZCC and had walked them round the sites. Thereafter, he was satisfied that church members respected the paintings.

In other cases, flakes of painted rock face – some small, some relatively large – appear to have been chipped off, as if someone had stood in front of the paintings and thrown stones at them. This might be natural flaking of the rock surface in some cases, but in most instances it seems to be deliberate. Whole flakes have been deliberately broken off the painting of the recumbent giraffe, for example, perhaps to obtain *muti*. Finding a solution is not easy, according to Alec Campbell. Many countries with a rock art heritage – from Algeria to Australia, and including the United States – have experimented with ways of protecting their paintings, but without much success: something as simple as a plastic skin does not seem to work. The answer, Alec Campbell believes, lies in a different direction: 'education and the involvement of local communities in their future conservation is vital,' he says.

At Tsodilo I felt I was in the presence of something which I can only describe as elemental, whether natural – the great rocks, the silence, the oppressive heat, the emptiness – or supernatural. On our last night I asked Andy if he believed Laurens van der Post's account of his misfortunes. 'Yes, I do,' he said, somewhat to my surprise. I asked him to explain. 'Well,' he said, 'something equally strange, and even worse, has happened to me.' Intrigued,

I asked him to go on. He then told me an extraordinary story. One day he and his wife had climbed to the top of Female Hill, where they found a cave with a view over the vast expanse of the Kalahari below. Bushmen must have lived in the cave, or at least used it as a lookout post, Andy guessed, judging by the number of pottery shards on the floor. He picked up one, rather handsomely decorated, and being interested in such things, slipped it into his pocket. 'From then on,' he said, 'everything started to go wrong.' That night he and his wife drove back to the small town of Shakawe, about 50 miles north of Tsodilo, where they were staying, and 'had the first row of our married life. And it was a terrible row.' It was also the night, Andy said, that his wife met the man 'to whom she is now married'.

His marriage having collapsed, the second disaster soon followed. As a dealer in African art and handicrafts, Andy was commissioned by a well-known London store to make a collection of artifacts for sale in England. 'I was paid up front,' he said, 'a lot of money.' He spent the next year or so assembling a large number of pieces from various parts of central and southern Africa, and all went well until the time came to ship the collection to Britain. Then things started to go wrong. His shipper's lorry broke down, and at the last moment, he had to find a substitute. He was in Malawi and choice was limited. 'I advertised in the local paper and got a reply. But when I saw the driver of the lorry I just knew it was wrong,' he said. 'He had a face that spoke of drink, drugs, and God knows what else besides. . . . He looked terrible, like the devil. I should have said no, but I was desperate so I hired him. We loaded the lorry, I went ahead to make the final arrangements, leaving this bloke to come on behind me, and never saw him again! He just disappeared, with all the stuff, £10,000 worth of it – gone, never to be seen again.'

It was a crippling loss and Andy became deeply depressed. He confided in a friend, wise in the ways of Africa, who urged him to return the piece of pottery. Andy had left it in a box in his warehouse, so he put the box in his car and drove to Tsodilo. It was only when he arrived that he found he had the wrong piece of pottery. 'The girls working in the warehouse must have been tidying up.' On his next visit to the warehouse, he found the original piece of pottery – and was dismayed to discover that somehow it had been broken. Only one shard remained. He returned to Tsodilo but, not having time to climb all the way to the top of Female Hill, left the piece of pottery in a crack in the rock, halfway up. That, he hoped, would end his run of bad luck, and for a time it seemed to have done so.

A year or so later, however, nemesis in the shape of the Botswana government dealt him another bitter blow. Although he had originally been given permission by the museum, which manages the Tsodilo site, to put up a temporary camp, another government department later objected that the camp was too permanent, and he was eventually evicted.

On the last occasion I saw Andy, I asked him if he had considered following Laurens van der Post's example by writing a letter of apology to the spirits. He confessed he had not. I suggested he should do so.

In the mid-1980s something else happened at Tsodilo which raised questions about the supernatural qualities of the 'sacred rock'. Whether one believes in such things or not, the facts are as follows: on 22 February 1986 a small detachment of SAS specialising in mountain warfare arrived on a training exercise. They made friends with the local Bushmen who took them on a tour of the hills and showed them some of the rock paintings. Even the SAS were impressed by the survival skills of the Bushmen. At one point, the Bushmen dug up a juicy root from deep in the Kalahari sand and offered it to their guests who were surprised at how good it tasted. That night most of the party turned in early, but the leader, Joe Farragher, and one or two others, decided to go hunting with a torch, apparently ignoring a warning from the Bushmen not to kill anything in the confines of Tsodilo – the same instruction that Laurens van der Post had been given by his guide. They killed a small animal, probably a spring hare, which they brought back to camp.

Next day, 23 February, was a typical Kalahari day, the sun blazing down on the ancient rocks from a clear blue sky. The SAS party split up into pairs, each pair choosing a section of

Male Hill as their climbing area. At about 2.30, Bill White (not his real name), a comparative novice, started to climb up over a huge rounded boulder at the foot of the hill. Having conquered the boulder he found himself at the foot of a sheer rock face, impossible to climb, and shouted to his companion that he was coming back. When he came to the last part of the descent he decided to jump to the rock where his companion was waiting on the rope. As he landed, he twisted his body to compensate for the steep slope – and dislocated his back. Paralysed, and in acute pain from a slipped disc, he was unable to move for what must have seemed an agonisingly long time before his companion was able to climb up and help him down. It took him about two hours to hobble back to camp, where the team's medic gave him an injection.

Soon afterwards, someone on the rock face was seen waving a red shirt, and word quickly spread that there had been a second accident, this time to Joe Farragher who, apart from being the team leader, was an exceptionally strong, experienced mountaineer. Farragher, leading his pair, had taken all the normal safety precautions, including using devices known as 'friends', which are pushed rather like fingers into the rock where they expand and anchor the climber. He was about to pull himself up by a handhold when the rock crumbled and gave way, not only the handhold but the 'friends' as well. He fell a long way, perhaps 90 feet down the face, ending up on a ledge. At that point, a heavy storm broke over Tsodilo, with thunder and lightning, a high wind and heavy rain which seriously hampered the rescue. In the two to three hours it took to get him down from the cliff ledge the temperature dropped sharply, from intense heat to bitter cold. A rescue helicopter arrived eventually, but too late to save Farragher, who died from his injuries. Later, Bill White told me: 'I wasn't superstitious before, but now . . .'

Alec Campbell points out that hunting in itself is not taboo: both the Bushmen and the Mbukushu hunt at Tsodilo. The crux of the matter, Campbell explains, is that before hunting 'a request must be made to the spirit in Male Hill'. This 'destructive spirit', of which Campbell tantalisingly adds that he has a 'fairly accurate description', is considered to have been responsible for the death in 2000 of a black herbalist who insisted on climbing the hills without a guide. He was found dead where he had fallen, having struck his head on a rock.

One day Kunta, a local Bushman who worked for Andy, took me to see a small rock, surrounded by bushes and small trees, which he called Baby Kama, just below the great, steep, soaring rock face of Male Hill. Kunta explained that before his father set out on a hunt, he and his companions would go to the rock to pray for success. This was taken seriously, because 'if we did not pray, it [the hunt] would not be successful.' Afterwards, if they had been successful, they would leave offerings to the spirits on the rock, either meat or honey – Bushmen love honey so much they will risk life and limb to get it. Kunta's habitual air of defeat and despair left him when he spoke of his life as a boy at Tsodilo, 30 or at most 40 years before. There was plenty of game then – eland, kudu, gemsbok – and a lot of Bushmen visited Tsodilo. Once when his father sent him to the spring on Female Hill to fetch water he found his way barred by a large snake, 'black and very thick', which he took to be either a python or a black mamba. So he ran back to tell his father, who 'invoked the spirits who called on the snake not to harm us'. When they went back to the spring, the snake had vanished.

'Then,' Kunta explained, 'I really believed in the spirits of Tsodilo, Nom and Chokxam, but we don't worship any more.' When I asked him why not, he replied, 'We don't believe it's ours any more, because the government, the white people, the tourists are there now. We go there only to take tourists. We think the spirits are dead. We feel very sad. We'd like it to be as it was in the old days. Those were the good days.' I persisted, asking him why he thought the spirits were dead. 'Because,' he said, 'of the arrival of the Mbukushu, of the white people, the people of the University [of Botswana] – we think they damaged the paintings – and the Batswana.* Our spirits . . . have either gone away or been driven away by the great wind of an evil spirit. They are nowhere now.'

---

* The ruling Tswana tribes.

At the end of their stay at Tsodilo, Samutchoso tells Laurens van der Post ruefully that the spirits of the hills are losing their power. Had van der Post and his party gone there in the same manner even ten years before, the spirits would have killed them all. It was a cry straight from the heart, van der Post says, and 'an example of the injury the coming of the European had done to the being and spirit of Africa'. Samutchoso's gods were dying from a contagion brought by the white man, and against which they had no immunity. He knew that, without his gods, life would lose its meaning. Fifty years later, Kunta was telling me the same thing.

Standing by the sacred well on Female Hill, Kunta spoke of the disaster which had overtaken his small band of 30 people.* Originally, they had lived in a small village near the base of the hills, but then in 1995, on the grounds that their camp was an eyesore, and that they were begging from passing tourists, but also because their cattle were inside the perimeter fence, which was intended to protect the environment and some of the lower paintings from the cattle, they agreed to move to another village, much farther away.

This meant that the men, who had previously acted as guides at Tsodilo, were worse off, and their wives had more difficulty selling their Bushman handicrafts. Although they had agreed to move – Alec Campbell attended the meetings at which they said they would go 'in their own time' – two of the elders complained to me about being pushed out. In the 1988 edition of *The Lost World of the Kalahari*, the same group of Bushmen are shown (p. 153) standing in the White Paintings Shelter, before several white, geometrical rock paintings, and are described in van der Post's caption as: 'A remnant of the true Bushmen, their evening shadows falling on the painted rock'. Gxauwe, in the middle of the picture, the only man in the village who still hunted, told me more than ten years later: 'We feel very bad in our hearts. They chased us out. The museum told us to move. We can't go back to where our grandparents are buried. I and my son were both born

---

* The present Bushman inhabitants are Juwa, who speak a Northern Bushman language, and arrived in Tsodilo comparatively recently, whereas the original inhabitants were Ncae, or Central Bushmen.

in the hills.' They were forced to move in the rainy season, he said with a rueful grin. 'We got very wet. When we arrived there were no houses.' For the loss of their homes, the elders said, and at least partial loss of earnings, each family was awarded 500 pula (£71), less than £10 a head. Alec Campbell disputes this, saying he was present when their huts and other belongings were assessed, and that they were paid in all 17,000 pula (£2428).

Kunta's genuine despair at the tragic decline in the Bushman way of life only became apparent when he talked about what had happened to the young men of the village. 'They don't hunt any more, they're like the Batswana, they like drinking more than hunting. They put their minds in the beer.' Every day they would go to the Mbukushu village to drink themselves silly, he said, returning late at night only to sleep. 'In the morning they go back to the Mbukushu village. We older people don't like what they're doing. We tell them not to do it, but it just causes a fight, and their parents are afraid of them. They are killing themselves.'

These young Bushmen made a small wage working on the roads, known in Botswana as 'drought relief', but immediately spent it on drink. 'They go straight to the Mbukushu [liquor seller] with 163 pula [£23.20], their month's wages, and give it straight to him for credit.' I asked Kunta how they bought food, or anything else. 'They almost never do,' he said. 'Only shoes.' For the rest, they lived off their parents or relatives. 'They are used to it now, the drinking, they like it now.' Even the missionaries were unable to stop them drinking, Kunta said. The police sometimes punished them, but they paid no attention. He could speak from experience. 'I used to drink. I stopped drinking after my first child was born. Now I've stopped, I have three cattle.'

In Alec Campbell's view, Kunta was exaggerating. Many of the young men, Campbell says, belong to an American mission-ary church and do not drink. It remains true, however, that alcohol has a destructive effect on Bushmen.* It also makes them fighting mad.

---

* In their allergic reaction to alcohol – or at least lack of tolerance to the effects of alcohol – Bushmen are similar to other indigenous peoples of the world, such as Australian aborigines.

'They are very violent,' Kunta continued. 'Last year, one chopped his wife with an axe and broke her jaw. She lost some of her teeth. Some relatives heard about it, and beat up the husband with their 'kerries on his head.' Both husband and wife were taken to hospital, and the two relatives who beat up the husband were fined 200 pula (£28.50) – more than a month's pay.

As we left Tsodilo, I wondered what fate awaited Kunta and his small band. They had already been reduced to the sorry state endured by most of the 50,000 or so Bushmen still left in Botswana: a people with no land, virtually no rights, no place in society except at the very bottom, and little if any future. Like the Bushmen of South Africa, once masters of all they surveyed, and now reduced to a mere handful, do they too face extinction? Or will the third millennium bring new life and hope to Africa's oldest people? These questions hung in the still air as we started our long journey across the deep sand of the Kalahari. From Tsodilo itself came no answer; only the eerie, plaintive calls of the grey and yellow-billed hornbills, as they swooped in their timeless trajectory through the acacia forests, as archaic and inscrutable as their surroundings.

CHAPTER THREE

The African Eve

The implications of DNA studies are that everyone in the world today can trace their ancestry back to an African origin. The unity of the human species is remarkable.

H.J. and Janette Deacon, *Human Beginnings in South Africa*, 1999

The origins of the Bushmen, as befits some of Africa's oldest people, are hidden in the mists of time or, as the anthropologists would prefer to say, in the fossil remains of their ancestors in sites all over southern Africa.

Small, mysterious, funny, brave and endowed with a beauty all their own, the Bushmen carry with them from their ancient past an innocence which has caught the imagination of many writers, poets and scholars. One of their mysteries is their click language. There are four main click language groups, none of them mutually intelligible. An offshoot of one of the four – Khomani – was thought until just the other day to have become extinct. Miraculously, it has survived, but only just: there are no more than a dozen speakers left. To hear Bushman men and women laughing and talking animatedly in a flurry of clicks, some as soft as an antelope's footfall, others as sharp as a stick snapping, delivered at such speed the untrained ear can hardly keep pace, is to step if only for a moment into another world.

Modern research can shed some light on their history, but much of their ancient world is now submerged, an African Atlantis. Today's Bushmen are almost the only surviving link with that pristine, pre-agricultural world of the hunter-gatherers, from whom we are all descended.

There are 100,000 or so Bushmen still left in southern Africa – just under 50,000 in Botswana, about 35,000 in Namibia, about 4,500 in South Africa, refugees* who fought for the South African

---

* There are also a few mainly in or near the Kalahari Gemsbok National Park.

army in Angola, and who were resettled near Kimberley, and a few thousand in Zimbabwe, Zambia, and finally Angola, where war has made any accurate assessment impossible. Bushmen are genetically distinct, according to anthropologists, because they were extremely isolated at 'the bottom of the bag' of Africa.

In their book, *Human Beginnings in South Africa*, Hilary John and Janette Deacon argue that at the earliest stage in their development, about 2.5 million years ago, the first 'true humans' were restricted to the African continent, and ventured into Eurasia only 1.8 million years ago. 'Africa,' they say, 'continued to be the evolutionary centre of humankind and to contain the bulk of the world's population until the explosive global expansion of our species, *Homo sapiens*, in the last 50,000 years.' We know this to be so, because it is in Africa that the oldest stone tools have been found, left behind in a 'trail of evidence' by our ancestors.

One of the most startling ideas to have emerged in the second half of the twentieth century is the suggestion that we are all descended from one 'African Eve'. This hypothesis, which is based on mitochondrial DNA research, claims that all humans are descended from one ancestor, a woman – because mitochondrial DNA is transmitted through the female line. Known as 'the lucky mother', she lived in Africa about 200,000 years ago. The final stone in the arch of the Deacons' argument is the astonishing conclusion: 'everyone in the world today can trace their ancestry back to an African origin.'

DNA research can even claim that the 'African Eve' belonged to a surprisingly small population of somewhere between 1000 and 10,000 women of child-bearing age, and that she came from Sub-Saharan Africa. Archaeological sites such as Klasies River and Border Cave have revealed not only the remains of the ancestors of modern humans but 'more specifically the ancestors of Khoisan [Bushman and Khoikhoi] peoples, who lived there more than 100,000 years ago'. It comes as no surprise therefore to learn that the genes of the Bushman hunter-gatherers, and of the Khoikhoi herders are, according to the Deacons, represented in all South African peoples. This must be true, too, of neighbouring countries including Botswana and Namibia, home of the Kalahari Bushmen. Indeed, writing of the Kalahari Bushmen, another scholar, Professor Alan Barnard of Edinburgh University, concluded: 'For our purposes, the present-day Bushmen ... can be regarded as the aboriginal inhabitants of southern Africa,' adding that the Gwi and Gana Bushmen of the Central Kalahari, whom he considers as being among the most isolated of all, have 'probably lived in their traditional habitat for many centuries if not millennia'.*

This is an important conclusion, because it unmasks the contention of today's Botswana government that *all* non-white inhabitants of Botswana are 'indigenous'. It also gives authority to demands from Bushman pressure groups for recognition of land claims to ancestral territory, including Botswana's Central Kalahari Game Reserve. One such claim may prove a landmark. In March 1999, after a five-year legal battle, the Khomani Bushmen of South Africa – who were believed to be on the verge of extinction – won a spectacular victory for the return of their traditional hunting grounds. This was a direct result of the Mandela government's decision to make good one of the many injustices of the apartheid regime, but it would never have happened if it had not been for the determination of two exceptional people, Cait Andrews, a Cape Town musicologist, and a human rights lawyer, Roger Chennells. By a series of remarkable coincidences they were able to exploit the key legislation, the Land Restitution Act, which the Mandela government introduced soon after coming to power in 1994. This enables tribes or communities who have been deprived of their land either to have it returned or to be given other land in compensation. In this case, the Khomani Bushmen, who were evicted from what is now the Kalahari Gemsbok National Park in Northern Cape Province, were given land next door to the park, bought for them by the federal government. The South African government's generosity was undoubtedly made easier by the fact that South Africa has very few Bushmen left: nearly

---

* From *Hunters and Herders of Southern Africa*, CUP, 1992.

all of them were exterminated in the course of more than 200 years of ruthless, mainly white colonialism.

The story of Cait Andrews begins in the dramatic setting of the Northern Cape. One hot sunny day in the early 1990s, she was walking across a bare, rocky hillside in the Karoo, a vast, semi-desert plateau which acts as a buffer between the great sand sea of the Kalahari, to the north, and the rich green vineyards of the Cape, to the south. The landscape held her in its spell. Cait was not alone, although her companion, a human rights lawyer, was out of sight behind a hill. Suddenly she stopped. Her eye had been caught by something moving in the bush. As she focused her gaze, a male springbok stepped into the open and stood looking straight at her. She stood equally still, mesmerised by the closeness and beauty of the animal, taking in his handsome brown and white coat, jet-black nose and liquid brown eyes. Judging by the spread of his horns, he was in his prime. But, as Cait well knew, once a springbok male has lost his harem of females to a younger, stronger rival, he faces a solitary and celibate future. Instead of turning and making off, as she expected, he advanced towards her. Then, calm and unhurried, he walked right past and disappeared into the bush beyond.

After a moment or two Cait herself walked on, thrilled by such an unusual encounter, with every sense alert. She climbed a small ridge, the slope leading her down into a shallow bowl-shaped depression where again her attention was held, this time not by a movement but by an inanimate object, or rather objects – four rocks. Something about their positioning and their relationship to one another drew her glance. Suddenly, the full realisation of what stood before her, as it had stood for perhaps thousands of years, rang in her mind with the sonority of the instrument itself. She knew intuitively, and beyond any doubt, that she was looking at a rock gong.

She had never before seen a rock gong, but as a musicologist she had read about them, and she knew they were created by Bushmen. She knew that sometimes rock gongs were merely single stones, sometimes they were composed of as many as four which was the case here. Recovering from her surprise, and in the grip of an excitement she had hardly ever experienced before, she picked up the stone beater lying next to the main rock and struck it. A few seconds later, startled by the majestic note of the rock gong, her lawyer friend came hurrying over the top of the adjoining ridge, to find Cait standing rapt in front of her discovery. For both of them it was a memorable occasion, but for Cait it was to prove a turning point in her life.

Cait knew that a rock gong can emit a note as clear and loud as a note on a piano. She knew, too, that it was probably man's oldest musical instrument, as mysterious as the blowing of the wind and as elemental as the earth itself. She also realised that the four stones she had found had been selected and brought to one place, and positioned so that a player sitting on the sitting stone could easily reach all the notes with the stone beater. The four notes were significant: doh, me, soh, and another doh, two octaves above the first. 'Just as a beam of white light can be split into a rainbow by a prism,' Cait says today, 'so a wave of sound can be split into harmonies by passing it through an echo chamber – the jaw harp, or Jew's harp, works like this. Just as the rainbow consists of a set and limited number of colours, so the "sound rainbow", the harmonic series, consists of a set and limited number of notes. Just as the primary colours are red, yellow and blue, so the primary notes of the harmonic series are doh, me and soh.' Her guess, at the time, based on the presence of some Bushman rock engravings nearby, was that the three notes of her rock gong were the three notes at the *root* of Bushman music. She was determined to find out.

A month or two later, drawn by what had become an obsession, Cait returned to the Karoo. It was as if she needed to reassure herself that what she had discovered really was a rock gong, and not a hallucination. She wanted to be sure that it was still there. This time she set out alone. She was nearing the hollow in the hills when, at almost exactly the same spot, a male springbok – possibly the same animal – stepped out of the bush and walked towards her. Cait stopped and watched motionless as the buck, calmly and unhurriedly, exactly as before, continued past her and without another glance disappeared from sight. To Cait, this was much more than a coincidence, it was a clear and unmistakable sign, and when a few minutes later she climbed the same small ridge and descended the same gentle slope and found the rock gong standing exactly as she had last seen it, as it had stood no doubt for centuries, she was both deeply moved and convinced that something of enormous importance had just happened to her.

In the weeks between her first and second visits, Cait had thought a lot about her discovery. It had intensified her real but rather vague interest in the Bushmen. She knew a little about their calamitous history and had always been strongly attracted by the spiritual side of their culture. This was hardly surprising as she came from a religious family – one of her ancestors was a well-known missionary in the Cape in the mid-nineteenth century, her father was a minister of the Anglican Church, and two of her brothers were also churchmen, one being Bishop of Cape Town. She was half Afrikaner, brought up to be bilingual – the family had a rule that one day a week only Afrikaans was spoken – and had been deeply impressed by the work of the great Afrikaner romantic, Laurens van der Post, and above all by his passion for the Bushmen.

Cait drove back to Cape Town across the Karoo with her thoughts in a turmoil, like someone who has just stumbled on a great secret. For mile after mile, following the road across the vast expanse of the high veld, the far horizon framed by purple mountains, her mood, she told me later, swung between doubt and euphoria. Uppermost in her mind was the question: were there any true Bushmen still left alive in South Africa, and if so, how could she find them?

Laurens van der Post had carried out his search for what he believed to be the last of the wild, or free, Bushmen in the 1950s. But that was in Botswana. In South Africa, as she knew, the Bushmen had been exterminated, mainly by Dutch settlers, commonly known as Boers or Afrikaners, and largely in the name of Christian civilisation. She knew too that some of her ancestors might have been involved. But, had any Bushmen survived this holocaust?

The question might have hung there unanswered, like some hidden Bushman cave painting awaiting revelation, had not something now occurred which was almost as strange in its way as Cait's discovery of the rock gong. Turning on the television one night, she found herself watching without much interest a popular current affairs programme called 50–50. Then in the space of a few seconds, her indifference changed to undivided attention as a group of small people appeared on the screen. A film report explained they had been found virtually starving in a squatter camp on the outskirts of the Kalahari Gemsbok Park, near the Namibian border. An Afrikaner farmer called de Waal had offered them food and lodging on his farm several hundred miles to the south, in return for staging a daily show for fee-paying tourists. The Bushmen had agreed – anything rather than starve. Dressed in skins, they sat round a camp fire, making bows and arrows and other Bushman handicrafts while the tourists looked on and took photographs. Cait listened with mounting excitement, noting down that de Waal's farm was at a place called Kagga Kamma in the Cedarberg, a spectacularly rocky area only a few hours' drive north of Cape Town.

As she switched off the television, she was already wondering about her next move. Should she go to Kagga Kamma? Were these 'true' Bushmen? Before she had decided on a plan of action, a friend told her that Laurens van der Post was arriving in Cape Town in a few days' time, and offered to effect an introduction. So it was that Cait found herself driving through the imposing gates of the Mount Nelson Hotel, and up the avenue of royal palms, to have afternoon tea with the great man in his suite. She told him of her discovery of the rock gong, and of her fascination with the Bushmen, partly as a result of reading his books, and asked for his advice. How should she, who had no knowledge of or experience in this sort of detective work, set about finding the 'true' Bushmen? What should be her next step? Impressed by her determination, van der Post encouraged her. 'Follow your nose,' he said.

Cait telephoned Kagga Kamma, booked herself in as an ordinary tourist, and played the 'honorary blonde'. 'Oh, I'm so interested in Bushmen, and I would love to meet them, do you think I could, apart from the tourist visit, just go and speak to them because I've got so many questions I want to ask them.'

Cait told me that it was still possible to do that at the beginning. Later, there were so many 'nut cases and cranks' who wanted to live like the Bushmen that the Kagga Kamma management actively discouraged personal contact between Bushmen and visitors. She managed, however, to 'squeak through', taking her two young children and paying 'the exorbitant price for a so-called chalet'. But she made certain she would be able to talk to the Bushmen on their own, without a guide. One of the staff drove her up to the small Bushman village in the hills, saying he would come back an hour later. He either forgot, or was busy, and left her there with the Bushmen for about three hours.

She arrived an hour before sunset. A little fire was burning outside one of the huts, and the head Bushman, Dawid, came out to greet her. He invited her in Afrikaans to sit on a sheepskin by the fire, appeared to change his mind, and then called two young girls over. 'He was on the other side of the fire from me, he was on the men's side, I was on the women's side of the fire, these two girls stood behind him and they watched me and their heads were moving and they were participating in some way, I wasn't sure what. At the end of this long conversation he dismissed them . . . and only as they moved away, the sun hit me full in the face.' The girls had been instructed to keep the sun out of her eyes. 'He'd wanted to move the sheepskin into the shadow but it was too late, I'd already started sitting. So he made a back-up plan . . . that's when I knew that they were true Bushmen, and I had goose pimples.'

Cait was struck by Dawid's good manners and his hospitality. She said: 'Always, anybody is welcome at a Bushman's fire.'

On the way to Kagga Kamma, she had passed a dead porcupine lying beside the road, and had stopped to pick up as many quills as she could, knowing Bushmen used them to make necklaces. They stank, so she had washed them. When Dawid stood up to say goodbye, Cait said she had some gifts, and gave him the porcupine quills. Dawid told her that a child had been playing with a candle in his hut two days before and a fire had started. Everything the Bushmen had brought from the Kalahari was burned. 'In fact they were wondering where they would find porcupine quills, and next thing here was a woman with what they'd asked for. So that put me on the list, so to speak.'

Dawid and some of the others listened to her description of the rock gong, and then, she told me, virtually said, 'Where the hell have you been all this time? We have been waiting for you.' When she asked them about the springbok they replied: 'It was either the god or the guard.' Later she asked about the trance dance, and altered states of consciousness, which interested her very much, but Dawid was evasive.

On her next visit, Cait bought some meat as a gift, and not long after she arrived a young woman started singing. It was Oulet, Dawid's daughter. 'She started the trance dance song. I'd never heard it before [but] I knew instantly what it was, and the first three notes to split the air were doh, me, soh, the three notes of the rock gong! They then proceeded to do a full trance dance . . . it was one of those occasions that could have been any time in the past 25,000 years, and there was trance and there was healing.' Cait had been told she could film and photograph anything she wanted, but as the trance dance began she was asked to put her camera away, not because they objected to it being filmed but because they were worried about damage to the camera – a strange echo of the experiences of Laurens van der Post's cameraman at Tsodilo.

Cait cannot remember exactly when the Bushmen raised the question of legal assistance. One day, however, she attended a meeting at which every household was represented, which meant that 'something was up'. Both men and women had their say, although the women preferred to stay in the background. 'It's not that the women are all disempowered. They don't like to have the front voice, they like to have the back voice. For them that is more powerful.'

Gradually, as they began to know and trust Cait, the Bushmen started to air their grievances. They believed that relatives were being turned away at the gate and that the management might be listening in to their telephone calls. They had been told by de Waal that they could hunt, but 'we can't follow a spoor over rocky ground.' They wanted more to eat. 'They didn't mention the *dop* or tot system . . . but they were given wine as part payment. They already knew, although they had been there only for a month or two, that Kagga Kamma was not going to be their home. 'They said, "Here we are *vasgedruk*, trapped between a rock and a hard place, and we don't know what to do. Please will you find us some land?" They not only needed land, they needed "a country to roam around in", and a *prokureur*, a lawyer, which I interpreted as a human rights lawyer, who could negotiate with de Waal. "We'll pay, we'll pay, we can pay, we Bushmen have money."

'I don't think they had any idea what a lawyer's fee might be,' said Cait. Dawid was aware of the Bushmen's powerlessness when it came to negotiations, admitting, '"We see now we can't read contracts. We can't, in other words, fight the West at its own game. We need a school for our children so they will be able to read. Will you help us?" So I said, "Yes, I will." And now, how many years down the track, and we're still at it, but getting somewhere.'

Cait's friend, who was with her when she discovered the rock gong, was also a musician, a fellow student of Zen Buddhism, and a human rights lawyer, who ran Lawyers for Human Rights at the Karoo Law Clinic. He referred to himself as 'the farmers' friend', Cait said with a laugh. 'So I immediately phoned him and said, "Can we do this?" and he said, "I'll come and see."' Cait booked herself and her lawyer friend into Kagga Kamma as ordinary tourists, and took him to meet the Bushmen. 'With his Zen mind, he was very easily able to get to the bottom of the story, to sum up what the position was, what their questions were, and what they wanted.' He lived too far from Kagga Kamma to take the case, but suggested instead another lawyer, Roger Chennells from Stellenbosch, who had already agreed to help in principle.

Once more Cait embarked on the now familiar, but always spectacular journey through the Cedarberg of the Western Cape to Kagga Kamma, where a surprise awaited her and Roger Chennells.

Working at the lodge, there was a new chief guide, Michael Daiber, whose job included responsibility for the Bushmen. 'We were sitting and I was assessing him to see if I dare tell him that my companion was a human rights lawyer. We were talking very quietly and pussy-footing around each other, and this guide turned to me and said: "Please don't blow this because I'll lose my job. But we need a human rights lawyer and I don't know where to find one."' When she had recovered from her astonishment, Cait introduced Roger Chennells. 'Everybody seemed to be at the right place at the right time at the right point.'

While Cait Andrews was engrossed in the problems of the Khomani Bushmen of the Northern Cape, 1000 miles to the north a very different personality was about to become caught up in the future of the Botswana Bushmen. John Hardbattle, a gregarious, forty-seven-year-old rancher with an infectious laugh, was the son of a Yorkshire father and a half-Bushman mother. Born in Bechuanaland and brought up in England, he had returned in 1973 to the country of his birth* where his mother Khwa still lived, to run the family farms. One day in 1992, on a farm named Jakkalspits, 15 miles from Ghanzi, the hot, dusty, beef-ranching capital of Botswana, a historic meeting took place. The man who came to see John Hardbattle that Sunday afternoon was a relative of his mother, a wise old Bushman called Khomtsa Khomtsa. Although he can hardly have realised it at the time, Hardbattle was being asked to give up his bachelor life of shooting and parties to devote himself to the daunting task of leading his mother's people in their struggle for equality and justice.

In the poetic phrases of his native Nharo (which Hardbattle had learnt from his mother as a boy) Khomtsa Khomtsa explained his mission. He had been trying to speak to people in authority for many years but nobody would listen to him. Hardbattle recalled later: 'He told me that he had written to Queen Elizabeth pointing out that when you [the British] came to our land you saw the eland and the gemsbok, the grasses and the trees, but you recognised only the black man. You never saw us – maybe because we are so small – but we were always there

---

* Now Botswana.

with the land and the grass and now you have given the black man our land and today we have no rights, no land. We would like you please to see us now and to give us back our land and our rights to live there.' Khomtsa Khomtsa then asked a question which was at least partly rhetorical. 'Whose land is this?'

There was little doubt in Hardbattle's mind about the answer, nor in Khomtsa Khomtsa's. They both knew that the Bushmen were the original inhabitants of much of Africa, and had hunted and gathered across these plains and deserts for longer than anyone could remember. Why was it, then, Khomtsa Khomtsa wanted to know, that the Botswana government persistently discriminated against the Bushmen, refused them their rights and took away their land? Even in the Central Kalahari, where Bushmen had lived virtually in isolation for thousands of years, the government was now saying they had no rights, and must leave and move to government settlements. He, John Hardbattle, Khomtsa Khomtsa said, was the only man who could put the Bushman case. The Bushman, who could not speak English and could neither read nor write, was being cheated by the white man and the black man alike. Would John Hardbattle accept the challenge?

At first, according to people who knew him well, John Hardbattle was very reluctant. He was already heavily committed, and Khomtsa Khomtsa had to use all his powers of persuasion. In the end, no doubt influenced by his mother, for whom he had a deep affection, John agreed. He knew from his own observations that most Bushmen had become a landless underclass, prone to disease, despair and alcoholism. He knew, too, from his own experience, the tragic history of the Bushmen of Southern Africa. And he knew, from his very own genes, what it felt like. Although his father, Tom Hardbattle, was in his lifetime one of the wealthiest cattle ranchers in Ghanzi, his children – John, his brother and two sisters – were classed as Coloured and looked down on as half-castes.

They began to make plans. An organisation, First People of the Kalahari, would promote the Bushman cause, presenting their case to the Botswana government at home, and to foreign governments and international organisations abroad. They would use a small house in Ghanzi, which belonged to the Hardbattles, and was only an hour's drive from the farm at Jakkalspits, as the First People's office.

John now threw himself into the new venture with all the energy and enthusiasm he seemed to be able to summon up at will. He travelled the country, talking to Bushmen round their fires, eating with them, hunting with them, sleeping under the stars. He made repeated visits to the Central Kalahari Game Reserve, telling the Bushmen there to stand firm against the government's attempts to move them from land their ancestors had lived on for centuries to bleak resettlement camps.

Hardbattle's name became increasingly familiar in the local press, especially in the liberal and outspoken *Okavango Observer* – later to be silenced – then on the radio and television in South Africa, Britain, and finally the United States, to the growing concern and irritation of the Botswana government. As the confrontation with President Masire's men became more acrimonious, John Hardbattle and First People came under increasing government surveillance as subversives; their telephones were tapped, and their visitors monitored.

First People's demand for land rights inside the Central Kalahari Game Reserve caused especial ire, since diamonds had been discovered at Gope. Hardbattle's crime, in short, was to challenge the supremacy of the ruling Tswana cattle barons, of whom Masire was a leading light.

In 1996, John Hardbattle undertook several important trips abroad. In London, Lucia van der Post, Sir Laurens's daughter, wrote an article about him in the *Financial Times*. 'You cannot imagine,' he told her, 'the discrimination which our people have suffered, the loss of dignity, of culture, of rights. We were regarded as less than human.' He remembered as a child running away from anthropologists who came from Witwatersrand University in Johannesburg to measure and study him because they could not believe that white people, 'real people', could breed with the Bushmen.

He also remembered 'the giving and sharing' among Bushmen, although, now, 'the links and the networking have been broken, and the Bushmen live in scattered, small, dismal settlements, which they called places of death. There is no work, no way of life, no hunting to be done, no journeys to be made, no singing, no dancing. They sit out their days doing what disenfranchised, dispossessed, nomadic people do all over the world: they drink, they beg, they rob, they somehow try to endure the endless barren days. Their children learn idle, thieving ways. They are deprived of dignity, of purpose, of language, of culture.'

In the short space of two or three years, John Hardbattle had blazoned abroad the threat to the Bushmen of the Central Kalahari Game Reserve, reaching a worldwide audience, and enlisting the support of many influential sympathisers and donors. Despite the hectic pace of his life, he somehow found time to fall in love with a number of attractive women, having a son by one, and a daughter by another. Alas, just as his daughter was being born in the summer of 1996, John was diagnosed with cancer, and died only a few months later.

The Botswana government, which had been forced by his campaign to postpone if not abandon its attempts to evict the Central Kalahari Bushmen from their ancestral lands in the Reserve, returned to the attack in early 1997. In the summer of that year about 1100 people including virtually the whole population of Xade, the biggest village in the Reserve, were deported, mainly to a bleak settlement called New Xade. There was no bush food, and water had to be pumped in from a borehole 40 miles away.

John Hardbattle's premature death – he was only fifty-one – was a grievous blow to the Bushman cause, and First People has never really recovered. But the flame of resistance he engendered, particularly among the Bushmen of the Central Kalahari, still burns brightly. He has also left behind an awareness of just how important is the survival of the Bushmen, not just to themselves, and not just to Africa, but to the entire world. Five years after his death, the real battle to save the Bushmen is now taking place.

Part Two

Village life

CHAPTER FOUR

Colonisation by Mistake

I find the thought of what black and white did to the
Bushman almost more than I can endure.

Laurens van der Post, *The Heart of the Hunter*, 1961

The end of the fifteenth and the beginning of the sixteenth
centuries were the high-water mark of European seafaring
exploration and discovery. While Portuguese navigators circled
Africa and blazed a trail to India and beyond, a brilliant Genoese
in the pay of Spain, Christopher Columbus, who also thought he
was opening a route to the East, was in fact sailing the Atlantic
to discover the Caribbean and South America. When Columbus,
who styled himself 'Admiral of the Ocean Sea', first sighted Cuba
he thought it was Cathay, and sent a delegation ashore to find a
representative of the Great Khan. But eccentric though his ideas
of geography may have been, Queen Isabella of Spain believed in
him, and in 1492 backed his expedition to 'the Indies'. His return
a year later with a cargo of gold and Indians caused a sensation,
not only in Spain but throughout the rest of Europe. The
Admiral of the Ocean Sea had indeed discovered a 'New World',
and confounded his critics.

At the time Columbus was discovering the 'West Indies' and
the Americas on behalf of Ferdinand and Isabella, Bartolomeu
Dias and Vasco da Gama were opening up Africa and the East
for the successors of Prince Henry the Navigator. In 1488,
Bartholomeu Dias became the first man to sail the length of
Africa. He was unable to get as far as India – a contemporary
said that like Moses he was prevented from entering the
Promised Land; but when he reached the southern tip of Africa,
he named it 'Good Hope, for the prospect it gave of the
discovery of India'. Ten years later, a fellow Portuguese, the
'fiery aristocrat' Vasco da Gama, completed Dias's great voyage

of discovery by sailing all the way from Lisbon to the Cape, up the east coast of Africa to the port of Malindi and from there, guided by a local pilot, across the Indian Ocean to the west coast of India. Thus was discovered the sea route from Europe to the East.

Between them, these two intrepid sailors revolutionised Europe's trade with the East, the newly discovered Cape route replacing the ancient Silk Road along which camel caravans had carried silk, ceramics and spices from China to the Mediterranean, and gold, silver and other products of European technology back again. In 1500 another Portuguese, Cabral, reached India by way of Brazil, sailing across the Atlantic and back again, rounding the Cape and finally reaching India. The year 1509 saw the arrival of the Portuguese in Malacca, a prosperous port on the south-west coast of the Malay peninsula. In 1512–13 Antonio de Abreu landed in the Moluccas, the Spice Islands. And from 1519 to 1522, in a crowning triumph for Portuguese seamanship, Ferdinand Magellan, and after his death, Juan Sebastian Elcano, a former mutineer, made the first circumnavigation of the world. By 1557 the Portuguese had established themselves as far afield as Macao, on the South China mainland.

In the second half of the sixteenth century the Portuguese began to run into stiff opposition. The British were the first to found an East India Company to exploit the rich pickings of the East, and were followed two years later by the Dutch East India Company, which established its company headquarters at Batavia, later Jakarta, on the island of Java in 1619. In the heavily-populated East, where large land empires controlled much of the trade, European sea power was crucial. Dutch maritime mastery enabled them to corner the hugely profitable trade of the Spice Islands, and by 1641, when they took Malacca from the Portuguese, they had succeeded in driving both the Portuguese and the British not only from the East Indies, but from Malaya and Ceylon as well. India was, however, another story: the Portuguese hung on to Goa, and the British to Bengal, eventually gaining dominion over most of India.

As their distant empire grew, the Dutch East India Company began to cast around for a suitable revictualling station where their ships' crews, always prone to scurvy, could take on supplies of fresh meat, fruit and vegetables as well as water, and recuperate from the long outward and homeward voyages. They did not have far to look. The obvious place, they decided, lying halfway between Holland and Batavia, was the Cape of Good Hope, a decision at least partly encouraged by the knowledge that the crew of a Dutch East Indiaman, wrecked in Table Bay in 1647, had built a fort and survived there for a year before being rescued. So it came about that on 6 April 1652, the envoy of the Dutch East India Company, Jan van Riebeeck, arrived from Holland at the head of a small expedition in his flagship, *Drommedaris*, and dropped anchor in Table Bay.

The ripples of his arrival were to spread farther, and have a more profound effect than either he or the solid Dutch burghers who sent him could possibly have foreseen. The impact on the indigenous people of the Cape was to prove catastrophic. In the course of the next 150 years van Riebeeck's settlers and their descendants, known as Afrikaners after their adopted country, impatient of any authority except God's and their own, expanded north and east relentlessly, in search of land and the holy grail of personal freedom. In the process, they destroyed the indigenous Khoikhoi and Bushman populations, slaughtering the men and enslaving the women and children, until by 1850 only a handful were left. All this was done, Bible in one hand – for these Dutch settlers were devout Calvinists – rifle in the other, in the name of Christian civilisation. Today we would call it genocide.

Ironically, the men who sent out van Riebeeck, the directors of the Dutch East India Company, had never intended to colonise the Cape of Good Hope. In fact, so strict were van Riebeeck's instructions that he should have no contact – apart from trade – with the local population that he planted a thick bitter-almond hedge all round the settlement, part of which you can still see today in Cape Town, most impressively in the Kirstenbosch Botanical Gardens, at the foot of Table Mountain.

Being traders who were interested almost entirely in profit, the Heren XVII – the seventeen directors of the Dutch East India

Company – repeatedly urged van Riebeeck to keep his costs down; he wanted 163 men to run the settlement and man the fort, the Company insisted on no more than 100. So in 1656, four years after his arrival, he complied with orders from Amsterdam and laid off the first nine 'freeburghers', settling them on 28-acre farms on the banks of the Liesbeeck River. The only people who were upset by this arrangement were the unfortunate Khoikhoi, whose traditional lands these were. As Allister Sparks explains in his history of apartheid, *The Mind of South Africa*: 'Any thought that the land might belong to the Khoekhoe, that their age-old usage gave them a prior right to it, or at least the right to be consulted about its expropriation, simply never occurred to the settlers. Van Riebeeck's instructions were not to become involved in disputes with the Khoekhoe, yet he commandeered their land for the "freeburghers" and was astonished and aggrieved when they took exception to this and rose up to fight black South Africa's first war of resistance. When the brief conflict was over van Riebeeck lamely claimed title to the land by right of conquest.'

In a remarkably frank account of the first Dutch-Khoikhoi war that he sent to his employers in Amsterdam, van Riebeeck wrote: 'The reason advanced by them for making war on us . . . [was] that they think they had cause for revenge . . . upon people who had come to take and occupy the land which had been their own in all ages.' They insisted so strenuously on the return of their land, van Riebeeck continued, 'that we were at length compelled to say that they had entirely forfeited that right, through the war which they had waged against us, and that we were not inclined to restore it, as it had now become the property of the Company by the sword and the laws of war.' Thus was established, Allister Sparks comments, the right of conquest and a tradition that the land was the white South Africans' for the taking – 'the first act in a long process of land dispossession that combined with slavery and cheap labour to create the institutions and the habits of the apartheid society'. Not long afterwards, more freeburghers began moving inland beyond the reach of the Company, 'gobbling up the land they believed they were freely entitled to'. As their numbers increased, there occurred at the southern tip of Africa, as Allister Sparks puts it, 'one of the most remarkable settlements in the history of colonialism. A small and scattered community of white men drifted beyond the effective reach of any law or administrative arm and lost themselves like so many Robinson Crusoes in the vastness of Africa for a century and a half.'

These were the trekboers. They had no books and no schools, only the great States Bible which each family carried with it and read from with increasing difficulty, as literacy dwindled, laboriously intoning the complicated High Dutch phrases in which the word of God was written. This was the God of Abraham talking directly to his people, and every word was taken as the literal truth. One South African historian, Leo Fouche, has argued that given the conditions of life in the first 50 years of the Cape Colony, the emergence of the trekboers was almost inevitable. The trekboers were oppressed by the Company and hungry for land. They suffered from labour shortages and agricultural difficulties. There was a limited market for their livestock. No wonder they succumbed to the 'relative ease of acquiring Hottentot cattle'. By the end of the seventeenth century these trekboers were already the spiritual fathers of the Voortrekkers, ready to achieve their historical mission, which was 'to make of South Africa a white man's country'. As they lumbered off over the veld in their creaking oxwagons they bore with them, along with the Bibles, their guns, a few essential household possessions, and a plethora of preconceptions. They were convinced, for instance, that the indigenous Africans they met were all 'savages'. This was exemplified to the primly Calvinist Afrikaners by their 'nakedness', 'dirtiness' and 'foul habits'. To European ears the word Hottentot itself sounded outlandish. But then it was a derogatory European invention, deriving – according to one early English visitor, Edward Terry – from their click language, which sounded like the 'clucking of hens or the gobbling of turkeys'. It was not the name they used themselves, which was Khoekhoe (or Khoikhoi) – 'the real people' or 'real men'.

The other indigenous inhabitants of the Cape, the Soaqua, or Sonqua, were hardy hunter-gatherers. They and the Khoikhoi probably shared a common ancestry – they both spoke click languages – but they had developed separately, the Khoikhoi as more sedentary pastoralists, the Soaqua as semi-nomadic hunters. When the Dutch discovered that they did not keep animals but lived by hunting and gathering, and were despised even by the Khoikhoi, they gave them the name of 'Bosjesmans' or Bushmen, and concluded they were less than human. Being Calvinists, the Dutch believed in predestination, the division of souls into the Elect and the Damned, the former being the few God would save and the latter the rest of mankind who would perish in the flames of Hell. To the simple Afrikaner settler, it was a doctrine easily translatable into Christian and heathen, white and black, and it followed all too naturally that those to be saved were God's chosen people. With an unassailable belief in their own superiority went a horror of miscegenation – adulterating the purity of their stock. 'There is no trusting the blood of Ham,' declared one group of wealthy Stellenbosch burghers in 1706, listing among these untouchables 'Kaffirs, Mulattoes, Mesticos, Casticos and all that black brood living among us, who have been bred from marriages and other forms of mingling'. It was hardly surprising that, given the settlers' bigoted and racist views of Africa and the Africans, friction between them and the local population should so easily and frequently turn to violence. The second Dutch–Khoikhoi war began in 1673 when a group of Dutch hippopotamus hunters were killed by a group of Bushmen allegedly in the service of a Khoikhoi chief of the Cochoqua clan. The Dutch retaliated with overwhelming force and at the end of hostilities the Cochoqua had lost nearly 1800 head of cattle and 5000 sheep.

Under van Riebeeck's successors, Governor Simon van der Stel and his son Willem Adriaan, and on orders from Amsterdam, the Company made a determined effort to become self-sufficient in food production, especially meat, thus reducing its dependence on Khoikhoi cattle owners. To attract new settlers, the Company offered Dutch families free passage to the Cape and free land on arrival. As a result, the colony found itself expanding at 'an irreversible and unprecedented rate', according to Nigel Penn, in his masterly history of *The Northern Cape Frontier*

Zone, 1700–c. 1815. As an added incentive, the freeburghers or trekboers who had always been forbidden to buy cattle from the Khoikhoi were now actively encouraged to do so, a policy which was to have disastrous consequences for the Khoikhoi, and ultimately the Bushmen as well. In 1700, Willem Adriaan van der Stel gave permission for new farms to be established and grazing licences issued in an area called the Land van Waveren, a fertile valley and ideal cattle country, some distance from Cape Town. Alarmed and angered by this new threat of dispossession, the Khoikhoi reacted with determination.

The third war, which began in 1701, established what was to become a familiar pattern; in retaliation for the theft of their land, the Khoikhoi launched bold, night-time raids on Dutch farms, stealing or killing as many of the settlers' livestock as possible. In revenge, the Dutch hunted down and killed the raiders, although they proved hard to catch, and seized their cattle, which inflicted crippling damage on the Khoikhoi economy. Governor van der Stel encouraged the policy of hot pursuit, sending soldiers on horses into the worst areas, and eventually the Company's tactics produced a string of successes. In one typical engagement a Company corporal and his men succeeded in killing and wounding 20 'Bosjesmans'. By 1705 the war was over. The governor decided it was time to hold peace talks and summoned a number of Khoikhoi captains – headmen backed by the Company – to his headquarters at the Castle in Cape Town. There, in return for an agreement to stop raiding and stealing Company livestock, the governor confirmed some captains in office, and appointed others, handing each a copper-headed staff of office. At the end of the meeting, he distributed gifts of beads and tobacco which he hoped would be enough to maintain 'the peace which that [Khoikhoi] nation calls Sam Sam'. Such hopes would soon prove illusory, not least because of the 'shocking' behaviour of the Company's settlers in the interior, as the governor learned from a secret report.

Gangs of colonists, 40 or 50 strong, armed and financed by freeburghers, had been raiding up to 100 miles inland, attacking Khoikhoi and Bushman communities with 'violence, murder and death' and stealing large numbers of their livestock. One group of 45 freeburghers of 'the worst sort' had returned with more than 2000 cattle, having sworn themselves to secrecy during what they euphemistically described as the Christian Voyage. Convinced that these raids were a direct cause of many of the attacks on Company property, being Khoikhoi acts of revenge for the theft of so much of their own livestock, van der Stel immediately suspended all livestock trading by freeburghers and ordered an inquiry. Nothing came of it, however, as by his own admission, 'so many of the settlers were implicated in the affair that half the colony would have been ruined.'

Having swallowed up practically all the Khoikhoi land, the trekboers were beginning to put pressure on the vast 'empty' spaces which had been Bushman hunting grounds for thousands of years. Like the Khoikhoi before them, the Bushmen retaliated in the only way that was open to them, by attacking the settlers' livestock. In 1715, Bushmen in the Waveren district raided cattle on several settler farms, and although a number were shot dead, they managed to wound one farmer in the leg with an arrow. As they retreated, they shouted defiantly that they would return and the farmers would not be able to catch them because they would hide in the highest mountains. A few weeks later, they raided another white farm, carrying off 700 sheep and kidnapping the shepherd, a slave. The freeburghers began to take reprisals into their own hands. The Bushmen launched yet another attack, stealing cattle and sheep and driving them at such speed across the mountains that the pursuing party, led by a Company sergeant, could not catch them. After a two and a half day chase they managed to recover only one wounded cow, and find six dead cattle and 200 dead sheep. Of the three herders who had been with the animals, two were killed and the third kidnapped.

Rumours swept the isolated settler community that *Bosjesmans* were planning a concerted attack on white farms. The mood grew panicky. The settlers of Waveren were so terrified they had to sleep with their firearms in their hands. Under mounting pressure the governor agreed that a commando of freeburghers should be formed to hunt down the robbers, and undertook to supply the gunpowder and the ammunition. He also, however improbably, counselled restraint, urging the commando not to do anything that might embitter any further this 'brutal and barbaric people'.

Freeburgher commandos had been operating in secret for some time, but this was the first time one had been officially authorised, with the government 'legitimising independent civilian retaliation' and paying for its members' ammunition. The commando, consisting of a leader, his deputy and 22 freeburghers, set off for the Kruis River in December 1715, and a week later found a *kraal*, or encampment, of 'at least' 14 Bushmen.* Next morning, the commando having crept up on the *kraal* overnight, fighting started. The Bushmen defended themselves with bows and arrows and assegais, but eventually numbers and firepower told, and despite one of the burghers being wounded when his musket exploded in his hands, the battle seemed over. As two members of the commando charged forward in thick bush, however, one was stabbed through the leg with an assegai, and the other had his belly slit open. Dragging him to safety, his comrades stuffed his entrails back in his stomach and crudely stitched him up, but to no avail – he died a few days later. The Bushmen meanwhile had disappeared, leaving behind 84 cattle, 214 sheep, 8 women and 9 children. One of the captured women was sent forward with an offer to make peace, but was sent back to deliver a defiant 'No'.

Although many of the Bushmen raiders had been shot, the survivors, according to Penn, were 'vengeful rather than vanquished'. A few days later the same group launched another attack on the commando, killing two cows with arrows and wounding several more and two horses. Again the settlers tried to parley, sending one of the women forward to ask the men why they refused to make peace. The answer she brought back was that as long as the commando continued to hold their women and children hostage, the white men would not get home alive, and since the approaching night was going to be moonless, they would have 'lots to think about'.

As a gesture of compromise, the commando released three of

---

* The real figure turned out to be considerably higher.

the women prisoners with gifts of tobacco – always the way to a Bushman's heart – but even that failed to mollify them, and they replied scornfully they would be waiting for their enemies when they returned to Roodezand, the farm belonging to one of the freeburghers. True to their word, when the farmer reached home a few days later all his cattle had gone. Eventually, honour perhaps being temporarily satisfied, a Company representative sent to patch up the quarrel reported that the Bushmen were tired of stealing and anxious for peace; and had even made a request to be given Company staffs of office. It would turn out to be a transitory interlude in the long-running frontier war. Nothing could stop the steady encroachment by the trekboers on what little land remained to the Khoikhoi and Bushmen.

In 1726 the Heren XVII of Amsterdam received a message from the Cape which stated that, apart from a single hut or two, no Khoikhoi were living within '50 or 60 miles' of the colony; many had died of European diseases, and the few survivors had 'receded far inland, in order to save their trifling herds of cattle from the mortality which has been raging here some years ago'. No recognition, nor indeed remorse, here for the role of the Dutch themselves in virtually wiping out the once flourishing Khoikhoi population of the Cape. In the second quarter of the eighteenth century, the settlement continued its 'irresistible expansion', and by 1732 the entire length of the Oliphants River – 150 miles north of Cape Town – had been colonised by white farmers.

Resistance continued, however, on the flat, coastal plains of the Western Cape, an area known as the Sandveld where, for at least 1500 years Bushman hunter-gatherers had co-existed for the most part peacefully with Khoikhoi pastoralists. Here were white frontier farms, owned mainly by rich freeburghers who lived in comfort – and safety – farther south, and who often left management of these remote properties and herds to sons or managers, or even Khoikhoi servants. Cattle-raiding was part of everyday life, and since the governor in Cape Town was simply too far away to be of any practical assistance, the frontiersmen were accustomed to taking the law into their own hands. When in 1731, for example, a Khoikhoi-Bushman group calling themselves the 'ten sons of Grebnan' attacked two farms in quick succession, a commando of 12 colonists immediately set off in pursuit. When they eventually tracked down the raiders, who immediately started to kill the stolen cattle rather than see them recaptured, the commando fired a warning shot. The response was a defiant hail of arrows, answered by a volley from the commando which killed six raiders, and wounded several others. A woman and three children were taken prisoner and sent 'over the mountains', the first recorded instance of what was to become a common practice, the deliberate capture of women and children who ended up as serfs on white farms. Despite their defeat one Bushman was defiant enough to shout to the departing commando: 'We Bushmen have still more people, and will not leave the Dutch in peace.'

Although Khoikhoi and Bushman resistance to white expropriation of their land and livestock had from the very beginning been determined and often recklessly brave, the rebellion which began on the Sandveld frontier in 1738 was, according to Penn, unique for 'its magnitude and ferocity'. Many of the rebels had lived with and worked for the settlers, could speak Dutch, and knew how to handle firearms. In many cases, former servants embittered by long-standing grievances were fighting their former masters, which gave a crueller edge to the conflict. The strength of the opposition, however, must have come to many settlers as a nasty shock. On one occasion, the members of one commando found themselves so outnumbered they were forced to parley by sending forward an emissary. The answer was blunt. The raiders told them they intended to drive the Dutch off their land, and that this was 'just the beginning . . . that they would do the same to all the people living there, and that if they would not leave, they would burn all the wheat that was growing in the veld as soon as it ripened so as to cause them to leave their land.'

Panic spread across the northern frontier, as colonists drove their stock southwards and abandoned their farms. 'Reports of robberies and rumours of murders swept from one lonely farm to another.' At the height of the disturbances 10 farms were burnt and a further 48 abandoned. Over 700 cattle and nearly 3000 sheep were stolen, and the raiders responsible for this had at least

13 muskets between them; the frontier was in flames. It was only after intensive commando activity, using 'ruthless search and destroy tactics', that the settlers regained control, driving home an unmistakable message: in the end, Bushmen and Khoikhoi alike were powerless to stop the trekboers invading and seizing their land at will.

Of all the brutal incidents which doubtless occurred on both sides, a massacre carried out by a settler commando stands out as particularly ruthless. Having made contact with a group of known rebels, the leader of the commando, Jan Gibbelaas, a senior Company official, persuaded them to parley by dispensing arak and tobacco. While he was doing so, a settler notorious for his aggressive behaviour whispered to him that some of the rebels were planning an attack on a particular farming district. That seems to have been enough for Gibbelaas. Fearing the rebels' 'evil intention' and seeing they were armed with 'muskets, bow and assegaai', as he wrote in his official report, he gave the order to open fire 'as soon as they ran away, when between 30 or 40 were killed'. The full horror of what ensued was not revealed, however, until O.F. Mentzel, a soldier who took part in the commando, published his account nearly fifty years later. Mentzel paints an altogether bloodier picture. 'Since the position had become serious,' he wrote, 'the Commander ordered grape shot to be fired from the field-cannon he had with him, and his men to fire their muskets in volleys of 10, thereby killing and wounding a considerable number of men and women. The war ended suddenly. The enemy fled, some of the women even abandoning their children in fright. Though this was a very weak Commando, some of the soldiers proved that if they were free to do as they pleased, they could be wanton and savage. Some of the most brutal ones seized the small children by their legs and crushed their heads against the stones. Others killed the wounded women and cut off their long breasts, afterwards making themselves tobacco pouches from these as tokens of their heroism.'

The rebellion had impoverished many of the frontier farmers, considerable numbers of whom were unable to pay their loan rent. Some had lost all their livestock and seen their houses burnt down. A few even lost their lives, although white casualties were only a handful, compared to more than 100 Khoikhoi and Bushmen killed. Those were the reported deaths, the real figure was almost certainly much higher; and the survivors had most of their livestock taken forcibly from them.

From the Piketberg to Namaqualand, and from the west coast to the Bokkeveld, the Khoikhoi and Bushmen of the north-west Cape had been finally 'shattered, dispersed and subjugated'. Those that remained were now 'cowed and broken people living in isolated *kraals*'. Their only hope of survival, says Penn, lay in their acceptance of Dutch overlordship symbolised by the staff of office given by the Company to *kraal* captains, and their promise to keep the peace.

As the frontier moved inexorably north and east, ever farther from Cape Town, the Company's control over it inevitably decreased, and 1739 probably marked the last time the Company was able to exert decisive control over the destinies of both white frontiersmen and indigenous Khoikhoi and Bushmen. The commando, by now firmly established as the settlers' main weapon for gaining and keeping possession of the frontier, became increasingly under the control of the frontier trekboers, and only nominally under the orders of the Company. Before 1739, as Penn points out, the government at the Cape had tried, albeit ineffectively, to protect the indigenous population from the worst excesses of the colonists. From now on, the influence of the state, when it was felt at all on the frontier, was to be placed completely behind the commandos in their drive to crush Khoikhoi and, above all, Bushman resistance.

CHAPTER FIVE

A Fight to the Death

'What are you doing on my land? You have taken all the places where the eland and other game live. Why did you not stay where the sun goes down, where you first came from?'

Koerikei, Bushman warrior

With the crushing of the 1738–39 rebellion in the south-western Cape, the way was now open for the trekboers to move forward again and satisfy, at least temporarily, their hunger for land, cheap labour and livestock. Intrepid as any mariner, they sallied forth to the north and the east in their creaking, clumsy but extraordinarily durable oxwagons, penetrating the Onder (Lower) Bokkeveld, the Hantam and the Roggeveld. It was a vast, arid region of rocky, stony high veld, sometimes known as the Cape Thirstland, but more commonly today as the Karoo. The mountainous areas were harsh and cold, cold enough in winter sometimes to kill livestock, especially lambs. The lower areas were much warmer but had a low rainfall and very little perennial water. To survive, therefore, herds had to be moved to the Onder Karoo in the winter and to the mountains in the summer, something the Khoikhoi pastoralists had been doing for centuries. The arrival of the trekboers on this environmental frontier, which separated the winter and summer rainfall regions of the Cape, complicated an already delicate balance. For the first time, the advancing Dutch were competing with both Khoikhoi pastoralists and Bushman hunter-gatherers who relied on the game for their survival; it was not just a question of land, but also of scarce grazing, and even scarcer water.

The impact of the trekboers on the indigenous population was at first, however, less drastic than might have been supposed, because there were so few of them in an almost limitless landscape. Not all of the interior was arid and waterless, of course. North of the Bokkeveld and the Roggeveld, two of the main settlement areas, is a mountain called the Hantam. Between it and the Roggeveld lies a plain which enjoys better than average rainfall and has several good springs. It was probably occupied by the trekboers as early as 1740 and the first loan farm – on the site of what is now the little town of Calvinia – was granted in 1750. It is excellent sheep country, and even better horse country; the first Dutch colonists found that horses which grazed on the Hantam were immune to horse sickness. Since horses were all-important to the trekboer economy, and since they formed along with firearms the strength of the commando, which in turn was the trekboers' power base, no one farmer was allowed to monopolise the grazing. By 1778, 14 farms had been established on the slopes of Mount Hantam.

The early settlers soon realised it was more sensible for them to exploit the local Khoikhoi as cheap labour, than to drive them out. Their herding skills and their knowledge of local conditions – they knew where the best water and grazing were to be found – made them virtually indispensable. Some Khoikhoi did, of course, find themselves being relieved of their stock by the 'characteristically colonial methods of force, fraud and unequal exchange'. But at least some trekboers were willing to play a paternalistic role in trying to protect their Khoikhoi labourers by opposing what was often sheer robbery by agents of the Dutch East India Company. The trekboer takeover was therefore, Nigel Penn suggests, gradual infiltration rather than shock tactics – although the end result was much the same.

The first recorded instance of resistance to the trekboer presence in the Roggeveld came, significantly enough, from Bushmen, not Khoikhoi. In 1754 the Stellenbosch magistrate and council received an SOS that roving bands of 'Bosjesmans' had stolen half the cattle and sheep belonging to a farmer called Roelof van Wijk. They had murdered a herdsman, and were threatening to burn down the farmers' houses. The Stellenbosch authorities immediately appointed two field corporals, told them to organise a commando, and instructed them to give all possible assistance to the beleaguered trekboers. They failed miserably on both counts; but a local Roggeveld commando was formed without their help and carried out a successful series of raids on four different *kraals*. Each *kraal* put up a fight, showering the commando with poisoned arrows, but the Bushmen suffered heavy casualties; 64 were killed, while only 3 members of the commando – 1 white farmer and 2 'tame' Hottentots – were wounded. Nearly all the stolen animals were recaptured. One *kraal*, however, which was particularly well-protected behind some rocks, held out all day, and when in the evening the commando finally withdrew, the defenders taunted them by shouting 'that they would not be able to hide their stock anywhere that they could not find it'.

Whereas the Khoikhoi were a known quantity, both as pastoralists themselves, and as vassals of the trekboers, the Bushmen were a different proposition – hunter-gatherers who were still roaming freely in the deep interior, largely unknown and untrammelled. To the trekboers, men of limited imagination, the Bushmen were wild and savage, barely human, in every sense beyond the pale. 'It was this perception of confronting a society that was even more "other" and "primitive" than the Hottentots,' Penn says, 'that encouraged the colonists to conduct a style of frontier fighting that approached the genocidal after 1770.'

The trekboers were now turning their eyes to the north-east, where the grass was good and there were plenty of cattle. This, however, was out of bounds as far as the Company was concerned, since its colonists were strictly forbidden to cross the Fish River and barter cattle with the Xhosa, Bantu-speaking pastoralists who had pushed their way south from central Africa in preceding centuries.

The Cape government did however give permission for the occupation of the Bushman Mountains and the strangely-named Camdeboo.* Its reasoning was that the area had 'no other inhabitants than wild Bushmen and Hottentots, who possess no cattle and who must subsist solely by the game in the fields, and therefore on that side also no evil is to be apprehended.' Nothing

---

* Green Hills in Khoikhoi.

could have been further from the truth. For beyond the Camdeboo lay the Sneeuberg, and the reason why it was empty of both Khoikhoi and Xhosa pastoralists was that the Bushmen were stronger there than anywhere else in the Cape. The entry of the trekboers into the Sneeuberg was to inflame the whole area and set off the most violent reaction in the colony's history. Things were made worse by the scale of the invasion. In just over three years, between May 1770 and August 1773, 109 farms were granted in the Camdeboo and Sneeuberg out of a total of 192 for the whole of the northern frontier. But by the end of 1773, such was the strength of Bushman resistance that not only had trekboer expansion stopped, but the very existence of the trekboer economy itself was at risk.

Field Corporal Adriaan van Jaarsveld, who had distinguished himself for the number of Bushmen his commandos had killed in the Roggeveld, and who had moved east in 1770, reported that there were so many Bushman attacks on farms in the Sneeuberg that livestock losses had become intolerable. No animals were ever recovered after a raid, since if they could not be driven off, the Bushmen always slaughtered them. He urged that the farmers in his district should be allowed to attack and destroy the Bushmen in the winter, when they had to light fires for warmth and so gave their positions away. The situation being equally grim in the Hantam and Roggeveld, the combined Board of Magistrates, the Council of Policy and the War Council met to discuss the crisis and decided on a response so severe that it would crush Bushman and Hottentot resistance once and for all. A General Commando – in effect a killing machine – would be set up and launched across the entire region. Thus, in the closing years of the eighteenth century the Bushmen were presented with a decisive challenge: submit, retreat or perish.

The man chosen to lead the General Commando was Godlieb Opperman, a farmer from the Roggeveld who in 1750 had forced a local Khoikhoi Captain, Oubaas, to barter four of his oxen for a pittance, and had then helped himself to another six. Although Oubaas had made an official complaint, nothing ever came of it, and 24 years later Opperman was deemed to have 'the necessary discretion and the greatest share of fitness and vigilance' of all the candidates. He was given draconian instructions by the governor: all opposition must be crushed, and as many Bushmen taken captive as were needed to provide an adequate supply of forced labour – it was made clear that the principal enemy was not the Khoikhoi but the Bushmen. Bushmen resisters who were not reduced either to 'a permanent peace or tranquillity or otherwise entirely subdued and destroyed' were to be taken captive. At the beginning, the commando's orders were to spare the women and defenceless males, the women being released and the young and adult males being given to the poorest colonists for a 'fixed and equitable term of years'.*

If, however, the Bushmen did not sue for peace, the governor stated, 'and should necessity thus demand that they should be entirely subdued and destroyed', it was permissible to 'attack and slay them in such a cautious manner, however, that our own inhabitants may be as little as possible exposed to danger, and not rashly led to slaughter; and also that no blood shall be spilled without absolute necessity, and that as much as shall be by any means possible, the women and defenceless males shall be spared.'

Once in the field, however, the brutal realities of guerrilla warfare made their own rules. The figures speak for themselves. The first section of the General Commando, under the command of Nicolaas van der Merwe, which left the Bokkeveld with 27 Europeans and 38 Khoikhoi auxiliaries in August 1774, and for the next 10 weeks swept through an area east and north of the Roggeveld as far as the Sak River, destroyed 167 *kraals*, killed 142 Bushmen, and took 89 prisoners. Only one commando member was killed, dying nine days after being shot by a poisoned arrow.

The second section, under Gerrit van Wyk, comprising at least 31 Europeans and a slightly larger number of Khoikhoi auxiliaries, was given the task of searching the area north and

* In practice, very few adult males were ever taken alive and it was also argued that it was heartless to release widows and orphaned children. Instead, they were to be incorporated into the labour force.

north-east of the Sak River, that is Bushmanland. Its body count was slightly smaller, but still fearsome: 96 Bushmen killed and 21 captured, as against no commando members.

The third section, under Opperman, which conducted operations in the key Sneeuberg and Camdeboo region, as well as the Nieuweveld and Koup areas, wreaked enormous destruction, killing 265 Bushmen, and capturing 129. Some of the commando members, including Opperman himself, were wounded but none fatally. Most of those captured were women and children, and it was common practice to give all children under the age of twelve to farmers as unpaid servants. The women were either released or given as wives to Khoikhoi commando members. Almost no men were taken prisoner, and the inescapable conclusion is that they were killed.

The commandos had superiority in numbers. They nearly always attacked individual *kraals* which contained on average an extended family of about 13 persons.* Secondly, thanks to their Hottentot spies and scouts, the commandos nearly always had the benefit of surprise: they specialised in dawn attacks on sleeping encampments. Thirdly, they had immensely greater firepower and mobility than the Bushmen: muskets against bows and arrows, and horses against men on foot.

There was a fourth reason for the extreme one-sidedness of the casualty figures, a reason at once heroic and tragic. The Bushmen never surrendered. They 'have never been known to demand quarter in any situation', reported Colonel Collins, a British officer, in 1795. A laconic entry in the record kept by Gerrit van Wyk's commando made the point more brutally: '17 Sept . . . they shot briskly arrows but would not come out when called; shot five and took a child. 22 Sept . . . the Bushmen having ensconced themselves behind the fence of a *kraal*, shot Gerrit Bastert Minie through the hat, therefore shot 8; they would accept no peace . . . the commandant marched up to the first fire

---

* The smallest group Nicolaas van der Merwe's section came across numbered 6, and the largest 30, which conforms with the average size of a Bushman hunter-gatherer band, whether calculated from the evidence provided by group portraits in the rock paintings of the south-west Cape, or anthropological research done in the twentieth century.

that was perceived, and had them called out to make peace, but instead of answering they shot their arrows, therefore shot 10.'

The commandos found it almost impossible to find any *kraal* captain with whom to negotiate peace terms, partly because the Bushmen did not have the same system of chiefs as the Khoikhoi, and partly, and perhaps more importantly, as Penn explains, because of 'a deep-rooted determination to reject unequal terms'. Even Khoikhoi captains were reluctant to co-operate with the General Commando, and in one instance one man whom Opperman wished to appoint and present with a copper-headed staff of office, declined the offer saying 'that he dared not undertake it, as his tribe would kill him'. If the Khoikhoi were frightened to accept the Company's blandish-ments, the Bushmen were contemptuous of them. They spurned the Dutch offers of peace and fought to the death, frequently displaying incredible heroism. 'When a horde is surrounded by the farmers, and little chance is perceived by them of effecting an escape, they will fight it out most furiously as long as a man shall be left alive,' according to John Barrow, the secretary to the British Governor, who visited the Sneeuberg Bushmen in 1797. In an account of his journey, *Travels Into the Interior of Southern Africa*, published in London in 1804, Barrow wrote: 'It frequently happens on such occasions that a party will volunteer the forlorn hope, by throwing themselves in the midst of the colonists in order to create confusion, and to give to their countrymen, concealed among the rocks or in the long grass, at the expense of their own lives, an opportunity of exercising more effectually their mortal weapons upon their enemies, and at the same time to facilitate the escape of their wives and children.'

Various reasons have been put forward to explain the Bushmen's suicidal courage. The short answer is that their resistance was born of desperation. On a practical level, in the Sneeuberg and the Roggeveld, they were fighting to retain their hold on an area where the environmental balance, which depended on managing the sparse rainfall of the Cape interior, was critical. If they lost this crucial escarpment and its irreplaceable resources, their way of life was doomed. Dispossession meant literally death. One has to remember, too, that the

Bushmen had not only the trekboers to contend with. Defeat on one front could mean a forced retreat into areas so arid that human existence was almost impossible, or into hostile territory controlled by Bantu-speaking Xhosa and Tswana. The Xhosa in particular were unlikely to be receptive to Bushman refugees. 'What happens to a Bosjesman-Hottentot who is captured by a Hottentot or a Caffer?' asked a Capetonian of a frontiersman in the 1770s. 'Is he killed or must he work as a slave?' 'They kill him,' was the answer, 'otherwise he would run away again.'

But there were other, deeper reasons why the Bushmen were so determined to resist. The land had for them not merely a practical, economic significance but a spiritual importance. Penn argues that the more we learn about Bushman culture the more evident it becomes that there was 'a profoundly spiritual connection between particular places and the system of meaning' that the Bushmen had constructed in order to explain their world. The stories, myths and legends contained in the Bleek-Lloyd archive* were in some ways, Penn says, evoked by the landscape itself. 'Thus, to lose land was to lose, literally, everything.'

Barrow also offers a rare, and sensitive, insight into the character of the Bushmen, and the difficulty if not impossibility of transforming them into obedient serfs. 'Such as have been taken very young and well treated, have turned out most excellent servants; they have shown great talent, great activity, and great fidelity. An opposite treatment has been productive of a contrary effect; and the brutal conduct of most of the Dutch farmers towards those in their employ has already been noticed. The poor Hottentot bears it with patience, or sinks under it; but on the temper and the turn of mind of the Bosjesman it has a very different effect. He takes the first opportunity that offers of escaping to his countrymen, and contrives frequently to carry off with him a musquet, powder and ball. With tales of cruelty he excites them to revenge; he assists them in their plans of attack; tells them the strength of the whole, and of individuals; the number of their cattle, and the advantages and dangers that will

---

* The famous record of Bushman language and myth translated and recorded by Wilhelm Bleek and Lucy Lloyd in Cape Town in the 1870s and 1880s.

occur in the attempt to carry them off; the manner in which expeditions are conducted against them; and, in short, every thing he knows respecting the colonists.'

As pure hunter-gatherers who, unlike the Khoikhoi, had never herded animals, and had no desire nor aptitude to do so, the Bushmen had no place in the trekboer economy. It is quite possible, therefore, that many male Bushmen were never given the chance to surrender but were simply shot out of hand. With their menfolk gone, the women were assimilated into the trekboers' households, either directly as domestic help, or indirectly as the wives of existing Khoikhoi servants. Children were often 'given' by one farmer to another, and could be ordered as 'items' from commandos in the field. One magistrate of Stellenbosch, Hendrik Bletterman, was 'given' two Bushmen children in April 1774, and a third by a commando sergeant a few months later.

Joshua Penny, an American sailor press-ganged into the Royal Navy, and who deserted in Cape Town after the British conquest, fled to the Koue (Cold) Bokkeveld, and lived among the trekboers for several months. In his memoirs, which Penn considers 'slightly unreliable', he recalls having served in a commando in 1796. After the shooting had stopped they 'found in the hostile camp 20 or 30 dead bodies, and a woman with nine children. The woman was shot, because no prisoner can be admitted into any settlement over the age of 11 years. . . . We returned to Cold Bokeveld with the nine captive children in baskets, slung on the oxen by a girth which passed round the bodies five or six times, and drawn taut by two Hottentots.'

By the end of the century, the continual fighting and raiding on the frontier had brutalised attitudes to such an extent that the colonists now considered Bushmen as 'vermin', fit only for extermination. John Barrow, as a humanitarian Englishman, was shocked to hear a settler from Graaff Reynet, in the Eastern Cape, when asked if the 'savages were numerous or troublesome on the road', reply that he had only shot four, 'with as much composure and indifference as if he had been speaking of four partridges'. Barrow said he had heard another of the 'humane colonists boast of having destroyed with his own hands near three hundred of these unfortunate wretches.' Even the women and children were expendable. Nicolaas van der Merwe, for example, did not think it unreasonable to order the shooting of Bushman women and children who had been wounded 'in order that their death might not be still crueller'.

Penn puts it like this: 'To European observers the San (Bushmen) seemed to possess neither property, political structures, religion, houses, literacy, decency, or even an intelligible language. Somatically, too, they were as far removed from the European norm as any people the Dutch had ever encountered. Conscious of the achievement of their own nation, and imbued with a sense of their own superiority under God's guidance, it was hardly surprising that the colonists should imagine the San to be completely "other" than themselves. Fear, contempt, hatred and almost unrestrained licence to violence, provided by the context of a legitimate war on the furthest frontiers of European expansion, ensured that the war against the San would be marked by genocidal atrocities.'

But despite the violence meted out to Bushmen, they continued to resist. The trekboers, a thin white line stretched across the veld, found the Bushmen an awkward and elusive enemy. There were too many of them, they were too spread out, and their raids were cunningly planned and costly. They nearly always attacked at night, often killing the shepherds before driving off the cows and sheep. As Barrow reported: 'Should they seize a Hottentot guarding his master's cattle, not contented with putting him to immediate death, they torture him by every means of cruelty that their invention can frame, as drawing out his bowels, tearing off his nails, scalping and other acts equally savage.' The raiders would then drive their booty into the high and dry areas where the Dutch on their horses found it hard to follow, either because of the rocky terrain or because there was no water. If the Bushmen thought they were going to be overtaken, they would kill or maim the livestock. Their objective was to strike the trekboers where they were most vulnerable. Unlike the Khoikhoi, the Bushmen had no use for livestock except of course to eat it, since they had no wish to become pastoralists.

It was when they were caught in the open, on flat ground, that the Bushmen were at a disadvantage. Keeping 100 to 150 paces from the enemy, the Dutch commando would dismount and fire with devastating effect, well out of range of the Bushmen's most feared weapon, their bows and poisoned arrows. The Bushman rate of fire was about five or six arrows a minute, accurate up to about 30 paces. But it was in the rugged hills and kopjes of the Sneeuberg that they were at their most dangerous. Able to spot the approach of a commando from a great distance – Bushmen have phenomenal eyesight – they would either take evasive action, or spring an ambush by rolling boulders down the hillside on top of the enemy.

In one incident in the Swartberg, a commando was camped for the night, having captured 82 Bushmen. Lack of handcuffs meant the prisoners were not as securely tied as they might have been, and they managed to break free, attacking their captors and trying to recover their bows and arrows. In the confusion, some escaped (though 19 were shot dead and 21 children recaptured). As a result, the commando leaders asked for permission not to take prisoners in future, as it was impossible, they said, to hold them securely. Even this extra turn of the screw did not lessen Bushman resistance, and indeed raiding intensified.

On 1 August 1775 Adriaan van Jaarsveld, one of the most ruthless commando leaders, took 77 men on a search and destroy mission to the Seekoei River. Pretending to be on a hunting trip, the party shot a number of hippopotamus and, leaving the carcases on the river bank, moved off downstream. Van Jaarsveld knew very well that Bushmen loved every kind of meat, especially hippopotamus. So when the commando came stealing back during the night they found, as they expected, a large number of Bushmen, women and children as well as men, busy feasting on the fresh meat. Biding his time, van Jaarsveld waited until they had eaten their fill and were sleeping it off. He ordered the attack at dawn. Taking the Bushmen completely by surprise, the commando massacred 122, and took 21 prisoners. Only 5 escaped.

Meanwhile, however, van Jaarsveld's own 'captain', the Khoikhoi to whom he had entrusted his farm and livestock during his absence, deserted 'to his accomplices in the field', taking 78 of van Jaarsveld's sheep with him. The Sneeubergers petitioned the Company to deliver them from 'the great assemblages of these heathenish evildoers' who now numbered 'in their thousands'. Indeed, one commando had the novel and uncomfortable experience of being surrounded and outnumbered by so many Bushmen that the Dutchmen were lucky to escape with their lives. There were other disturbing signs. Khoikhoi servants were deserting their 'masters' to join the Bushman resistance, horses were being stolen instead of killed, and by expanding their bands into larger groups the Bushmen were making it more difficult for the settlers to pick them off piecemeal.

All across the Northern and Eastern Cape, the same pattern of stock raiding and killing was repeating itself. Commandant Opperman, who had led the 1774 General Commando, asked the government for at least 200 men and large quantities of powder and shot. By the time the authorities in Stellenbosch had agreed, the trekboers had already been forced to abandon the Sneeuberg and the Camdeboo. This was one of the most serious setbacks suffered by the Dutch, and was caused largely by lack of ammunition, but also partly by the difficulty of recruiting men to the commando. The experiment of arming 'faithful Hottentots and Bastaards' to operate as independent units had proved unsuccessful, the 'faithful' often defecting, guns and all, to the enemy. In one case, a field corporal was obliged to lead a commando against a Khoikhoi captain to whom the Company's highest accolade, the copper-headed staff of office, had been given. The number of Bushmen in the resistance had grown so large that trekboer commandos were unable to defeat them. Colonel Robert Gordon, commander of the Cape garrison, who visited the Sneeuberg in 1777, was taken to the site of a battle where a member of the commando, a certain van der Walt, had been shot by a Bushman bowman from a distance of 24 paces. Gordon reported that although the farmers shot many of the Bushmen, they could not take the hill which the Bushmen had fortified with piles of stones.

With the departure of a dispirited van Jaarsveld, the Camdeboo and the Sneeuberg were left open to attack. The new field sergeants, the brothers Carel and David Schalk van der Merwe, soon ran into the general reluctance of the local farmers to do commando duty. One farmer who was instructed to send his wagon on commando duty did so without the tilt, the canvas wagon-cover. When the field sergeant wrote asking for the tilt he received a reply saying, 'You write me to send my wagon tilt tomorrow, which is impossible that I can do, as it is the bolster of my bed. I am not unwilling, if I had enough bed clothes, to give the tilt, but I am deficient in these. I remain, therefore, after compliments, your friend, Cornelius de Clerk.' On the back, de Clerk had added a postcript. 'The tilt of which I write you, is the bolster for my head, and my wife is my mattress, so if you claim the tilt by force, order the mattress with it, as cook.'

David van der Merwe complained of being able to kill little more than 70 Bushmen in four months, and when his commando returned it was to find that in its absence many farms had been attacked, stock stolen and herdsmen killed.

The Bushmen, or Chinese as the settlers called them, had a famous 'chief' called Koerikei, the bullet-escaper. Van der Merwe told Gordon that, after an action which he commanded, 'this Koerikei, standing on a cliff out of range, shouted out to him: "What are you doing on my land? You have taken all the places where the eland and other game live. Why did you not stay where the sun goes down, where you first came from?" Van der Merwe asked why he did not live in peace as before, and why he did not go hunting with them [he had been living with the farmers] and whether he did not have enough country as it was? He replied that he did not want to lose the country of his birth and that he would kill their herdsmen, and that he would chase them all away. As he went off he further said that it would be seen who would win.'

By the end of 1779, farmers in the Camdeboo were complaining that: 'There has never been such an irruption of the Bushmen as now, for here we see Bushmen daily, and though we make every exertion, we cannot overtake them, the country is so rugged and hilly. They light fires in the mountain before our eyes; and as the Bushmen have now such free access, please to see, sir, the number of cattle that have been carried off recently.'

The figure mentioned in official reports for 1779 was 750 cattle and more than 3000 sheep, one of the worst records for livestock losses.

The settlers who were still holding out in the adjoining area of Bruintjieshoogte were also being constantly harassed. Bushman raiding parties were so large that one commando took to its heels in the face of the enemy. More and more Bushmen were using guns, and fewer and fewer frontiersmen were willing to do commando duty. 'I get more excuses than men,' reported Field Sergeant David van der Merwe of the Camdeboo, and his brother Carel complained that the time seemed to be approaching when 'I shall at last have to do a commando with none but Hottentots, which cannot be.'

In the older settled areas, such as the Roggeveld and the Nieuweveld, Bushmen and Khoikhoi were co-operating. Field Sergeant Adriaan van Zyl was given permission to raise a commando, which he did, but a Khoikhoi captain in the Bokkeveld, whose loyalties might have been presumed to lie with the government, tipped off his Bushman friends, and the planned operation was a resounding failure. Meanwhile, the new Field Sergeant of the Klein and Middle Roggeveld, Carel Kruger, was writing in his turn to Stellenbosch: 'It has never before been so as now, from January to the present time with stealing and surrounding the houses by night, and discharging arrows at them, so that the people dare not venture out to protect the cattle; and we cannot take the field with a commando because of the prevalence of the horse distemper, but must await a suitable season.' The settlers could have been forgiven for concluding that even their very own Calvinist God had turned his back on them. The colonial frontier was in retreat everywhere in the northern districts, despite more than a decade of constant commando activity. The Bushmen and their Khoikhoi allies were gaining the upper hand.

The government panicked, issuing instructions that all farmers who had deserted their farms must return to them within four months or forfeit them. Combining persuasion with threats, and in a rare show of generosity, it also promised to make loan-farms available free of charge for ten years provided they were in a *cordon sanitaire* stretching from the Plettenberg River (formerly the Seekoei) to the Sak, where they would block Bushman incursions to the south. Finally, yet another commando was organised, but despite killing nearly 500 Bushmen and capturing 112 in the period between 1787 and 1788, it did not seem to bring a military solution any closer. The mood on the frontier was now degenerating into something which Penn found essentially evil: 'The pervasive violence, the hatred and contempt of trekboers for Bushman life and an ethos of unfree labour encouraged white farmers to treat all non-whites who were not actually in the commandos with them as potential enemies or bondsmen.' As life on the white farms grew more and more unbearable, an increasing number of Khoikhoi labourers ran away from their brutal masters to join the Bushman resistance, often taking the farmers' guns and horses with them. These 'desertions', as they were called by the infuriated trekboers, sometimes led to personal tragedy, as when a family fleeing from a particularly violent farmer suffocated their baby in case its cries betrayed their hiding-place. This was the lawless state into which the frontier of the Dutch colony had sunk when a British government, increasingly concerned to safeguard the Cape route to its Indian empire, decided to intervene.

CHAPTER SIX

Failure of the British Peace Plan

What are the missionaries doing in this country, why don't they stay with the other Dutch people ... he could not endure the Dutch living in his country.

Gerrit Maritz quoting Captain Vigiland, 1800

In September 1795, as Dutch power waned and the shadow cast by Napoleon grew longer – he was to invade Egypt three years later – Britain felt impelled to take possession of the Cape. It was done in a gentlemanly manner, at the request of the Prince of Orange, who had remained loyal to his British ally, whereas the Dutch republic, aligned with France, was at war with Britain.

British ships had been using the Cape route to ply their lucrative spice trade with the East since Drake had put in there in 1580 on his epic circumnavigation, calling it the 'fairest Cape we saw in the whole circumference of the earth'. In the last years of the dying century, and first two decades of the new, however, the balance of power was changing radically. The old enemy under a new disguise – an imperial France under the dynamic leadership of Napoleon Bonaparte – posed a real threat to British interests. French control of the Cape would be disastrous for Britain, since it would cut the lifeline to India, Britain's most important overseas possession now that the American Colonies had gone. Napoleon had had his eye on the Cape for some time.

The main concern of the British was to secure the Cape as a naval base, and at first they were reluctant to become involved in governing the interior. Events, however, soon forced their hand. In 1797 the governor, Lord Macartney, sent his private secretary, John Barrow, to the eastern border to discover the reasons behind the Bushman rebellion, and to negotiate a settlement. Barrow's brief was 'to bring about a conversation with some of the chiefs of this people, to try if, by presents and persuasion,

77

they could be prevailed upon to quit their present wild and marauding way of life.' Unfortunately for him, the Bushmen did not have 'chiefs' because of their egalitarian, hunter-gatherer way of life, and the Dutch settlers were uncompromisingly hostile. General Craig, the British commander, had already suggested to the Dutch authorities that it was impractical to try to exterminate the Bushmen and had urged a more humane approach, freeing Bushman captives and letting them return to their homes. The Dutch disagreed, the new magistrate in Graaf Reinet, Bresler, advising Lord Macartney that in his opinion the Bushmen were 'a nation of thieves'.

Barrow went ahead all the same, travelling with Bresler to Graaf Reinet and touring the troubled areas of the Sneeuberg, the Tarka and Bruintjieshoogte. For most of the journey, and like Gordon before him eighteen years earlier, Barrow hardly saw a single Bushman, the only exception being a group which his party managed to approach only after stalking and surprising them by standard commando methods. Although Barrow had insisted that bloodshed was to be avoided at all costs, and guns were to be used only in self-defence, his Dutch escort took no notice. Barrow's description of the ensuing encounter is one of the most moving passages in his *Travels*, and it turned out to be as influential as it was harrowing. Indeed, it would be no exaggeration to suggest that British policy towards the Bushmen, on both the eastern and the northern frontiers, was shaped by Barrow's grim experience that day.

After describing how the party stole up on the sleeping Bushmen, Barrow wrote that 'my ears were stunned with a horrid scream like the war whoop of savages; the shrieking of women and the cries of children proceeded from every side.' He rode with the commandant and another farmer, both of whom opened fire on the *kraal*. Barrow immediately accused them of breaking their word not to shoot, to which the commandant replied, 'Good God . . . have you not seen a shower of arrows falling among us?' Barrow retorted that he 'certainly had seen neither arrows nor people, but had heard enough to pierce the hardest heart; and I peremptorily insisted that neither he nor any of his party should fire another shot.' One more Bushman was shot, however, allegedly for trying to kill a member of Barrow's party by creeping up behind him with drawn bow. 'It had been hoped,' Barrow added, 'the affair would happily have been accomplished without the shedding of human blood, and that the views of the expedition would have met with no interruption from an accident of such a nature.'

It was only with the greatest difficulty that Barrow was finally able to approach the terrified remaining Bushmen, whom he describes as 'mild and manageable in the highest degree'. He concluded they were forced to retaliate as best they could against 'the brutality and gross depravity of the boors', who enslaved their women and children and 'ceaselessly' tried to drive them from their land. Barrow asked to speak to 'the captain or chief of the horde, but they assured us there was no such person, that everyone was master of his own family, and acted entirely without control, being at liberty to remain with, or quit, the society as it best suited them.'

Barrow came away convinced that the real cause of the war between the Bushmen and the colonists was the commando system, which exacerbated bitterness and hatred.

Despite their courage, the strain was finally beginning to tell on even the stoutest Bushman heart. The Xam of Bushmanland, for example, were running out of territory to which they could escape when they needed to recoup their losses. In the west, the colonists had closed Namaqualand to them; the way to the south was also barred; and to the east lay the battle zone of the Sneeuberg. Even in Bushmanland itself, the environment was suffering from the trekboers' habit of driving their herds and flocks into the area after the rains, causing serious damage to the vegetation and driving out the game which also depended on the grazing and water. Dutch hunting parties were slaughtering vast quantities of antelope to satisfy the almost insatiable demand for *biltong*, the sun-dried venison which still has an almost mystical significance for Afrikaners. By the 1790s, the eland, the largest of the African antelopes and central to Bushman culture, was being hunted almost to extinction. The great herds of eland which used to roam the Cape savannah were now to be found only beyond the Sak River. In Bushmanland, where whole wagon-loads of dried meat were being hauled out to satisfy settler demand, the Xam saw their material and spiritual patrimony being relentlessly plundered. In his *Travels in Southern Africa*, H. Lichtenstein describes the return of a hunting party to the Roggeveld in 1803, having shot 17 eland weighing 700–800 pounds apiece, which meant each hunter's share was 'about four thousand pounds of pure, excellent flesh'. This was cut up on the spot, salted, packed in the skins, and then carted home in a wagon the hunters had brought with them. 'The great muscle of the thigh, smoked, is more particularly esteemed,' Lichtenstein explained. 'These are cut out at their full length, and from the resemblance they then bear to bullock's tongues, are called thigh-tongues. They are often sent as presents, or for sale, to Cape Town, and are there eaten raw, and cut into very thin slices, with bread and butter. Thus prepared, they are esteemed an excellent *gourmandise*.'

Faced with rape of their land and its resources, despite what would be seen today as heroic resistance, the Xam suddenly found themselves being proferred the hand of friendship by a most unlikely benefactor: a farmer with a somewhat violent reputation, named Floris Visser. Not only was Visser a trekboer, but he was a Company field sergeant into the bargain. Visser first recommended himself to the British authorities at the Cape in May 1797 when he arrived in Stellenbosch after a 40-hour ride on horseback to report the arrival of a group of about 300 Koranna tribesmen in the Roggeveld. Although they seemed peaceful and said they wanted to 'dwell with the Christians', Visser was worried because the Koranna group included both Bushmen and Bantu-speaking Xhosa, neither of whom were particularly popular with the colonists. Furthermore, none of them had any cattle, which made Visser suspect they might have been planning 'to plunder the inhabitants of his district'. Visser had come for advice from the British on how he should deal with the situation, his own view being that peaceful persuasion should be tried first to get the Koranna to go home, and only if that failed should force be used. The governor, Lord Macartney, promptly agreed, since he wanted to avoid bloodshed, and Visser was sent off back to the Roggeveld to see what he could achieve. He seems to have been successful; so when in 1798 Visser approached the British again, this time with a plan for a peaceful settlement with the Bushmen, Macartney responded enthusiastically.

The Visser plan was revolutionary. First, the Bushmen would be given livestock by the government, to encourage them to become pastoralists; second, they would have the 'exclusive and uncontested right' to certain tracts of land; and third, the government would appoint 'mutually acceptable captains' among the Bushmen.

In July 1798, Macartney issued a proclamation which was based on Visser's proposals but went far beyond them. The first article gave a good idea of its ambitious scope. 'It appears that one of the first steps towards civilising and conciliating the Bosjesman, would be to impress them with a sense of the benefits arising from permanent property, preferable to casual and predatory supplies, and to make a free gift to them of such a quantity of Cattle, as may be sufficient for their immediate subsistence.'

To 'civilise' the Bushmen by acquainting them with the 'benefits' of owning property, and to turn them into a pastoralist society by giving them cattle, would seem at first sight to be an attempt to square the circle, and as such doomed to certain failure. Such a change, says Nigel Penn, from 'a form of primitive communism to a form of private property' clearly had far-reaching implications for Bushman society, and if implemented would have meant the extinction of the hunter-gatherer way of life. Even if it were possible to transform the Bushmen into pastoralists like the Khoikhoi in the space of a few generations, which was doubtful to say the least, such an existence was no longer viable in the conditions of the Cape in 1798. If the Khoikhoi, who were expert herders and drovers, could no longer survive in that role, what hope was there for the Bushmen? Given the almost total ownership of the means of production by the colonists, Penn observes, 'the proposal to wean the Bushmen from their "casual and predatory supplies" was but a prelude to their wholesale incorporation into the colonial economy as labourers – the likelihood of which the authorities could not have been unaware.'

Was then the Macartney-Visser plan no more than a cynical exercise in subjugating the Bushmen by kindness? The French Revolution, with its clarion call of Liberté, Egalité, Fraternité and its proclamation of the Rights of Man, was barely ten years old. Barrow, who had already learnt at first hand that Bushman society was essentially democratic and individualist, and did not approve of chiefs or captains, should perhaps have known better. But both Barrow and Macartney were deeply committed to stabilising the border, stopping the cattle-raiding and the killing, and establishing a Pax Britannica in the Cape.

What is not at all clear is whether the Bushmen were aware of what they were being let in for. The proclamation promised that they would be confirmed in the possession of their own land, 'a sufficient District beyond the Sak River towards the Kareeberg', that they were to be 'left in possession of their just rights and habitations', and that they were 'not to be molested, nor their Children taken from them or made slaves or servants of, on any pretence whatsoever'. What is more, in a passage that seemed to reflect the hand of Barrow, field sergeants were expressly forbidden to lead commandos against the Bushmen, or take any violent action against them except in self-defence. In his attempt to reach a comprehensive peace settlement, Macartney had the northern and eastern borders of the colony – the latter for the first time – demarcated more clearly. In future no colonist would be allowed to hunt, settle or graze livestock beyond those borders. The express purpose of this was to protect the 'Caffres and the Bosjesman' – the former being tribes such as the Xhosa – from being reduced, as in the past, to 'misery and want' which, in turn, had led them into 'robbing and various other irregularities in order to support life'.

The intentions were excellent but, alas, impractical. For example, anyone wanting permission to hunt across the border was supposed to obtain a pass from the governor, which would have meant trekking hundreds of miles to Cape Town and back, clearly an absurd piece of red tape which no frontiersman would dream of complying with. More seriously, the new borders tended to include only areas which were permanently settled, thus excluding in the north-west the vital summer rainfall grazing which the trekboers depended on for the seasonal movement of their livestock.

To begin with, however, the peace initiative seemed to be working. In January 1799 Visser was able to report from the Roggeveld that a Bushman captain by the name of Vigiland had agreed to the peace terms and had persuaded another Bushman leader, Danser, to visit Visser's farm where he was also promoted to captain and presented with a staff of office. They in turn knew of two other captains, by the names of Orlam and Ruijter, who were also anxious to make peace. Thus encouraged, Visser and a party of colonists set off in February to trek to the Kareeberg, stopping to parley with various captains on the way, and at the final treaty ceremony distributing largesse in the form of livestock, beads, knives, tobacco, mirrors, flints and tinder-boxes. Visser reported later that a total of 471 Bushmen took part in these peace ceremonies, of whom 284 were women and children, and 187 men. Some Bushmen, however, did not approve of these developments, and the members of one great *kraal*, three days' journey away, which contained 'many people, many guns and much livestock' were said not only to be against making peace but to have threatened to destroy the colonists.

Even such dark threats did not spoil the final occasion, according to the representative of the London Missionary Society, Dr J. van der Kemp, who was not present but wrote later that Visser kneeled down in a field, leading his men in prayer and hymn-singing. When the Bushmen asked with surprise 'the meaning of this solemnity and having received for answer that it was thanksgiving to God, and a demonstration of joy on account of the peace with the Bosjesmen,' they 'begged that instructors might be sent to them, to teach them the Christian religion'. Even if missionary fervour led Dr van der Kemp to exaggerate, the Bushmen must have been intrigued by the sight of Visser and his Dutch fellow farmers at prayer. Hymn-singing, accompanied by brandy-drinking, was the usual prelude to a commando attack.

Visser was by all accounts an unusually 'pious colonist', and his Christian beliefs may well have motivated him to try to make peace with the old foe. The advent of evangelical Christianity, introduced by the Moravian mission, a German Protestant organisation, was beginning to have a profound effect on the Khoikhoi and Bastaard communities, and word may have spread to the Bushmen. But it is doubtful if that is what brought them to the peace talks in the Kareeberg. Other, more pressing considerations, were driving them into the arms of Visser. The wholesale slaughter of the game in Bushmanland by Dutch hunting parties, and the destruction of the grazing by trekboer livestock, were pushing the Bushmen to the brink of starvation. Unable to feed themselves, a group of 'about 85' told Visser they wanted to work for the Dutch, and one group under a Captain Platje wanted to work for Visser himself. In his role as protector of the Bushmen, Visser agreed to allow destitute Bushmen to work for the colonists provided they were paid the same wages as Khoikhoi labourers, that contracts were properly drawn up and observed, and that their wives and children were not mistreated.

In April Visser despatched three of the Bushmen captains to Cape Town to meet the governor at his request. As luck would have it their arrival coincided with that of Dr van der Kemp and his three colleagues from the London Missionary Society who had been sent out from England to preach the gospel to the heathen. Since the territory they would have to cover was so vast, and they were so few in number, the British party decided to divide its forces. Dr van der Kemp, a Dutchman and the leader of the group, and an English colleague, Edmond, decided to go east to minister to the Xhosa, but the other two, Johannes Kicherer, another Dutchman, and William Edwards, an Englishman, who had intended to visit Namaqualand, were forced to change their plans because of serious unrest in the area. Providence now came to their aid, or so it seemed to these men of God, because the three Bushman captains 'expressed their earnest desire that proper persons might come and reside among them, who would afford them those valuable instructions which would enable them to become as rich and happy as their neighbours'. Dr van der Kemp was at first hesitant since he believed like most of his contemporaries that the 'Bosjesman' nation was 'perhaps the most savage and cruel in the whole earth'. On the other hand he was impressed by the Bushman captains' 'ardent desire to leave off all acts of criminal violence for ever and to be instructed in the knowledge and service of the God of the Christians'. So it was decided that the Namaqualand mission should be diverted to Bushmanland.

The government gave the men of God every assistance, and in return expected William Edwards 'not only to take their spiritual concerns at heart, but also to correspond about their political concerns'. During the fortnight it took Kicherer and Edwards to reach the Roggeveld they attracted a large congregation en route. At Visser's farm, where they stayed for two or three weeks, their Sunday services attracted 22 wagon-loads of churchgoers, 'besides many on horseback, some of whom came from four days' journey to hear the word of God'.

In early July, the two missionaries left for Bushmanland accompanied by 50 men, 6 wagons full of provisions, 60 oxen and 200 sheep. Visser, who travelled with the party, planned to continue farther north to the great *kraal* to try out his powers of persuasion on the still hostile Bushman inhabitants there. A month later, having crossed the Sak River, the missionaries found a suitable site for a settlement. The local Bushmen seemed friendly, but not all the white farmers were as welcoming. One Roggevelder, Martinus Coort, gave vent to his feelings by declaring 'that he would do nothing for the peaceful Bushmen nor the missionaries but [wished] that the missionaries would be killed and that all the Bushmen were dead'. There were others, less outspoken but equally critical of missionary endeavour, who believed that the spread of literacy would undermine their authority, and – to use a South African phrase common in the apartheid period – produce a crop of 'cheeky Kaffirs'. Kicherer, in his personal account of his experiences, said that farmers who opposed the missionaries' presence were 'generally uncivilised and ungodly men. . . . The better sort of the Settlers instruct their Hottentots and their Slaves, and . . . some have been savingly converted. But those Farmers who are notoriously wicked are afraid that the heathen will become too wise by instruction, and so reprove them for their wicked works.'

In August the main body of colonists departed, leaving the missionaries to fend for themselves, although Visser's son Gerrit, and a farmer-cum-missionary, Cornelis Kramer, volunteered to stay. More Bushmen arrived at the mission station, although it soon became clear that they were attracted more by 'handouts of the "irresistible herb," tobacco than by the magnetism of the Christian message', as Kicherer frankly admitted. Being great meat-eaters, the Bushmen were also drawn by the missionaries' mutton supplies, and the 'little presents' which Kicherer doled out to 'excite the spirit of industry'. Soon, about 30 Bushmen were living beside the mission, and Kicherer was able to observe them closely. He was not impressed. 'They delight to smear their bodies with the fat of animals, mingled with a powder [probably specularite] which makes it shine. They are utter strangers to cleanliness, as they never wash their bodies, but suffer the dirt to accumulate, so that it will hang a considerable length from their elbows.' Describing their sleeping arrangements, Kicherer said 'they lie close together like pigs in a sty. They are extremely lazy so that nothing would rouse them to action, but excessive hunger.' He admitted they were 'dexterous in destroying the various beasts which abound in the country; but when they cannot procure these, they make shift to live upon snakes, mice, and the most destestable creatures they can find. There are some spontaneous productions of the earth of the bulbous kind which they also eat ... There are also some little berries which are eatable, and which the women go out to gather, but the men are too idle to do this.'

Other criticisms voiced by Kicherer were that Bushmen have 'no idea whatever of the Supreme Being' and 'practise no kind of worship'. He was even more dismissive – and inaccurate – about their family life, claiming they were 'total strangers to domestic happiness. . . . They take no great care of their children, and never correct them except in a fit of rage, when they almost kill them by severe usage. . . . Bosjesmen will kill their children without remorse on various occasions, as when they are ill shaped, when they are in want of food, when the father of a child has forsaken its mother or when obliged to flee from the Farmers or others; in which case they will strangle them, smother them, chase them away in the desert, or bury them alive.' There were cases, Kicherer claimed, of parents throwing their 'tender offspring to the hungry Lion, who stands roaring before their cavern, refusing to depart until some peace-offering be made to him'. Kicherer also repeated the well-worn cliché that Bushman treatment of the old was cruel. 'The Bosjesmen frequently forsake their aged relations, when removing from place to place for the sake of hunting,' and would 'leave the old person with a piece of meat and an ostrich egg-shell full of water; as soon as this little stock is exhausted, the poor deserted creature must perish by hunger, or become the prey of the wild beasts.' He ended his diatribe with a sweeping denunciation: 'Many of these wild Hottentots live by plunder and murder, and are guilty of the most horrid and atrocious actions.'

Penn dismisses Kicherer's portrait as a 'heartless distortion of certain practices which, doubtless, occurred occasionally within the hard-pressed hunter-gatherer communities'. In periods of terrible drought, there would be times when there was not enough water to keep everyone alive. In those extreme conditions, if an old or very weak member of the band could not walk to the next water hole, and the survival of the rest of the band was at stake, he or she might be left in the desert with only a scrap of food and a mouthful or two of water. This was the harsh but ineluctable law of survival in the world of the hunter-gatherer in southern Africa.

No doubt the Bushmen had as distorted a view of the missionaries as the men of God did of them. What, for example, could they have made of Kicherer's habit of identifying them by a method which smacks more of the boot camp than the seminary? As the numbers of would-be converts increased, Kicherer found it necessary 'for the sake of distinguishing one from the other, to give them names, which I wrote with chalk on their backs; accordingly when any one of them approached me, the first thing he did was to show me his shoulders.'

In March 1800, partly because of the threat of attack by Bushmen of the great *kraal*, and partly because of the unpredictable behaviour of Captain Vigiland, the mission made a strategic withdrawal to the Sak River. Kicherer was anxious to keep on good terms with Vigiland – after all he was the first Bushman captain to have made a peace agreement, he was an influential figure among the Xam, and his *kraal* was near the new site of the mission – but it became increasingly difficult.

Things came to a head when Vigiland seemed to change overnight into a man of violence, knifing and killing Captain Orlam with whom he had been in Cape Town, and inciting his followers against the missionaries. Kicherer asked Visser to intervene and detain Vigiland on his farm, which Visser did. But when Kicherer left shortly afterwards on a visit to Cape Town, Vigiland was released and appeared at the mission, where he ordered one of the Khoikhoi servants to bring him one of the missionaries' sheep. Kramer, the missionary-cum-farmer who had been left in charge, thought this was stretching Christian charity too far and refused. In a rage, Vigiland stabbed the sheep and would have stabbed Kramer as well if a Bushman girl had not intervened by throwing her *kaross* – a blanket made of antelope skin – between them.

Vigiland was then 'seized by Brother Kramer, who the Lord on this occasion endowed with unusual strength and intrepidity', and who bundled him off to Sergeant Visser. Once again, Visser seemed reluctant to detain Vigiland for very long, and soon afterwards he was at liberty once more, intent on making more mischief. In desperation, Kicherer appealed to Visser's old rival Gerrit Maritz, who had recently been made Field Cornet of the Middle Roggeveld, asking him to send a commando to deal with Vigiland. Although Maritz moved with caution, not wishing to disrupt the fragile truce in Bushmanland, he and his men succeeded in capturing the renegade captain, but as he was being taken to Stellenbosch under escort, Vigiland managed to escape, 'foaming with rage, and calling upon his numerous horde to assist him in revenging the affront'.

It was Maritz who was able to explain what was at the root of the trouble. 'When I asked him why he did this,' he wrote in his official report to the Stellenbosch magistrate, 'he answered what are the missionaries doing in this country, why don't they stay

Chief 'Fritz' Aribib, with his wives and bodyguards. In 1895, he signed a treaty with the Germans, ceding large tracts of land in the Etosha area to the Reich.

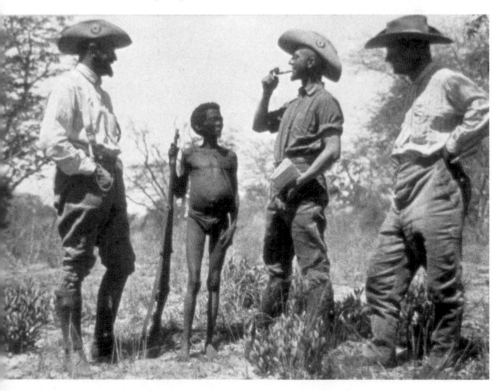

Hauptmann Müller (with pipe) on patrol at Gautsha in 'Bushmanland' in 1911. The smallness of Bushmen was often emphasised, for example by picturing them holding rifles rather than bows.

Wilhelm Bleek in 1862. He and his sister-in-law, Lucy Lloyd, were the first to record the myths and beliefs of the Xam Bushmen and to translate their language. They obtained permission to interview Bushmen prisoners from the Breakwater gaol in Cape Town.

One of their informants was the story-teller, Kabbo. He was among the last of the Xam, who are now extinct.

Bushman prisoners in 1911 in Swakopmund Prison where conditions were said to be 'abominable'. The German geographer, Franz Seiner, protested that the two armless men (marked with crosses) were unlikely to have engaged in stock theft.

Emaciated 'wild' Bushmen
from the Kalahari, circa 1912, the
victims of drought, famine and
repressive German colonial policy.

Three Kung Bushmen
wired by the neck, Amme,
Gane Goa and Guntsa. Taken
during the German occupation
of Namibia, in 1910.
The original listed their skin
colour, height and height when
seated. The semi-erect penis
was normal among Bushmen.

German justice, circa 1914. This photograph was sold as a postcard among the German settler community and appeared in the South African Blue Book, documenting German atrocities in South-West Africa.

Pregnant Bushmen women and malnourished children. Taken in the 1930s, the photograph was republished in books and newspapers, often with deliberately misleading captions such as 'Bushmen after a feast'.

Bushmen captured by police during the South African Mandate in the late 1930s. They are wearing burlap sacks and chains.

F. P. Courtney-Clarke, the secretary for South-West Africa, liked to boast that his young Bushman servant Ngani, a Haikom who spoke nine languages, could mix a good cocktail. Later, Ngani acted as interpreter for the Marshall family.

In 1936, the South African big-game hunter Donald Bain led a group of Bushmen through the streets of Cape Town to Parliament, in an attempt to persuade the government to restore their hunting rights – part of his campaign to save 'the living fossils' of the Kalahari.

P. J. Schoeman (right), Chairman of the Commission for the Preservation of the Bushmen, recommended the creation of two Bushman reserves. In 1952, he exhibited a group of 'wild' Bushmen from Namibia at the van Riebeeck Festival in Cape Town.

Toma, the great hunter and leader of the Bushmen at Nyae Nyae who befriended the Marshall family.

'Beautiful Ungka'. Sadly, she died of malnutrition and tuberculosis, along with many of the Marshall's friends in Tshumkwe.

Bushman mother and child, Nyae Nyae, early 1950s.

A Bushman soldier with an officer of the South African Pied Crow battalion at Omega in the Caprivi Strip, in the 1980s during the Angolan War. The photographer has gone out of his way to emphasise how tiny the Bushman is.

with the other Dutch people, [and] that he could not endure the Dutch living in his country.'

Vigiland undoubtedly saw the missionaries as posing a threat to the Bushman way of life, and he wanted them kept out of his territory. In that, he was reacting in very much the same way as Koerikei, the 'bullet-escaper'. A month later, Maritz led a commando to the Sak River but declined to pursue Vigiland, as Kicherer had hoped, into Bushmanland.

Meanwhile, the Dutch were angry because the British governor had put Bushmanland out of bounds to them, and the loss of its seasonal grazing at a time of serious drought made their resentment all the sharper. When crop failure overtook the Roggevelders, the days of pacification – and the mission to the Bushmen – seemed to be numbered.

At about this time, Kicherer had done his best to broaden his charges' horizons by taking nine of them on a visit to Cape Town. The programme was heavily stage managed. The Bushmen made a little speech, written no doubt by Kicherer, thanking the governor 'for permitting Missionaries to come and teach them, no man before having cared for their souls'. Propaganda aside, they seem to have been amused by some of the sights of Cape Town, likening the 'genteel auditory' of the Calvinist Church to a nest of ants, and the sound of its organ to the noise of a swarming bee-hive. Other sights must have made them wonder about the attractions of the Christian religion and British colonial rule. 'Some of the first objects which presented themselves to their affrighted view ... [were] several men hung in chains for atrocious crimes, and many of the Bosjesmen were conscious of having deserved the same punishment. Their terror was soon increased by beholding in a few days the public execution of another malefactor.' Somewhat tactlessly, Kicherer went on to explain to his guests 'the nature and excellence of European Justice, as an ordinance of God'.

Kicherer undoubtedly had a talent for self-deception, but the missionaries were beginning to discover that their flock, like Bushmanland itself, was stony ground on which the seeds of faith sprouted with difficulty. Other races and peoples, for example the Khoikhoi, the Bastaards (Coloureds), and the

Bastaard-Hottentots, were much more receptive to the Christian message, and, not unnaturally, Kicherer and his assistants now began to turn their attention away from the Xam and towards these more rewarding converts.

But why were the Bushmen such unfruitful soil for these harvesters of souls? The answer seems to lie in the very nature of the hunter-gatherer psyche. Professor Alan Barnard, examining the missionary record from the vantage point of the second half of the twentieth century, says that 'only a very small fraction of Bushmen have in any sense been converted to Christianity, and I doubt whether many of these, except at one or two permanent mission settlements in north-eastern Namibia, have displayed even the pretence of giving up their traditional beliefs.' The problem seems to be not one of receptivity, rather of over-receptivity to myths and stories. 'Ideas and stories are easily assimilated without threat to the belief system as a whole,' says Barnard, and Penn agrees. For the Bushmen, the latter adds, 'religion is an integral part of the specific ecosystem in which they operate, and the natural, the social and the spiritual are all closely intertwined.' Flexibility and fluidity are part and parcel of a hunter-gatherer society. But there is also, Penn believes, a 'fundamental inflexibility at the heart of this easy acceptance of other people's stories. No belief is allowed to interfere with the traditional flexibility which is so necessary if hunter-gatherers are to continue to exist as hunters and gatherers. Thus those aspects of the Christian message which encouraged a sedentary life; or a life devoted to the production or exchange of commodities; or a life of service as a bondsman in someone else's employment, or even the adoption of a pastoralist life-style, were rejected as inappropriate.' The wind would eventually blow the Bushmen away completely, but they would die unconverted.

As for Kicherer, he was right in one thing. When one of his converts, Carolus, a Bastaard-Khoikhoi, warned him that 'wicked Bosjesmen' were planning to kill him, Kicherer told him 'not to be afraid, for that the Lord Jesus will preserve us'. Soon afterwards, Kicherer was sitting at an open window one sultry evening, when 'a concealed party of Bosjesmen were just about to discharge a volley of poisoned arrows at me; but, by the same girl who saved the life of brother Kramer from the dagger of Vigiland, they were detected and made off in haste.'

The attempt to kill him seems to have been his final disillusionment and shortly afterwards Kicherer set off for the Orange River where, after the stony ground of Bushmanland, he found 'a great hunger for the bread of life'. But after a year or so there, Kicherer had to return to the old mission on the Sak River. Many of his Khoikhoi entourage were impatient to go back to their familiar haunts, although the reception they received when they did so must have disappointed them deeply. Some of the local Xam Bushmen, who according to Kicherer had expressed 'a great desire for our return', played a rather spiteful trick on them, assuring the new arrivals that there had been plentiful rains, whereas in fact there was a drought. After three days without water the missionary herds and flocks were in considerable distress. Then, when they reached the first spring, they found the water had been poisoned with 'serpents' heads', and soon afterwards 80 of their oxen were stolen. Although Kicherer's Khoikhoi herdsmen managed to recover 73 of them, it soon became clear that during the missionaries' absence, many of the Xam had reverted to their bad old ways of 'reiving and raiding'.

Three years of severe drought had forced the Xam to travel great distances in search of water, and even the Bushmen on Visser's farm had deserted him, disappearing into the veld in classic hunter-gatherer style. Before leaving, however, they had broken into the school house which he had built, and into the grain store of a neighbouring farmer. Visser was forced to ask Maritz – how humiliating that must have been – to send out a commando against them; and adding insult to injury, another group of Bushmen raided his son Gerrit's farm and stole his cattle. That all this should happen to the two architects of reconciliation with the Bushmen, Floris and Gerrit Visser, demonstrated, more dramatically than anything else could have done, the final breakdown of the peace policy.

CHAPTER SEVEN

A Voice in the Wilderness

During the last ten years a wholesale system of extermination of the Bushman people had been practised.

Louis Anthing, Magistrate of Namaqualand, 21 April, 1863

After the Treaty of Amiens in 1802, which brought together Britain, France, Spain and the Batavian Republic – Holland – in a brief respite from war, Britain withdrew from the Cape.* The new Dutch administration was more pro-settler and anti-missionary than its predecessor, and even more determined to exert control over the frontier. Hendrik van der Graaf, the magistrate of the new district of Tulbagh – Stellenbosch having been split up as too cumbersome – was sent north to start negotiations with the Bushmen. His brief was 'to put an end to the robberies and plunderings of these savages by mild and kind treatment, and by this means gradually to remove the ancient hatred borne them by the colonists.' Such sentiments, although laudable, were in reality little more than whitewash.

However high-minded the aspirations of the Batavian Republic, like the Dutch East India Company before it, the harsh realities of life on the frontier soon made them unattainable. Confirmation was not long in coming. In August 1804 Magistrate van der Graaf received a message from one of his field commanders reporting that a Dutch farm manager had killed four followers of a Bushman, Captain Goedhart, and that Goedhart was threatening revenge. So seriously was the news taken that the governor, Janssens, ordered the despatch of a 'solemn commission', headed by van der Graaf, to investigate the

---

* Britain would return to the Cape in earnest in 1806 when Napoleon's continuing military adventures had the statesmen of Europe trembling in their chancelleries.

matter on the spot. While the commission was trying to start negotiations with Goedhart, two Khoikhoi servants of another local farmer were killed by a different group of Bushmen. Despite the inflamed situation, Gerrit Visser, thanks to his negotiating and linguistic skills, managed to achieve a settlement which offered the Bushmen an amnesty and an 'annual tribute' of cattle, providing that they kept the peace. During the negotiations the Bushmen were entertained, given presents of sheep and promised that the magistrate would visit them in six months' time to seal the pact.

However fair and generous the settlement might seem, it probably never had a real chance of success, since suspicion and dislike, and hatred too, were so deeply ingrained on both sides. The events that followed had about them a tragic inevitability. Word spread among the Dutch that Captain Goedhart, on whom van der Graaf had pinned so many of his hopes, appeared to have gone back on his promise to keep the peace, by allegedly stealing 400 cattle. Just as one of van der Graaf's men, Field Cornet Olivier, was setting out at the head of a commando to investigate, he discovered that Goedhart and his men had crossed the Sak River and killed a white farmer, Christian Koopman: '43 arrows were found in his body, together with some wounds from an assegai, and his head had been dashed to pieces with a stone.' The brutality of this murder led van der Graaf to propose to the governor a harsh plan: soldiers would be sent in to protect the colonists, and Bushman lawbreakers would be arrested and sentenced to forced labour, possibly on Robben Island. In this way, van der Graaf hoped, the Bushmen might be led 'though perhaps not till the second generation . . . to adopt more active and civilised lives'.

There would be two benefits, van der Graaf suggested: the borders would be free from 'a terrible evil' and the Bushmen, 'these poor creatures', would be encouraged to aim at a higher degree of cultivation. As a reward for good behaviour, the magistrate generously added, the best behaved might gradually be released, and allowed to go home, where they might 'introduce something like civilisation among their countrymen'. The plan came to nothing, initially because Governor Janssens did not have enough troops to implement it, and, subsequently, because he and his government were thrown out the following year by the British, when they reassumed control of the Cape. The immediate reason for the collapse of the peace policy, however was something that no one, except God, could control: drought was the final blow. There was no water in the Sak River, which had been dry for five years and would be dry for a sixth year too. There was no grazing, neither for the trekboer livestock, nor for the game. Violence between the Xam Bushmen and the trekboers intensified. With little or no game remaining to hunt, since the settlers had shot out virtually all the eland, buffalo and quagga – a kind of zebra, now extinct – the Bushmen were forced to turn to the only animals left, the trekboers' livestock.

Many farmers left the heights of the escarpment for the Karoo much earlier than usual because of the drought, horse sickness, and attacks by Bushmen, including Kicherer's own mission Bushmen. In 1805 a large group of Xam fell on a flock of 200 sheep which the missionaries had just bought and which were being driven to the mission by two Bastaard shepherds. In the melee, both shepherds were wounded by poisoned arrows, one fatally. A commando was called out and the Bushmen tracked to beyond the Sak River, where nine were killed. The commando also recovered more than 100 oxen stolen from another farm, but not the missionaries' sheep, which had all been killed, as if in a final act of revenge.

That same year, Napoleon, newly-crowned as emperor, had defeated Austria and (despite Nelson's destruction of the French and Spanish navies at Trafalgar) was on the march again in 1806, this time routing the much-vaunted Prussian army; he was beginning to look invincible on land, if not on the high seas. Britain therefore moved with some haste to reoccupy the Cape and safeguard the vital sea link to India. Although the British government is unlikely to have known it, Napoleon had already ordered the French admiralty to prepare plans for an expedition to the Cape in 1812, the year, as it happened, when he decided to invade Russia instead.

The new British governor, the Earl of Caledon, a twenty-nine-year-old Irish peer, arrived in southern Africa in 1807 to be faced by a number of pressing matters. The most urgent were the running sore of the Bushman war and settler unrest at what they claimed was an acute labour shortage, brought about by Britain's recent abolition of slavery. The settlers' grievances were given priority, in the shape of legislation known as the Caledon, or Hottentot, Code, since it was the first attempt to regulate relationships between the colonists and the Khoikhoi, who still provided the colony's main labour force. Although the Code improved conditions of service for Khoikhoi farm labourers, it also, in the opinion of Dr John Philip of the London Missionary Society, condemned the Hottentots 'to a perpetual state of servitude'. It forced them, willy-nilly, on to the labour market, and introduced for the first time a pass system, the forerunner to the infamous pass laws which, much later, were to become one of the most hated instruments of apartheid.

But the Bushman problem would not wait. Soon after his arrival, Caledon received an alarming letter from Magistrate van der Graaf, informing his Lordship that in the first four months of 1807 Bushmen in his own district had stolen 818 sheep, 200 goats, 93 cattle and 20 horses, and killed 14 Khoikhoi and 3 whites. He also reported that local commanders were complaining about a shortage of ammunition and demanding the right to mount full-scale punitive commandos without first having to obtain the governor's permission. Caledon refused to be rushed, and decided (like Macartney before him) that he would commission his own review, by his own trusted observer. Just as Macartney had despatched John Barrow to the frontier, Caledon sent out Colonel Richard Collins in 1808 on a tour of inspection that would last more than a year. At the end of it Collins came to much the same conclusion as Barrow; the best way to advance 'the cause of peace' was to encourage state-supervised mission stations whose task would be to transform the Bushmen into 'useful wage labourers'. It was a mistake, he argued, to give them gifts of sheep, knives, tobacco, tinder-boxes, and so on; rather these things should be obtainable only from the mission stations, and in return the Bushmen would be expected to barter skins, ostrich feathers, ivory and possibly, as the Governor himself suggested, *biltong*.

Lord Caledon left the Cape in 1811, and Collins's recommendations were never carried out. Even if they had been, it is hard to believe they would have succeeded. Bushmen had no interest in the Protestant work ethic. They had no wish to be labourers in a white man's vineyard, Boer or British, or to be herders of his cattle. They wanted to remain free and independent, 'lords of the desert', as they had been before the coming of the white man. If they had to fight to preserve their ancient way of life, they would fight. If they had to die for their beliefs, they would die. Even as Lord Caledon and Colonel Collins were devising means to tame the Bushmen, and bring them within the settler economy – now just as much the preoccupation of the British authorities as it had been of the Dutch – the Bushmen were still determinedly at war, trying to keep the trekboers off their land.

The callous indifference with which the Bushmen were being exterminated appalled George Thompson, a British traveller in the Cape at around the turn of the century. 'In the afternoon,' he wrote in his journal, 'I left Beaufort in a waggon drawn by six horses. I was accompanied by three Boors [sic], one of whom informed me . . . that he had lately been out on commando against the Bushmen, in which 30 of those unfortunate creatures were shot; namely 26 men, 2 women and 2 children! This is truly a shocking system . . . still continued under the beneficent sway of England.' Worse was to come under successive British administrations. In the years before the Great Trek of 1835, when the Voortrekkers finally launched themselves in considerable numbers across the Orange River, the Bushmen fought and lost the battle for the Sneeuberg. They were defeated and 'pacified' by both almost non-stop commando activity and the more insidious practice of gift-giving. Even though missions to the Bushmen had been a failure, Bushman resistance, says Nigel Penn, was 'fatally undermined by the infiltration of seemingly peaceful colonists into their territory'.

Once the colonists were able to establish themselves beyond

the Sneeuberg, the Bushmen were unable to prevent the destruction of their society and their way of life. Every man's hand was against them, everyone wanted their land, whether Dutch farmers, or Bastaard and Khoikhoi-Bastaard pastoralists. Those who were not killed or taken prisoner retreated deep into the most inhospitable parts of Bushmanland in an attempt to survive, and to avoid becoming virtual slaves on colonial farms.

Their numbers declined dramatically as they were hunted down by Boer or Bastaard commandos who were determined to turn the Cape interior into a Bushman-free area. Under 'intolerable pressure' from white colonists, more and more Hottentot and Bastaard pastoralists began to move into Bushmanland. In 1847, the entire north-western Cape as far as the Orange River was annexed to the Cape Colony. Bushmanland was declared a communal grazing area in which white, Khoikhoi and Bastaard farmers had equal rights. Only the Bushmen – supreme irony – had no rights. By the middle of the nineteenth century, the world of the independent Bushmen had shrunk to the most arid areas, and even there they were not safe. The killing continued.

Thomas Pringle, described by Allister Sparks as South Africa's first journalist, had arrived from Britain with the 1820 settlers who established themselves at Grahamstown in the Eastern Cape. He has left a vivid description of one commando raid, based on an interview with a Boer farmer who took part in it. After taking the 'hapless little tribe' by surprise, the commando opened fire, killing most of them. When the firing stopped, five women were found to be still alive. 'The lives of these, after long discussion, it was resolved to spare,' writes Pringle, 'because one farmer wanted a servant for this purpose, and another for that. The unfortunate wretches were ordered to march in front of the commando, but it was soon found that they impeded our progress – not being able to proceed fast enough. They were, therefore, ordered to be shot. . . . The helpless victims, perceiving what was intended, sprung to us, and clung so firmly to some of the party that it was for some time impossible to shoot them without hazarding the lives of those they held fast. Four of them were at length despatched, but the fifth could by no means be torn from one of our comrades, whom she had grasped in her agony, and his entreaties to be allowed to take this woman home were at last complied with.'

Pringle, who brought an impartial eye to the genocide which had become an everyday occurrence, also tells of an army commander who was returning from a commando raid when he saw a figure wrapped in a *kaross* lying beside the path. 'Without uttering a word or asking a question,' Pringle recounts, the commander 'levelled his musket and fired. The *kaross* heaved up – and an aged female, in the agonies of death, rolled out of it. And the party rode on, without considering the matter worthy even of a passing remark.'

Out of this morass of brutal indifference emerged one day in the early 1860s a hitherto unknown but quite remarkable figure; a man much ahead of his time, an important local government official and an Afrikaner. His name was Louis Anthing, and he was the magistrate of Namaqualand, with his office in Calvinia, a pretty little town built in the Cape Dutch style, 3000 feet up in the foothills of the Hantam mountains. Anthing made himself highly unpopular with the British authorities at the Cape for daring to demand justice for the Bushmen. His single-handed campaign on their behalf was to cost him his career, and almost certainly his health, but his courage and his determination to see justice done never wavered. His involvement began in 1861 when he received a complaint from Jaco Fluik, a Bushman, stating that his people were being slaughtered by mixed commandos of whites, Bastaards and Khoikhoi. Anthing investigated Fluik's charges and uncovered evidence of many horrific massacres of Bushmen in the previous ten years. On 21 April 1863 he wrote a long report to the Colonial Secretary in Cape Town, which was laid before the Cape Parliament the following June. In it, he said: 'During the last ten years a wholesale system of extermination of the Bushman people had been practised. Corannas from the Orange River, Kafirs from Schietfontein, coloured and European farmers from Namaqualand, Bokkeveld, Hantam, Roggeveld, the districts of Fraserburg and Victoria, and doubtless Hope Town too, all shared in the destruction of these people ... the killing of the Bushmen was not confined to the avenging or punishing of [stock] thefts, but that, with or without provocation, Bushmen were killed – sometimes by hunting parties, at other times by commandos going out for the express purpose.'

Anthing then listed a number of the case histories he had researched, and which still make gruesome reading.* The first dealt with the activities seven or eight years before of a commando consisting of local European farmers, accompanied by a number of Bastaards, which entered Bushmanland to 'punish the Bushmen for alleged thefts'. The commando was split into two wings, the left made up of Europeans, which headed for the Hartebeest River, and the right wing, consisting of the Bastaards, taking the direction of the Kareebergen. The European wing attacked the Bushmen at a place called Boschduif, killing the entire community with the exception of one man who managed to escape, and either one or two small children, who were found alive and were taken away by the farmers. 'They then proceeded to a smaller *kraal* and killed every soul. From what I can learn,' wrote Anthing, 'upwards of two hundred must have been killed.'

Meanwhile the right wing came upon the Bushmen at a place known since then as Bushmanskolk. 'They allured the Bushmen to their wagons with professions of peace, and then massacred them, only two women escaping. The number killed by the right wing is said to have been more than that killed by the left wing.' Similar atrocities – Anthing wrote 'occurrences' – took place in several other places in Bushmanland in the same period. 'Hundreds must have been killed in each of these affairs.' Anthing then quoted the words of one of the witnesses whom he does not name, but who presumably was a Khoikhoi servant. 'They surrounded the place during the night, spying the Bushmen's fires. At daybreak the firing commenced, and it lasted until the sun was up a little way. The commando party loaded and fired, and reloaded many times before they had finished. A great many people [women and children] were killed that day. The men were absent. Only a few little children escaped, and

---

* Reprinted in *Miscast*, edited by Pippa Skotnes, Capetown, 1996.

they were distributed amongst the people composing the commando. The women threw up their arms, crying for mercy, but no mercy was shown them. Great sin was perpetrated that day. I was taken by my master to hold his horses. I did not join in the shooting. I had no gun.'

Anthing's letter, which was a long one, gave details of other, smaller but 'equally horrible' incidents. A Bushman herding some rams belonging to a Bastaard killed them and ate them, saying they had died from other causes. His employer told him to repay him in ostrich feathers, then a valuable commodity, which the Bushman did. 'The feathers were taken, but he was told they were not enough, whereupon he went home. The same day a party of six men – two Bastaards, two Europeans, and two Hottentots – proceeded to the Bushman's place of abode, with the avowed intention of killing him. They surrounded his hut during the night, and at daybreak shot him and his wife and child, leaving the bodies to be devoured by wild animals.' The Bushman had eaten the rams, 'doubtless, from hunger, not having enough to eat'.

In the cases Anthing had described, he went on, there was certainly some provocation, 'but I am assured that many Bushmen have been killed without any pretext whatever. The evidence I have taken states that parties were in the habit of going out to hunt and shoot any Bushmen they might find.' He had no reason to doubt the reports, because only a few days before he had been told of a Roggeveld farmer, who had admitted how in his younger days, he and other young farmers were in the habit of going out to shoot Bushmen 'for the fun of the thing'. The farmer described how, on one occasion, 'three Bushmen whom they had met, and who were quietly pursuing their way, were deliberately shot when their backs were turned to them.'

Magistrate Anthing listed one more case history which, he said, would reveal 'the desperation of the Bushmen'. It concerned a Bushman named Hercules, a leader of a guerrilla band who had given himself up to Anthing. On the day of the Boschduif massacre, described above, Hercules' entire family was slaughtered – his parents and all his brothers and sisters except one brother, who had gone hunting with Hercules. He had also lost all his wife's family in the attack on the smaller *kraal* by the same commando. Yet, Anthing goes on, 'all this does not appear to have driven him to any act of revenge. Probably his spirit was broken by the destruction of the whole of his clan.' Hercules continued to work for the Bastaards, despite being very badly treated, until one day 'his son and two other young Bushmen stole, or, by their account, took some sheep which they found straying in the veld. The young men were pursued. One escaped with a bullet wound in the neck; the two others, of whom Hercules' son was one, were killed. Hercules told me that his son had crept into a hole after being wounded, and had afterwards been dragged out and ripped open whilst he was still alive.' This drove Hercules to resistance. 'He ran away from his master and went into the bush, where he was joined by others, and they then resolved to resent their grievances.'

Hercules was eventually persuaded by other Bushmen to give himself up to Anthing, to whom he showed 'a little hair clotted with blood which he carried near his heart and said that that had belonged to his finest boy who had been killed, and that it was that which had led him to the same course he had been pursuing.'

In another letter to the colonial secretary, dated 29 May 1863, Anthing suggested that a farmer from the Lower Roggeveld, Floris Steenkamp, who was 'perfectly acquainted with all the facts', should be called to Cape Town. Steenkamp had taken part in commando operations from boyhood. He knew that parties of Bushmen who had never done any harm had been 'wantonly and treacherously massacred; that other Bushmen with whom he had been personally acquainted, and who had done him and others many kind services, had shared a similar fate; that the Bushman people had been hunted down and exterminated; that commandos with which he was present had shot down men, women and children when these had begged that the firing might cease so that they might surrender, and that he, Steenkamp, had been upbraided by the Field Cornet for interceding on behalf of the women and children; that on occasions there had been no necessity at all for violence as the Bushmen would in all probability have surrendered.' Steenkamp offered to give evidence, but his offer was ignored.

By the end of his inquiry, Anthing estimated that only about 500 Bushmen were left alive in the whole of the Cape, and that many of the dead had not been shot but had starved to death. He recommended that to protect this remnant a magistrate should be established in Kenhardt, and land set aside for the Bushmen. The government approved the first of these recommendations, but never implemented it because of lack of funds.

Anthing continued to campaign tirelessly and doggedly in the cause of the doomed Bushmen, not only to no avail, but to the annoyance of his superiors. Nothing further was done to protect the Bushmen. No magistracy was established, no land was set aside for them, they were given no food or other assistance, and none of the perpetrators of the genocide was ever prosecuted and brought to trial. Anthing was transferred to Cradock, and eventually his salary was stopped. In 1865, in poor health, he was forced to resign. To its lasting shame, the British colonial government could finally wash its hands of the Bushmen, and forget about Louis Anthing.

The miserable remnant of a once proud people, now starving, was forced to steal livestock to stay alive. If caught, they were murdered by local farmers or sent to Cape Town's Breakwater Prison and condemned to forced labour. Even when they were released, few survived for very long because their families had been uprooted and destroyed. A few joined the Korana uprising of 1868, but as Nigel Penn says 'there was no place left for them on earth'.

It was while a number of Xam were serving their sentences at the Breakwater that a remarkable German churchman, Wilhelm Bleek, obtained permission to record their myths. Finally Bleek and his sister-in-law, Lucy Lloyd, were allowed to have several of the prisoners stay at their house in Cape Town so that they could spend more time on their research. So began the first scholarly attempt to translate and record the Xam language and beliefs. One of the prisoners, Diakwain, described to Bleek and Lloyd what the Xam believed happened after death. Using the

Bleek-Lloyd translation, Stephen Watson turned his words into verse.

> The wind when we die, our own wind blows.
> For we, the Xam people, each of us owns a wind;
> each one has a cloud that comes out when we die.
> Therefore the wind when we die, the wind blows dust
> covering the tracks, the footprints we made
> when walking about living, with nothing the matter,
> when we still knew nothing of sickness and death.
>
> If not for this wind, our spoor would still show,
> our spoor would still show us, as if we still lived.

CHAPTER EIGHT

German South-West Africa

Within the German boundaries, every Herero, whether found armed or unarmed, with or without cattle, will be shot.

General von Trotha, 1904

Towards the end of the nineteenth century, the German Reich was the only major European power not to have embarked on the 'scramble' for Africa. Prince Otto von Bismarck, the cunning, arrogant and all-powerful imperial Chancellor, had always argued that Germany did not want any colonies. To maintain colonies one needed a big navy, and Germany's was tiny; moreover, colonies were expensive and Germany could not afford them. But in 1883 Bismarck changed his mind. A civil servant named von Kusserow, whom he was later to curse, persuaded him that being a colonial power need not be expensive – provided one followed the British system of using charter companies to foot the bill. Being devious as well as dictatorial, the Iron Chancellor concealed his intentions so skilfully that when on 7 August 1884 Germany took possession of a small, rocky, windswept island, halfway along the coast between the Cape Colony and Angola, christened Angra Pequena by the Portuguese, the British were taken completely by surprise. Togo and the Cameroons had been claimed by Bismarck's secret envoy, Dr Nachtigal, in July, and Bismarck had now added German South-West Africa, today's Namibia, a vast swathe of mountain, desert and rolling grassland, with a long, inhospitable coastline where diamonds would be found in staggering quantities. German East Africa followed a year later.

The ogre, as Disraeli called Bismarck to Queen Victoria, had done the insufferable English in the eye. Lord Derby, the

Colonial Secretary, accused him of 'sharp practice', but Gladstone, the Prime Minister, a convinced Liberal opposed to imperialism in all its forms, saw no harm in giving a slice of Africa to a 'good neighbour' like Germany. He went further, as Thomas Pakenham points out in his epic history, *The Scramble for Africa*, saying he looked 'with satisfaction, sympathy and joy upon the extension of Germany in these desert places of the earth'. Opinion in the cabinet was divided into what Mrs Thatcher would have called 'wets' and 'drys'. The chief wet was Gladstone himself, but some of his ministers, above all the radical, Joseph Chamberlain, were distinctly dry. 'The Cameroons!' he raged to fellow radical, Sir Charles Dilke. 'It is enough to make one sick. As you say, we decided to assume the protectorate eighteen months ago, and I thought it was all settled. If the Board of Trade or Local Government Board managed their business after the fashion of the Foreign Office and Colonial Office, you and I would deserve to be hung.'

The establishment of German South-West Africa was a direct threat to British interests in southern Africa. Not only did German South-West have a common border with the Cape Colony on the Orange River, it shared a frontier with Bechuanaland, now Botswana, another vast, semi-desert territory also destined to become fabulously rich through diamonds. Bechuanaland stretched half across Africa as far as the Transvaal, a Boer republic whose Afrikaner subjects were only too eager to twist the British lion's tail. If the Boers from the Transvaal were to link up with the Germans from South-West Africa, both Natal and the Cape would be at risk. There were other considerations too. A year earlier, the young member for Barkly West, the diamond millionaire Cecil Rhodes, had told the House of Assembly in Cape Town that Bechuanaland must be secured for Britain because it was 'the Suez Canal of the trade of this country, the key of its road to the interior'. Gladstone, despite his reluctance to make any move which smacked of imperialism, finally agreed, and 4000 colonial troops under a British officer were ordered north from the Cape to take possession of Bechuanaland. To sighs of relief all round, they did it without firing a shot. At the same time, Britain annexed St Lucia Bay on the east coast, north of Durban, to block the Transvaal's access to the sea. German territorial ambitions were thwarted in terms of an east–west link.

It was one thing to run up a flag, however, and another to run a colony from scratch, especially one as big as South-West Africa, nearly two and a half times the size of the Fatherland. The first governor, Colonel Theodor von Leutwein, supported by a mere handful of officials, servicemen and settlers, was so desperately short of money that his field of manoeuvre was extremely limited. Although the Reich had the best army on the continent of Europe, von Leutwein's budget would not stretch to more than a few hundred troops. Indeed, the poverty of the the new colony was so crippling that at one stage in the 1890s Bismarck even thought of abandoning the whole enterprise, and handing it over to the British. A sealed letter lay in a desk in the Foreign Ministry in the Wilhelmstrasse in Berlin which said: 'The Emperor is prepared to give up South-West Africa if necessary, so that all energies may be focused on East Africa.'

The crisis passed, largely because of the negotiating skills of the governor, a stolid but humane soldier. His policy of personal friendship with the tribal chiefs, although despised by most of the now 5000-odd settlers, paid off. There was peace, although the 'barbarous' behaviour of the settlers not only made von Leutwein's task of conciliation doubly hard, it was storing up a deep well of resentment and hatred. The Herero people, Bantu-speaking pastoralists who had migrated south over the centuries from central Africa, and to whom their cattle were sacrosanct, suffered most. Floggings, and even murders of Herero farm servants and rapes of their women, were almost everyday occurrences. Pakenham quotes one Herero tribesman's remark to a German settler: 'The missionary says that we are the children of God like our white brothers . . . but just look at us. Dogs, slaves, worse than baboons on the rocks . . . that is how you treat us.'

In 1904, the Hereros rose in open rebellion. Von Leutwein, who prided himself on knowing what the Africans were thinking, was caught completely unawares. When the news reached him, he was in the south, busy putting down a revolt by the Bondelswarts, a branch of the Nama, the other big pastoralist tribe in the colony.

The Hereros' paramount chief, Samuel Maherero, was not a fighting man and had always had good relations with the governor, but he was egged on by his young warriors, itching to 'wash' their spears in German blood, and by the general desperation of his people. The mood is made clear in the appeal he sent to another tribal leader, Hendrik Witbooi, chief of the Witbooi Nama: 'All our obedience and patience with the Germans is of little avail for each day they shoot someone dead for no reason at all. Hence I appeal to you, my Brother, not to hold aloof from the uprising, but to make your voice heard so that all Africa may take up arms against the Germans. Let us die fighting rather than die as a result of maltreatment, imprisonment or some other calamity. Tell all the Kapteins [chiefs] down there to rise and do battle.' This letter, with its rousing appeal to 'all Africa', went astray, although it is unlikely that Hendrik Witbooi, who was aged eighty and a born-again Christian, would have answered the call. Instead, in loyalty to von Leutwein, Witbooi sent a token force to support the Germans against his hereditary enemy. For two weeks, however, Maherero's warriors had it all their own way, ransacking isolated farms and murdering about 100 settlers, some of whom were ritually tortured before being put to death. Although every adult German male, apart from the missionaries, was considered fair game, the Herero spared the women and children, as well as all other whites, including the British and Afrikaners.

By the end of January, thanks to the call-up of reservists, and to a dramatic dash from the south by mounted troops to relieve Windhoek and other garrison towns, the tide had turned; the Germans had recaptured the initiative.

By mid-February von Leutwein was back from the south, ready to negotiate a peace settlement with Chief Maherero, but Berlin had other plans. The Kaiser, in his role as commander-in-chief, demoted von Leutwein as military commander, although he remained governor, replacing him by the iron-jawed General Lothar von Trotha, who was instructed to stamp out the rebellion 'by fair means or foul'. When von Trotha arrived in

Swakopmund in June – he had gained his reputation for ruthlessness in the Boxer Rebellion in China four years before – he brusquely told von Leutwein there would be no negotiations. Instead, the war would continue and the Herero would be put down by force of arms. By August, the Herero had withdrawn to the Waterberg, a rocky plateau on the edge of the Omaheke sandveld, the western limit of the Kalahari Desert. General von Trotha's plan was simple. He would drive the Herero out of the Waterberg, and force them to move to the east, into the Omaheke. Von Leutwein and some of his officers were horrified, since they knew the destruction of the Herero and their cattle would impoverish not only them, but the whole colony as well. Von Trotha was adamant.

By the end of August some 8000 Herero men, and twice as many women and children, with what was left of their cattle, horses and other animals and possessions, had fled into the great waste of sand which stretches 200 miles east from the Waterberg to the then Bechuanaland border. In the Omaheke there was no water, no food, no shade, and it was so hot the sand burned their bare feet in the middle of the day. The only people who could survive in the Omaheke were the Bushmen, and even they sometimes died of thirst. Once the trap was sprung, von Trotha sealed the wells, and blocked all escape.

At the beginning of October he issued a proclamation that was breathtaking in its arrogance and barbarity. 'I, the Great General of the German soldiers, address this letter to the Herero people. The Herero are no longer considered German subjects. They have murdered, stolen, cut off ears and other parts from wounded soldiers, and now refuse to fight on, out of cowardice. I have this to say to them . . . the Herero people will have to leave the country. Otherwise I shall force them to do so by means of guns. Within the German boundaries, every Herero, whether found armed or unarmed, with or without cattle, will be shot. I shall not accept any more women or children. I shall drive them back to their people – otherwise I shall order shots to be fired at them. Signed: the Great General of the Mighty Kaiser, von Trotha.'

'Drive them out – or wipe them out,' as Pakenham comments.

Von Trotha did both. By the end of October he was saying he had a plan to eliminate the entire Herero tribe. This went too far. His *Vernichtungsbefehl* (extermination order) caused consternation when it became public knowledge in Germany. Bismarck's successor as imperial chancellor, Count von Bülow, appealed to the Kaiser for permission to cancel it on the grounds that it was 'demeaning to our standing among the civilised nations of the world'. The Kaiser thought about it for five days, and then suggested that von Trotha should be told to 'show mercy' to the Herero. Von Bülow protested this was too vague, and the Kaiser spent another eight days agonising over that. Finally he gave in: instructions were sent to von Trotha to cancel the extermination order and offer the Herero surrender terms.

While all this was going on, Hendrik Witbooi, the octogenarian Nama chief, decided that, despite his earlier refusal, the time had come to take up arms against the Germans. He told his fellow chiefs: 'I have now stopped walking submissively and will write a letter to the [German] Captain saying that I have put on the white feather [the Nama war emblem] and that the time is over when I will walk behind him. . . . The Saviour himself will now act and He will free us through His grace and compassion.' Alas for the Nama, although they were brilliant natural guerrilla fighters and ran rings round the clod-hopping Germans, Hendrik Witbooi's death brought about the collapse of the rebellion. By then von Trotha was on his way home, and the tragic tally of his campaign was being totted up. More than half the 80,000 Hereros had been driven into the Omaheke, and most of them had died of hunger and thirst – no one knows exactly how many. About 5000, including Samuel Maherero, the paramount chief, managed to escape to Bechuanaland or the Cape. Many ended up in forced labour camps, where more than half the 15,000 Herero and 2000 Nama prisoners died. Conditions were even worse on Shark Island, near Angra Pequena, where Hendrik Witbooi's closest companions were sent. In the space of seven months, 1032 out of a total of 1732 prisoners had died of cold and ill treatment. When the 1911 census was taken, it was found that only half the Nama – 9800 out of 20,000 – and less than a quarter of the Herero – 15,000 out of 80,000 – had survived. In

Berlin, General von Trotha was awarded the Order of Merit – the Blue Max – by the Kaiser, for services to the Fatherland.

Although the Bushmen of South-West Africa were not the prime target of the Germans in the Herero-Nama war, its impact on them was 'devastating', according to Robert Gordon in his masterly history, *The Bushman Myth*. In some cases Bushmen were directly caught up in the conflict. One Bushman 'chief', Korob, allied himself with the Herero and fought alongside them at the Waterberg. Korob and his men somehow escaped the disaster of the Omaheke and continued afterwards to raid white farms in the area of the Okarusu mountains. They also made a living by ambushing and robbing Ovambo tribesmen on their way home from working on European farms. The local newspaper, the *Südwest Zeitung*, described them as 'cruel, cowardly, and cunning' and said 'fighting them was extraordinarily difficult.' They could vanish without trace and 'still have numerous rifles which we have not been able to remove'.

The war radicalised white opinion among both settlers and officials, something which drastically affected all non-whites, especially the Bushmen. All were the victims, one might say, of von Trotha's extermination policy. By 1905, for example, the life of a Bushman had come to be considered as of less value than that of any other black or coloured in the colony. The state had started making an 'ominous distinction between *eingeborenen*, indigenous inhabitants, and *Buschleute*, bush people'. Gordon cites the following case of a twenty-two-year-old German farmer from the Outjo district. The farmer, Wiehager, who was also a reserve officer in the army, killed two Herero women and a child for 'deserting his service' – in other words, running away from his farm. He was tried and sentenced to three years' imprisonment. While out on bail he captured three Bushmen – a common method of acquiring cheap labour – and later killed them. In the subsequent trial, he was found not guilty and discharged, despite having admitted in a private letter to the local military commander that he had killed them. The verdict was such a blatant miscarriage of justice that the government was forced to appeal, and this time Wiehager was sentenced to five years. As a rich young farmer he was able to retain a Berlin lawyer who called numerous witnesses, including the chief surgeon of the army, who testified that Bushmen had a 'treacherous' nature and that the army had orders to shoot any Bushman who did not stand still when told to do so.

Another consequence of the Herero-Nama war was a sharp increase in white settlement in the Grootfontein area north-east of the Waterberg. Grootfontein, always considered one of the best farming areas in the colony, was just south-east of Tsumeb, a rich copper-mining area which for centuries had been controlled and worked by the Bushmen, a surprising achievement for supposedly primitive hunter-gatherers. More settlers meant the need for more cheap labour, and very soon Bushmen began to be conscripted in considerable numbers into the colonial economy, including, ironically, the copper mines which they had once owned. The Germans were not fussy about how the recruitment was done. In November 1908, the *Südwest Zeitung* reported that a patrol from the Waterberg had arrested 50 Bushmen in the Tsumeb area and transferred them to the copper mines as, in effect, slave labour. To the west, in 1910, the Outjo district council voiced its concern at the number of grass fires being started, and, blaming the Bushmen, ordered all of them to report for work. A police patrol managed to round up more than 100 of these alleged 'arsonists', but all escaped shortly after the patrol reached Outjo.

In the same period, the authorities established three game reserves, all on Bushman land, and introduced strict game laws; hunting of giraffe, buffalo, eland and female kudu was banned. Forbidding them to hunt was as effective in exterminating the Bushmen as anything ordained by General von Trotha.

At Namutoni, in today's Etosha National Park, then Game Reserve No. 2, patrols were sent out regularly to round up Bushmen who were forcibly removed to a 'permanent' home elsewhere, meaning a white farm on which they would have to work for little or no pay. When the Germans first arrived, Etosha was controlled by Fritz Aribib, with whom the colony's first governor, von Leutwein, signed a treaty in 1895. This recognised Aribib as chief of all the Western Bushmen. Bushmen did not have chiefs, and it is therefore not clear how much, or how little, control Aribib actually had over his fellow Bushmen. Three years later, in 1898, one of von Leutwein's officers, Captain von Estorf, signed another 'protection treaty' in which Aribib ceded a huge piece of land including Grootfontein, Tsumeb and the Etosha Pan, for an annual payment of 500 marks. In return he was given German protection, and his people had the permanent right to forage for bush foods.

This raises an important point of international law. The signature of the two treaties, which implicitly recognised that Etosha and the whole surrounding area belonged to the Bushmen, would seem to establish that Aribib and his successors, the Haikom of Etosha, were the legitimate owners not only of Etosha Pan, but of the Tsumeb copper mines as well. The Haikom Bushmen would therefore appear to be entitled to benefit from a land rights claim to Etosha, at the very least, similar to the one conceded to the Khomani Bushmen of South Africa in 1999.

Aribib received his 500 marks every year as long as he lived. After his death the government declared the northern part of the treaty area a game reserve, now the Etosha National Park. The Bushmen living there were expelled from the reserve and forced to work for white farmers, who had the legal right to administer corporal punishment with a *sjambok* (rhinoceros-hide whip) – up to 25 strokes – and frequently did so.

In 1911 the Bushmen rebelled. The colonial press was full of headlines trumpeting 'Bushman Plague', 'Bushman Danger' and 'Yellow Peril'. The incidents that inspired this outburst were a spate of livestock thefts and, subsequently, the murder of white settlers in the Grootfontein area. One Bushman bandit leader, Namagurub, was active north of Grootfontein, between Tsintsabis and Kavango. He and his band, who were well-armed with rifles, were believed to have killed one white farmer and to have stolen 150 head of cattle from another. It took the police four years to catch him, and then only after receiving a tip-off from other Bushmen that he was planning an attack on the police station at Blockfontein, on the Kavango road, well outside his usual territory. The Germans finally managed to raid his large *werft* (*kraal*), setting the huts on fire, and causing a big explosion as Namagurub's arsenal, well stocked with gunpowder and ammunition, went up.

There was also a sharp increase in Robin Hood-style raids on comparatively rich workers going home from the copper mines with bulging tin trunks. Groups of three to five Bushmen armed with bows and arrows and the occasional muzzle-loader would hold up and rob parties of up to 60 unarmed Ovambos and Kavangos. By 1912 the situation was so serious that the Luderitz Bay Chamber of Commerce sent a peremptory note to the government demanding action. 'Be so kind as to proceed without delay in cleaning-up the Bushman rabble in that district.' But the rabble proved hard to catch and miners started to send some of their more valuable possessions by oxwagon or through the post.

The terror the Bushmen inspired was luridly portrayed by the *Südwest Zeitung*. 'They have been overtaken by such fear of the Bushmen, that a group of 30 strong people will throw away its belongings and flee, even if only two Bushmen show themselves with bow and arrow. For this reason the District Office is taking serious action. Mobile police stations have been set up, which pursue the marauding mobs.' When a sergeant called Alefelder was killed, settler reaction became almost hysterical. The supposedly liberal governor, Theodor Seitz, ordered police to shoot any Bushman guilty of 'the slightest case of insubordination'. Police were also instructed to open fire when a 'felon' was caught in the act or failed to stop 'on command'. Any who were arrested – rather than shot – were sent to work in the diamond mines at Luderitz Bay. The district commandant of Outjo wanted to include in these draconian measures Bushman women as well, since they were 'just as dangerous' as the men.

In the eight years from 1906 to 1914, it became 'explicit German colonial policy to wipe out Bushmen', in Gordon's view. Indeed, events in Namibia, Gordon believes, 'anticipated those in Nazi Germany to an extraordinary degree', while Hannah Arendt* placed 'the origins of totalitarianism in the colonial

---

* Hannah Arendt was a political philosopher, and mistress of the German existentialist philosopher, Martin Heidegger, author of *Being and Time* (1927).

experience'. German administrators continued to differentiate between *Eingeborene*, indigenous inhabitants, and *Buschleute*, bush people, arguing that one alleged difference was the Bushmen's 'unassimilability' in which 'genital distinctiveness' played a central role. Gordon draws a parallel with the way Hitler came to regard the Jews, and finds the resemblance 'uncanny'. Shortly before his death, Hitler dictated his political testament, in which he said: 'The Jew is the quintessential outsider. The Jewish race is, more than anything else, a community of the spirit. In addition, they have a sort of relationship with destiny, as a result of the persecutions they have endured for centuries. . . . And it is precisely this trait of not being able to assimilate which defines the race and must reluctantly be accepted as a proof of the superiority of the "spirit" over the flesh.'

The climax of the pre-war 'putsching' of the Bushmen came in 1911 and 1912, when the German authorities sent out 400 anti-Bushman patrols, which covered a distance of 37,500 miles (60,000 kilometres), and involved the arrest of hundreds if not thousands of people. Although the law stated clearly that Bushmen living peacefully, especially those outside the Police Zone (the white settled areas) should not be interfered with, police simply ignored the regulations. *Werfts* outside the Police Zone were raided as a matter of routine, and as many Bushmen brought in as the police could lay their hands on. Captives were then distributed to whichever white farms were short of labour, in the hope, according to Gordon, that they would become accustomed to the 'dignity of civilisation through the sweat of their brows'.

It was a vain hope. Most Bushmen ran away from the white farms at the first opportunity. The district commandant of Outjo complained that all attempts to educate Bushmen as workers had failed, and would continue to do so 'until the opportunity to hunt and rob was taken away from them'. The only solution, he felt, was to remove all Bushmen from the farming area, and send them somewhere where they could not rob anyone and had to labour for a living, such as the diamond mines – a work ethic similar to that expressed above the gates of the Nazi concentra-

tion camp at Belsen, which greeted new arrivals with the words
Arbeit Macht Frei – Work Makes Free.

White farmers remained heavily dependent on Bushman
labour, so Bushmen trouble-makers, who stole or ran away, as
Governor Seitz told the members of the *Landesrat* in 1912,
would have to be punished more severely. 'As if sentencing a 14-
year-old youth to a year's imprisonment and two times 15
strokes was not severe enough!' Gordon exclaimed. Corporal
punishment was the basic deterrent, followed by imprisonment,
either with or without chains, and deportation. Murder and
armed robbery merited the death penalty. Fourteen different
crimes were listed, few of which would stand up in a court of law
today. They included laziness, disobedience, vagrancy, insult,
drink and incitement. Desertion, predictably, was the commonest crime, followed by theft. Bushmen were the main offenders.

Many of the Bushmen who were deported were sent to
Swakopmund, a desolate seaport on the edge of the Namib
desert, where conditions in the prison camp were 'abominable'.
One survey showed that of 32 Bushmen held there at one time,
15 died within a year, one had syphilis, and another was said to
be suffering from scurvy – and that was after the government had
tried to improve things following a protest by an Austrian
academic, Franz Seiner. Seiner had influence, and was able to
complain directly to Berlin, which made the governor and his
officials understandably nervous. In line with most academics of
his day, Seiner did not make his protest on humanitarian
grounds, but only because of what he regarded as the unneces-
sary waste of valuable Bushman labour.

Official statistics for one group of Bushmen deported to
Swakopmund just before the First World War showed just how
severe Governor Seitz's new penalties were. Of the 16 cases
listed, 8 were for vagrancy, the penalty for which was banishment, 7 were for stock theft, and 1 for 'resistance and
provocation'. The lightest of the stock theft sentences was six
months' imprisonment, the heaviest six years in chains; resistance and provocation merited five years in chains. Since it must
have been well known to every official and settler in German
South-West Africa, as it was in Bechuanaland and South Africa,

that any prison sentence, even as short as a few weeks, was tantamount to a death sentence for a Bushman, one wonders how many of the poor wretches assigned to the Swakopmund jail survived German justice.

Not many German officials could have been accused of being liberals. One, however, Beringar von Zastrow, the commandant of Grootfontein, seems to have been a genuine exception. Intelligent and well-informed, he not only controlled the richest white farming district, but also the area where most Bushmen lived. Von Zastrow came to the conclusion that most Bushman attacks occurred in the oldest and most heavily-settled farming areas. Districts with a lot of Bushmen but few farms were relatively free of brigandage. Most of the trouble was caused by the Haikom, 'Chief' Aribib's people who were mainly in the Etosha area, and whose land had been taken by white farmers. Patrols, in von Zastrow's view, only made matters worse – very much what John Barrow, Lord Macartney's secretary, thought of the commando system in the Cape more than a century before. Banditry, von Zastrow insisted, resulted from 'ill-treatment on farms'. Most stock thefts were committed not by 'wild' Bushmen but by 'tame' Bushmen who had previously worked on white farms and were motivated by revenge.

Von Zastrow gave instructions that for minor misdemeanours such as leaving a job without notice, letting a farmer's cattle stray, or gathering bush food, first offenders were to be cautioned only. For second offences, however, and more serious crimes including stock theft, the punishment was deportation to the coastal towns of Swakopmund and Luderitz Bay. But his leniency infuriated the local German settlers who wanted all Bushmen, regardless of their behaviour, deported to a big reservation well to the east of Grootfontein, on the edge of the Kalahari. Anyone captured outside this reserve, they demanded, should be deported to Luderitz Bay, and to forced labour in the diamond mines. Von Zastrow dutifully attended Farmers' Association meetings and tried to talk sense into the angry audience. 'More than half of the farmers would not be able to carry on their business were the available Bushman labour to vanish,' he wrote later.

Von Zastrow also advocated the setting up of Bushman reserves, although for different reasons, a policy that successive administrations had shelved. 'There they can live and do as they please, as long as they do not break the laws. Thus, there are now over 200 people living at Otjituo and some in Nurugas and Namutoni.' He noted that the suggestion had been made to 'push them out of the inhabited areas back to the Sandfeld'. But he was convinced this was impractical because 'the animosity between the old and the new inhabitants would flare into violence . . . and the loyalty which Bushmen have to their lands is great: they won't give up their homeland even when their lives are at stake.' He dismissed the wilder extremists with contempt: 'Other proposals, such as extermination or the deportation of whole tribes, are so absurd as to merit no consideration.' Von Zastrow's wise words fell not so much on deaf ears as on minds inflamed by prejudice. He had to suffer much verbal abuse from angry farmers, and even his senior officials wrote to Windhoek disagreeing with his views. Despite his disapproval of corporal punishment for Bushmen, his instructions were simply ignored. The archives show that more than twice as many Bushmen as any other ethnic group were given corporal punishment for deserting white farms in Grootfontein District in 1913. Bushmen also received more strokes than other prisoners. Whereas between 5 and 15 strokes was normal, one Bushman received 40.

One of the frankest accounts of what really happened on Bushman patrols was recorded by a German trooper in a 60-man *Schutztruppe* sent to the Grootfontein area in 1915. Their orders were brutally simple. Armed Bushmen were shot on sight; captured Bushman women were used to carry supplies ('and for other purposes', Gordon notes). Even unarmed Bushmen were liable to summary justice. Walbaum described how the patrol came on a *werft* where two Bushmen were digging a warthog out of its hole. The Bushmen denied having received any message supposedly given to them by Walbaum's guides, so they were seized, bound and hanged. While they were swinging from a nearby tree, Walbaum's men finished digging out the warthog, killed it and cooked it, and enjoyed a 'superb' meal. On another occasion, Walbaum wrote, the patrol surprised and captured two

Bushmen and two women. 'We sent both women ahead and when they were five yards away, by arrangement, Falckenburg and I shot them in the head from behind.'

Much of Corporal Walbaum's time was spent in the pursuit of a particularly daring group of Bushmen, known as the Hans Gang. At its peak, it numbered between 30 and 40 members who, between them, had up to 17 rifles and a large supply of ammunition, mostly captured by successful raids on white farms. Hans was a Haikom, a well-known hunter, who was employed by a German farmer named Wegener. When Wegener was called up for military service against the South Africans, Hans took to the bush with a small band of followers. At Easter 1915 they killed a German farmer named Ludwig who had stolen the Bushman wife of Hans's friend, Max. After the murder Hans and Max were marked men, living as outlaws in the bush. Hans recruited new members of the gang by telling them the Germans intended to kill them all. As one member said later in court, 'We ran away because we were frightened of the white man. White people shoot Bushmen so we were frightened of them.'

Not long afterwards, Hans shot and killed another farmer, Muller of Knakib, who used to boast about the large number of Bushman concubines he had. It was common for German – and Afrikaner – settlers to abduct Bushman women for use as unpaid servants and this was a cause of deep resentment among Bushmen. Indeed, it was the chief cause, according to that dossier of German atrocities, the *South African Blue Book* (*Report on the Natives of South West Africa and Their Treatment by Germany*, 1918). Stock thefts, it argues, were committed largely by Bushmen who had been 'badly fed and flogged' by white farmers; but the chief cause of all 'Bushman trouble' was the settler practice of taking Bushman wives as concubines. The South African magistrate who replaced von Zastrow in Grootfontein, a Lieutenant Hull, was equally convinced. 'It seems that the Bushmen have lost all faith in the white man's methods [of justice], more especially as their women were being constantly interfered with by both farmers and police.'

German farmers in the area where the Hans Gang operated

were living in a state of siege, and did not dare to burn lights in their houses at night. In May 1915 Hans carried out a daring raid on the farmhouse at Sus, which the police were using as a temporary headquarters in their hunt for the gang. He chose his moment well. The farmer and his family were away, and the police were out hunting. Hans and three armed companions, including Max, attacked the farmhouse and killed three Herero labourers in their huts, but did not touch their women. 'The whole house was demolished,' Walbaum recorded. 'Every window was broken. In the house nothing was left: suits, clothing, laundered children's clothes, food, tobacco, schnapps, and 200 marks in money: everything was stolen.' The gang also took ten head of cattle and a Mauser rifle.

German reprisals were swift. Walbaum's patrol captured four Bushmen and two rifles in a surprise raid, helped by the fact that the Bushmen were 'totally soaked from the schnapps'. The prisoners 'said nothing. I hit them until the blood was running down [in streams]. They behaved badly and said their brothers would kill us all. I told them I would get them all. At night I tied each one naked to a tree. It was ice cold and they stood far from the fire; they tried to untie themselves with their feet. The watchman hit them all over with a *sjambok*. At 4 o'clock in the morning – the coldest time of the night – they started begging: "Mister, if you bring us to the fire we will say everything." I told them they had to wait because I was sure they were not mistreated enough.

'At five o'clock we untied them. Jonas told us everything but his bad behaviour he did not change. The woman stayed near the fire with her child during the night. All the men had bad lacerations on their shoulders from trying to untie themselves by rubbing their shoulders on the bark of the tree. At 8 o'clock we took the scoundrels to the bush where we found the right trees in no time. A few boxes were piled up, ropes were tied onto branches – the men were put on the boxes with their hands tied and ropes placed around their necks. We kicked the boxes over and they were dead in seconds, because their necks were broken. All four of them had burst veins in the lower leg after they died. In twenty minutes they were dead.'

Walbaum's patrol also managed to capture Max's wife, and because of her value as a hostage Walbaum asked a farmer, Regelen, to deliver her personally to headquarters in Grootfontein. Regelen was warned to be on his guard against possible attack on the road, but none the less was surprised one morning at dawn, 17 miles from Grootfontein by Max, who killed Regelen and rescued his wife.

Soon after the attack on Sus, Hans planned a daring raid on another white farmer, Eckstein, who had kidnapped some Bushman women from Tsebeb and taken them to his farm. An ambush was laid, but instead of Eckstein, two other white farmers, Ohlroggen and Korting, walked into the trap and were killed. Finally, in October 1916, Hans's luck ran out. Early one morning, he was walking along with some companions – in fact he was hobbling because of an infected foot – when a horseman appeared, galloping towards them. Everyone except Hans ran off, including a follower who was carrying the only rifle. The horseman, a former post-office clerk named Feuerstein, pulled up, and 'emptied his pistol' at Hans, shooting him dead. Feuerstein cut off Hans's head so that he could claim the reward and rode off in triumph. In due course he was tried for murder by a South African court, found guilty, and sentenced to death, to the outrage of the German settler community. But Feuerstein was as lucky as Hans had been unlucky. He and another German farmer, Voswinkel, who was also in prison for murder, made a daring escape to Europe, by way of Angola, and finished up as folk heroes.

Hans's gang was taken over by Max, but soon afterwards, tipped off by a Bushman informer, South African troops took Max by surprise and fatally wounded him. Not for the first time, nor the last, a Bushman resistant was betrayed by another Bushman. This particular Judas, according to Gordon, 'received the princely sum of 1 pound'.

Savage as German colonial justice was in the early part of the First World War, it was extra-judicial action by German settlers which assumed genocidal proportions. Contemporary photographs of terrified, ragged, starving scarecrow women and children, and dead men hanging by the neck, issued at one stage as postcards by the German colonial authorities, tell the brutal story all too convincingly. Settler commandos, operating more or less outside the law, shot down whole Bushman communities with impunity. Other farmers went out to capture Bushmen in the veld, and 'sold' them to the police for 30 marks a head. But the commonest settler strategy, according to Gordon, was to shoot any Bushmen suspected of stock theft. German colonial courts had on the whole turned a blind eye to these murders, and the perpetrators were rarely if ever brought to justice. That was soon to change, with the arrival of the South Africans.

CHAPTER NINE

Smuts and Botha

White South Africans believed that land was available virtually for the asking in an area they dubbed 'Bushman land and baboon country'.

Robert Gordon, *The Bushman Myth*, 1992

On 29 June 1914, the day Britain declared war on Germany, the South African government, as a fellow member of the British Empire, sent to London a message of military support, which contained a loyal and generous offer: to replace British troops assigned to imperial duties inside southern Africa, thus freeing them for service elsewhere. In reply the Colonial Office asked if South African ministers were willing and able to 'seize such parts of German South-West Africa as will give them command of Swakopmund, Luderitz Bay, and the wireless stations there or in the interior.' If the answer was in the affirmative, they would be doing Britain 'a great and urgent Imperial service'. There was no hesitation on the part of the prime minister, Louis Botha, or the defence minister, Jan Smuts, both staunch supporters of Empire, although both had fought against Britain in the Boer War. Within three days, they cabled their acceptance, on the basis that Britain undertook the naval side of operations while South Africa provided the ground forces. It was a decision, however, that was to prove highly unpopular with many Afrikaans-speaking South Africans, including the army commander, General Beyers, and a number of his senior officers.

Before committing itself to action, the South African government called a special session of parliament at which Botha declared that in virtue of her allegiance to the Crown, South Africa was automatically involved in what was to become known as the Great War. Smuts also spoke in support, pointing out that the Germans had already committed aggression by sending troops across the South African border in the remote north-west. The small Nationalist Party opposed the decision, arguing that South Africa should remain politically and militarily neutral, but to little effect; the government won the vote handsomely by 92 votes to 12. That same night, 14 September, troopships sailed for the ports of German South-West Africa.

The parliamentary vote, however, did not represent popular feeling in the country. The Boer War, which had ended in 1902, was a recent, and very bitter memory. Afrikaner opposition ran deeper and stronger than perhaps either Botha or Smuts had expected, and very soon they had rebellion on their hands. Beyers resigned his commission and his command, and one of his officers and protégé, Salomon Maritz, deserted to the Germans with his commando, handing over as prisoners of war those who refused to fight on the German side. Maritz then promoted himself general, proclaimed the independence of South Africa and declared war on Britain. Another rebel, General de Wet, a Boer War veteran, supported him, saying he planned 'to trek to Pretoria, to pull down the British flag, and to proclaim a free South African Republic'.

Botha and Smuts tried conciliation without success, and fighting broke out between de Wet and government troops in which de Wet's son was killed. Botha and Smuts now knew they would have to act. Botha personally took the field and defeated de Wet's commandos at Mushroom Valley. De Wet escaped but was captured in Bechuanaland trying to get through to Maritz and the Germans. Maritz escaped to Angola, but Beyers was drowned trying to escape across the Vaal River: his horse was shot under him.

Botha and Smuts both realised they must heal the political wounds as quickly as possible, and were far-sighted enough to adopt a policy of clemency, with one exception. Commandant Joseph Fourie, who deserted to the Germans without resigning his commission and still wearing his uniform, was court-martialled, and shot.

The fighting, mainly among Afrikaners, delayed the invasion, and on New Year's day 1915 the Germans were still in control of the whole of South-West Africa except for the two ports of Swakopmund and Luderitz Bay. To show just how serious he was, Botha himself took command, arriving in Swakopmund in February, having left Smuts to run the government in Pretoria. He was confronted with enormous problems of supply and transport, and although the Germans were outnumbered by four to one – less than 10,000 men, mainly reservists, against 43,000 South Africans – they might have given Botha a run for his money if they had been half as well led as their fellow combatants in German East Africa. Smuts, Botha's old comrade-in-arms, arrived in April to take charge of the southern front, and in three weeks of 'blazing action' advanced to the gates of Windhoek, although it was Botha who actually took the capital in May. The Germans, who had been delaying Botha's advance by blowing the bridges, now tried to bully and bluster him into a ceasefire, with both sides retaining the areas they held until the future of the colony could be decided at the peace conference. Botha swept the proposal aside, determined to push on as fast as he could to the north, where 4000 German soldiers were still at large. In a brilliant finale of forced marches and battles, the Boer cavalry came into its own. When the German commander saw the apparently disorganised horde of Boer horsemen materialising out of the bush to surround his troops he said: 'This is not a war, it's a hippodrome.'

Botha took the German surrender on 9 July and three days later Smuts announced that the conquest of German South-West Africa was the 'first achievement' of a united South Africa, in which 'both races have combined all their best and most virile characteristics'. Nevertheless, as Smuts's biographer, W.K. Hancock, notes, Botha was 'harassed to the very end by tension between the English- and Afrikaans-speaking elements of his army'. This tension, a legacy of the Boer War, proved a 'special curse' when the time came to take over the running of the country. Botha and Smuts were determined the Germans must never regain control of South-West Africa; part of the case against them would be that their administrators were 'men of low quality who had failed to treat the Native population justly'. This put the onus on South Africa to employ men of high quality. Under normal circumstances, perhaps half would have been

English-speaking South Africans: but Botha felt that, because of their 'bitter feelings' towards both the Germans and the resident Afrikaans-speaking Boers, most of whom had sided with Maritz, he could not appoint English speakers.

For electoral reasons too, Botha was keen to encourage more Boers to settle in South-West Africa, not only as farmers but also as policemen and administrators. He was lucky to find as his administrator a man of ability and experience named Gorges, although in the years ahead Gorges would often complain to Smuts about the 'poor quality' of his officials, some of whom might well have had a sneaking sympathy with the views of men like de Wet, Beyers and Maritz.

The new South African administration did feel obliged, however, to prosecute whites for killing Bushmen and other non-whites. The case of *Rex v. Becker* is a good example. Shortly after the South African invasion, a German farmer named Becker, of Hedwigslust, rode out one day accompanied by his 'boy', the Bushman Max, in search of 32 stolen cattle. They surprised a party of Bushmen who had killed one of Becker's oxen and were busy eating it. Without even dismounting Becker raised his rifle and shot the two men, two women and two small children, although they had offered no resistance. Max, the sole witness, ran away. 'I did not report the matter to the police,' he said in evidence, 'because I was afraid the *Baas* would have killed me if I did so. . . . I ran to the Sandveld because if I went towards the police station the master might get me in the road and shoot me.' Becker made the mistake of bragging about the incident to the newly-arrived South African police, who promptly started an investigation. Becker was tried and eventually given ten years' imprisonment, a sentence that profoundly shocked the German settler community.

Similarly, a farmer named Voswinkel was jailed for murder.* He was accused of torturing and killing a young Bushman, Xuiseb. Voswinkel, like many bachelor settlers, lived with a Bushman concubine; she in her evidence said she had heard

---

* Voswinkel later escaped to Germany with Feuerstein, the German who had killed the rebel Hans.

Xuiseb, whom she described as a little boy, being beaten, and later saw him in Voswinkel's room. 'He was fastened around his neck, arms and legs with Bushman rope. . . . He had marks on his back where he had been beaten and he was bleeding freely. I had to wash the blood from the floor afterwards. Accused and Wilhelm later took Xuiseb away. Xuiseb was fastened to accused's horse with Bushman rope. He had no clothes on, only a lappie [loin cloth] hanging in front.' Her statement was corroborated by numerous other witnesses. The boy was not seen again.

Then there was the case of Lieutenant Venuleth, a reserve officer, who in the early days of the war was in command of a patrol which came across a band of fifteen Bushmen. The Bushmen immediately scattered and ran, leaving behind only an elderly man and woman who were captured. When he returned to his farm, Venuleth organised a court martial with himself as president, assisted by his two sergeants, and duly sentenced to death and executed the elderly couple. Later, when he was tried by the South Africans, Venuleth admitted that the court martial 'was held in order to shoot the natives'. One of the two sergeants, Schultz, told the court he thought 'being Bushmen they should have been shot at sight. I had the right to shoot because they would not stop, because they had arms, and were suspected as spies. . . . It is quite sufficient if they do not stop when called upon.' In a sworn statement Venuleth sought to justify his decision by arguing that 'the accused were Bushmen, not vagrant Hereros . . . in the north Bushmen are a great nuisance and always stealing cattle.' He also claimed that he recognised them as 'the Bushmen who had stolen and slaughtered a sheep in October 1914 on my own farm'. The South African judge who heard the case pointed out in his judgement that Venuleth was at once President and complainant; no charge was made against the accused; they were not present; no evidence was led. He concluded: 'Now it is difficult to mention any principle of justice and law which has not been violated.' Yet Venuleth got away scot free on the basis that a South African court had no jurisdiction in a case which should have been tried under German martial law.

Robert Gordon, however, remains sceptical of the claim that South African justice was more severe on whites than that of the Germans. Superficially it may have seemed so, he writes, because South African courts imposed more death sentences on whites. None, however, as far as he could discover, was ever carried out. Despite the South African authorities' willingness to prosecute, many things did not change. Early in 1916, a number of Bushmen, including women and children, were arrested in Grootfontein on charges of stock theft. The magistrate gave orders for them to be taken to Windhoek by train, in case they tried to escape. Accordingly, the men were transported 'wearing a complete set of German chains'. When the jailer at Windhoek prison inspected his new charges, he observed of one: 'The said prisoner was completely chained and roped around neck, wrist and body. He left his teeth marks on the chain.'

Botha was anxious to settle more Afrikaans-speaking South Africans in South-West Africa to reduce the size and influence of the German settler majority and, also, to find a solution, or part solution, to the 'poor white' problem. The 'poor whites', South Africa's white underclass, almost wholly composed of unedu-cated, often illiterate Afrikaners, were renowned for being ultra-racist in a country that was to become a byword for racism. Gordon says the 'poor whites' were the tail that wagged the dog. 'White South Africans believed that land was available virtually for the asking in an area they dubbed "Bushman land and baboon country".' The Afrikaner popular press pandered to this view with articles such as 'The People Eaters of South West', which claimed that 'so-called wild Bushmen are complete cannibals.' The article was illustrated with two photographs, one showing a plot of land captioned: 'Where a Boer drove in his first stakes.' The second, of the same plot taken a year later, is captioned: 'Beautiful dam and fruit trees.' The inference is clear to even the 'most thick-skulled reader', Gordon says. Bushmen are inhuman and thus whites are justified in taking over and 'developing' land which 'they' are 'wasting'. The influx of 'poor whites' from South Africa, bringing with them a whole farrago of ignorant and extremist ideas, introduced a new mood of racial intolerance which was crystallised by the murder of a senior South African official.

There are several versions of how F.J. van Ryneveld, the Gobabis magistrate, met his death. The one which gained most credence among whites, and which was to leave a lasting impression on the settler mind, was that van Ryneveld went 'unarmed' to talk peace with a group of Bushmen, that he was treacherously shot down with a poisoned arrow, and died an agonising death soon afterwards.

In 1922 the farmers of Gobabis, a ranching area east of Windhoek, had reported heavy cattle losses, and blamed Bushmen who had moved south from Grootfontein. One of the farmers, a Mrs Bullick, wrote movingly to the administrator explaining she was a widow with six children, trying to farm on her own, and was being preyed on by Bushmen who were stealing her cattle. The administrator ordered an immediate inquiry. A police patrol was sent to the area, but was attacked by Bushmen and forced to withdraw with the loss of a vehicle. Magistrate Ryneveld was then told to talk to the Bushmen.

As it happened, possibly the best-known Bushman rebel of the inter-war years, an Aukwe Bushman from the north, Zameko, had originally lived and worked on the Bullicks' farm. When Mr Bullick was alive, relations were reasonably friendly. But after his death in 1921 things deteriorated, with Mrs Bullick claiming that livestock thefts had increased dramatically. On one occasion, when she protested to Zameko about a particularly blatant case, he allegedly threatened her and her daughter.

By the time van Ryneveld reached the scene, Zameko, whose gang was said to number between 150 and 300, was breathing fire. Ryneveld reported that Bushmen on the Bullick farm 'say straight out they are going to make war'. However, despite the frequency of stock thefts, and the number of Bushmen who had joined the resistance, van Ryneveld's first impressions were, as he put it: 'Bushman's attitude all bluff when a number but dangerous when 2 or 3 . . . [and] must be vigorously dealt with.'

Four days later, van Ryneveld and a small party of three native policemen, a tracker and a white sergeant called Viljoen, set out to talk to Zameko. Van Ryneveld was warned by one of the policemen, Corporal Saal, that he was running a serious risk because the Bushmen would think they were a police patrol – everyone, apart from the magistrate, was in uniform – but van Ryneveld decided to go ahead. As Saal predicted, the Bushmen were highly suspicious when they saw the official party, and some ran. The tracker and the native police shouted at the remaining Bushmen not to shoot: they came in peace. But the police uniforms and the cocked weapons must have suggested a trap. In the confusion that followed, shooting broke out. Four Bushmen were killed, and van Ryneveld was wounded by a poisoned arrow. Immediately he saw the magistrate was hit, Corporal Saal rode to his help and offered to wash out the wound. Incredible as it may seem, van Ryneveld waved Saal away. He simply could not bring himself to let a black man tend his wound, even at the risk of his life. Several vital minutes ticked away before Sergeant Viljoen appeared, by which time it was too late. 'Viljoen, I am finished,' was all van Ryneveld could say. The sergeant removed the arrow and then they all awaited the inevitable. The poison had worked very fast.

Retribution was almost as swift. A strong patrol was sent out in pursuit of the gang and eventually tracked it down. Morton Seagars, one of the policemen involved, described the action in his memoirs: 'We captured about a hundred-and-fifty Bushmen . . . when we arrived back at the base camp with them, they made a determined effort to get away, and a running fight took place in which a dozen or so of them were killed.' Zameko himself was captured; but managed to survive a prison sentence, eventually returning to his old haunts near the Bullick farm. Mrs Bullick continued to complain about stock thefts, and police posses rode out regularly to protect her. Her attitude did not change. In one of her many letters to the long-suffering administrator, she wrote that she had been shocked to find on a recent visit to Gobabis hospital that 'four Bushmen, who had received lashes in gaol, came into the operation room. They pulled down their trousers and a white nurse administered to each one of them a white cloth with ointment thereon. That was enough for me!' Bushmen arrested for killing cattle, she went on, should be lashed with a *sjambok* 'tipped with the same poisoned arrowhead. If they have wounds, these should be covered with arrow poison ointment, so that the wound can also hiss and foam and so that Mr Bushman can also feel the pain.'

In the wake of the murder of van Ryneveld, many Bushmen were reported to have crossed the border into Bechuanaland. A German writer, B. Voigt, while beating the nationalist drum, came near the truth: 'an evil time emerged for the entire Bushman population. Everywhere . . . the British-Boer soldiers and the police were instructed to prepare to flush out the Bushmen and to destroy the hordes. . . . None of them remained alive: neither man nor woman nor child were spared . . .'

By the end of the First World War, the South Africans were treating the Bushmen as brutally as the Germans had done. Torture, treachery and deliberate manipulation of the judicial system were normal practice. In 1918 a Lieutenant Burger reported how he rounded up a group of Bushmen by the old trick of extending the hand of friendship, sweetened by a gift of tobacco. When he arrived at the Bushman village at 6.30 one morning, the Bushmen ran away, but he persuaded them to return. 'I called them back and said they need not be frightened for I was looking for Germans. Two of them returned. I gave them tobacco to smoke as I did not intend doing them any harm, then all the Bushmen returned . . . they had a smoke and I gave instructions to have them arrested and charged for murder . . . as I was putting on the handcuffs the Bushmen ran away. I caught three, Corporal van der Merwe caught three, and three ran away. I then gave instructions to fire but not to hit, which was done. Native Constable Fritz killed one Bushman by accident.'

The police themselves continually flouted the regulations by wrongfully arresting Bushmen. In 1922 Grayson, the Gobabis magistrate, complained: 'Some years ago the Administrator ordered that Bushmen should not be prosecuted for game law contravention in outlying portions but with personnel changes this has started again. Bushmen argue that they cannot live without meat and since they are prosecuted for killing game and cattle, it is easier to kill cattle.' Fourteen years later his successor in Gobabis found it necessary to reissue instructions that 'police are not to prosecute a Bushman for shooting game, and if the Bushman knows that, it is possible it will reduce stock theft.'

Such a sophisticated and humane view was rare. The vast majority of settlers and police officials thought that the only good Bushman was a dead Bushman. Apart from calling for more police patrols to 'harass Bushmen constantly', the settlers wanted all Bushmen to be deported well to the east of the white farming area, and cattle theft to be made a capital offence. When police Subinspector Mason found that Bushman crime had increased 'by leaps and bounds', he recommended harsh counter-measures until such time as all 'Bushmen were dead, in gaol, or were outside the Police Zone'.

In a climate of such intolerance, the torture of Bushmen became routine. In one case, a Grootfontein farmer who suspected a Bushman of stealing, tied a *riem* (leather thong) round his neck and made him run in front of his horse for two and a half miles. He was then laid over a cart and thrashed, after which he was hauled up by his neck until his feet barely touched the ground – the position the police found him in when they arrived to investigate the theft. The farmer was fined £5, or one month's imprisonment.

German and South African farmers who were short of labour had a simple method of remedying the problem – 'manstealing' or 'blackbirding'. One case, *Rex v. Brand and two others*, 1929, became a *cause célèbre* and was raised before the Permanent Mandates Commission of the League of Nations. This involved the capture of about 50 Bushmen by three young, white farmers from the Gobabis district. After setting fire to the Bushman *werfts* at night, the farmers drove the terrified Bushmen in front of their horses back to their farms, where they were divided up, regardless of family ties. A police constable who happened to pass through the area a few days later took no action about the manstealing, but arrested and jailed several Bushmen for being in possession of jackal skins.* When the case eventually came to trial, the court held that manstealing could not be proven because 'the Bushmen could easily have escaped'. It found the

---

* After five days in jail, the Bushmen were returned to their 'employers'.

farmers guilty on an alternative charge of assault and fined them each £5.

At the League of Nations hearing, the Secretary for South-West Africa, F.P. Courtney-Clarke, tried to gloss over the affair, stating the farmers 'had been immediately arrested and a very serious view had been taken by the Administration – so much so, that they had been tried by the High Court and sentenced.' He was challenged by Mr Ruppel, of the Mandates Commission, who pointed out that the sentence had amounted only to a fine of £5. Mr Courtney-Clarke said 'this might seem lenient, but the judge had probably taken into acount that their actions had been due mainly to youthful exuberance.' Another member of the Commission, Mr Sakanabe, 'was curious that nearly one year had elapsed before the trial'.

South Africa's post-war role in South-West Africa began at the Peace Conference at Versailles in 1919, when the victorious Allies met to divide the spoils and establish a new international organisation, the League of Nations, whose purpose was to preserve the peace and 'make the world safe for democracy'. Former colonies of the defeated nations were declared 'mandates' of the League and placed under the 'tutelage' of one of the victorious powers – in the case of German South-West Africa, the victorious power was South Africa. The tutelary powers were responsible to the League for the well-being and advancement of their mandates, regarded as 'nations on the road to independence', and as long as Jan Smuts, one of the founding fathers of the League, was prime minister of South Africa, there was little criticism of South Africa's stewardship. When, however, the League of Nations was replaced by the United Nations in 1945, at the end of the Second World War, and Smuts was defeated in elections in 1948 by the right-wing Afrikaner National party, things changed. Alone of all the tutelary powers, South Africa refused to place South-West Africa under the United Nations' Trusteeship Council, the successor to the League's Mandates Commission, and far from leading South-West Africa along the road to independence, incorporated it instead into its apartheid system. This started a long and rancorous struggle with the

United Nations which lasted until 1988, when South Africa was finally obliged to withdraw from what is now Namibia.

The increasingly intolerant attitude of South African officials in South-West Africa was typified by a case quoted by Robert Gordon, when a judge trying a case in which Bushmen were accused of having robbed Ovambo labourers, described the Bushmen as 'savages who know no law and are comparable with children who are *doli incapaces* [incapable of guilt] . . . waylaying [of the] much needed supply of native workmen cannot be allowed to continue. A beginning of punishment must be made. A commutation might be misunderstood.' The judge went on to sentence them to be publicly hanged in front of other Bushmen specially brought into Windhoek for the occasion, in the hope that the spectacle would be a deterrent.

Men like F.P. Courtney-Clarke, the Secretary of South-West Africa, may have been kind to their Bushman servants, including the famous Ngani, a Haikom who spoke nine languages and could mix a good cocktail. Yet, he refused to agree to repeated suggestions that a special reserve be set aside for Bushmen. Perhaps the most extreme example of how far South African Nationalist opinion had moved away from the moderation of a Smuts was expressed by Eric Louw, later South African foreign minister, but in 1934 his country's representative to the Permanent Mandates Commission of the League of Nations, when he declared that: 'Nothing more could be done with the Bushmen than to punish them when they made depredations.' They were 'parasitic', 'like wild animals', 'a low type' and a 'deteriorate race'.

Meanwhile, the wholesale dispossession of Bushman lands continued. Huge areas were expropriated for use as game reserves, and equally vast areas were handed over in the form of native reserves to other tribal groups, mainly the Herero, who in turn had been dispossessed by white settlers. All the reserves the Herero were given were in the Kalahari Sandveld, which was considered unsuitable for white ranching, but had always been traditional Bushman territory. The Herero were adept at lobbying the government, vociferous in their demands, and each increase in their reserve area was made at the expense of the Bushmen. Bloody battles took place in the sandy wastes of the Omaheke between the Herero and the Kung; the Herero would attack on horseback, striking at the Kung from the saddle with their lethal knobkerries.

The Waterberg Massacre of 1947, which only came to light by chance, was a horrifying example. In the resulting court case, *Rex v. Majerero and twenty-three others*, 24 Herero were found guilty of cold-bloodedly massacring 13 Bushmen: 2 men, 4 women and 7 children. The trouble began when a 15-man Herero commando was chasing some cattle allegedly stolen by two Bushmen and one of the Hereros was shot and killed by a poisoned arrow. The following day a Herero commando, mounted on horses and donkeys, set out in pursuit of the Bushmen. Describing the ensuing bloodbath, Robert Gordon writes: 'They managed to surround the band of fleeing Bushmen, and while those on horseback patrolled the periphery to prevent escape, the donkey brigade dismounted and went in for the kill on foot. Using clubs and assegais, they ripped open stomachs and severed hands. In this well-planned and cold-blooded atrocity, not a single Herero was wounded.' Three Bushmen managed to escape, and were later apparently murdered, but no charges were brought because of 'lack of evidence'.

What had happened to the Haikom Bushmen of Etosha was a classic example of dispossession. In 1907, two years after the death of the Haikom 'chief' Aribib, the Germans simply tore up the treaty they had signed with him and proclaimed the northern part of the territory Aribib had ceded to be the Etosha Game Park. The Bushmen who lived there, and who had been promised 'protection' and the right to forage for bush food, were simply rounded up and sent to work on white farms. In addition, giraffe, eland and other large antelope were declared 'royal game'.*

The South African occupation, however, brought about a distinct change for the better, as the park came under the

---

* It was forbidden to hunt royal game and anyone who did so faced severe punishment.

enlightened control of two men who understood the Bushmen: Captain Nelson, who was game warden until 1928, and his successor, 'Cocky' Hahn, who was also the native affairs commissioner in Ovamboland. In 1922 Nelson informed the local Haikom they would not be interfered with in the Reserve 'providing they did not poison the waters or trespass on occupied farms'. After four years Nelson was satisfied that his policy had worked. As a result of not punishing Bushmen for killing game, stock-theft on neighbouring farms had been reduced, and there was no decrease in the number of game in the park. Bushmen were able to move in and out of the park with ease. There was even 'active encouragement' of Bushman resettlement in the park by both Haikom and Kung. 'Cocky' Hahn, a legendary figure who played rugby for South Africa and was nicknamed *Shongola*, Ovambo for *sjambok*, followed Nelson's example in encouraging a Bushman presence in the park. In a pamphlet produced for the Wembley Exhibition of 1935, he wrote that 'the wild Bushmen resident there ... form part and parcel of this sanctuary and afford an interesting study for those anxious to acquaint themselves with their life and pursuits. For small quantities of tobacco these Bushmen will keenly collect firewood, help visitors to establish their camps and are most useful and clever in erecting "skerms" [hides] for close-up game photography.'

One's heart warms to both Captain Nelson and 'Cocky' Hahn. They both obviously understood and liked the Bushmen, although collecting firewood and putting up hides for tourist photographers was a bit of a come-down for people who had once been 'lords of the desert'. Still, they were considerably better off than their kinsmen living south of Etosha, in the white-settled Police Zone. Hahn certainly thought so: 'The Haikom,' he wrote, 'have perhaps suffered more than any other Bushmen tribe. . . . Their various family clans or groups . . . have been pushed further and further north ... latterly by our own settlement schemes. Their hunting grounds and *veldkos* [bush food] areas have either been completely taken from them or have shrunk to such an extent that in very many cases the wild or semi-wild Haikom today find it almost impossible to eke out an existence . . .' It was surprising, Hahn thought, that they did not 'indulge in more cattle and stock thieving'.

In 1935 a Lutheran missionary, Heinrich Vedder, argued before the South-West Africa Constitutional Commission for the establishment of two Bushman reserves, one for the Haikom in the Etosha area, and one for the Kung in the north-east. He pleaded the Bushman case eloquently: 'Their language alone justifies the preservation of this primitive race ... You have reserves for game, you have reserves ... for the Hereros, the Ovambos, and the Okavangos, but you have no reserve for Bushmen, yet historically and scientifically Bushmen are entitled to far greater consideration than any other of our native tribes.' Yet, the opposite was happening: 'his lands are gradually being taken from him ... he has been prohibited from trapping or shooting in parts which he regarded as his own for generations.'

Vedder, an ethnologist as well as a missionary, was not the first academic to propose the creation of a Bushman reserve. Like Nelson and Hahn, he knew a great deal about the Bushmen, and on this issue, at least, he showed himself to be a man of intelligence and vision, a rare combination in a world of narrow-minded bureaucrats.

Vedder's ideas received enthusiastic public support, mainly because of a campaign by a South African big-game hunter, Donald Bain, who wanted to establish a reserve for the last of the South African Bushmen, whom he called the 'living fossils' of the southern Kalahari. In 1936 Bain collected a group of Bushmen and led them through the streets of Cape Town to Parliament, in an attempt to persuade the government to restore their right to hunt. As part of his publicity campaign, Bain invited the universities of Cape Town and the Witwatersrand to send expeditions to his camp in the Kalahari to study his Bushmen.

In 1949 the government of South-West Africa appointed a Commission for the Preservation of the Bushmen, with a well-known Afrikaner author and anthropologist, P.J. Schoeman, as its chairman. There were several reasons for the creation of the commission, the most important being South Africa's desire not to offend the United Nations, now that it had taken over the League of Nations' responsibility for the mandated territories. Schoeman had recently retired from his chair at Stellenbosch University, where he had been active in providing an academic

Tom Hardbattle in the uniform of the South African police in the early 1900s.

In his sixties, Tom Hardbattle took as his wife sixteen-year-old Khwa, whose mother was a Nharo Bushman and father an Afrikaner farmer.

Khwa with her children: Andrea, Polly, John and Tom. Baby Christina was born of a Herero father, after old Tom Hardbattle died in 1960.

Yorkshire-born, Tom Hardbattle joined the City of London Police, before emigrating to South Africa, where he eventually became a pioneer cattle rancher in Bechuanaland.

(*Below*) John Hardbattle (left) and his younger brother Tom in England where they were educated after their father's death.

(*Facing page*)
John Hardbattle (first left) as a recruit in REME (Royal Electrical and Mechanical Engineers). (*Inset*) John, an expert tank mechanic, during his service in Germany.

Bushman woman the worse for wear in the Omaheke, Namibia. Despair has driven many Bushmen, of both sexes, to seek oblivion in alcoholism.

The 'Magnificent Seven': the original members of First People of the Kalahari on 18 May, 1992, before their disastrous meeting with the Botswana government.
Left to right: Tsau and Gomme Kgao, John Hardbattle, Aaron Johannes, Roy Sesana, Saikuta, Khomtsa Khomtsa. All except Aaron and Roy are now dead.

(*Facing page*)
Khomtsa Khomtsa, the Bushman elder who in 1992 approached John Hardbattle with the question: 'Whose land is this?' which eventually persuaded John to join First People of the Kalahari, and to lead the fight for the survival of the Bushmen.

A Bushman on a horse showed us the way to Gope, a remote village at the edge of the Kalahari Game Reserve, the site of a disputed diamond mine.

Only five Bushmen families are left in Gope. Ketlhalefang has refused to be moved because she will not leave the graves of her ancestors.

rationale for the new Afrikaner nationalist doctrine of apartheid. Since tribal homelands, or Bantustans, were an essential plank in the edifice of apartheid, which was to dominate the politics of southern Africa for the next 45 years, it was inevitable that the Schoeman committee should recommend the creation of a special Bushman reserve. In 1952, like Donald Bain before him, Schoeman promoted his ideas for a reserve by exhibiting a group of 'wild' Bushmen from South-West Africa in Cape Town, at the van Riebeeck Festival, held to celebrate 300 years of white settlement. No one, presumably, asked what there was for the Bushmen to celebrate.

The Schoeman commission produced two reports, an interim report in 1952 and a final report a year later, the difference between the two being quite astonishing. The interim report called for the creation of two reserves, one for the Haikom adjoining the Etosha Game Park, where they had 'traditional hunting rights', and the other for the Kung in the old Game Reserve No. 1, with headquarters at Karakuwisa. The final report, however, dropped the idea of a Haikom reserve altogether, and altered the site of the Kung reserve from Karakuwisa to Nyae Nyae. Why such sweeping changes in so short a space of time? There were a couple of pointers. For one thing, while still chairman of the commission Schoeman had accepted an appointment as chief game warden of Etosha; and secondly, Karakuwisa turned out to have potential for development by white ranchers. Nyae Nyae, on the other hand, was well to the east, near the Bechuanaland border, and the prevalence there of *gifblaar*, a poisonous shrub, made it highly undesirable for cattle ranching.

But that was not all. The final report sounded the death knell of the Haikom. It recommended the expulsion of the Bushmen who had lived in the Etosha Game Park since the days of Captain Nelson and 'Cocky' Hahn. The first task of the newly-formed Game Catching Unit was to round up all Bushmen living in the park, of whom 300 'unemployed' were given the choice of moving either to Ovamboland or, because they were such good workers, entering the service of 'selected farmers'. There was a catch to this generous offer, however. All these farms were south of Windhoek, at least 250 miles away, making it extremely difficult for the Haikom to 'desert' back to Etosha. The local press gave sycophantic approval, claiming that the Bushmen were 'threatening' to exterminate all the 'zebras and wildebeest' in the area. All of them, about 500, were removed from the park and eventually 'absorbed as herdsmen and farm labourers into the economy of the country'.

The Schoeman commission, which originally looked as if it might be the Bushman's saviour, turned out to be yet another station of the cross on the long road to final dispossession. Twelve years later, in 1964, another government body, the Odendaal commission, was sent to South-West Africa to draw up the final boundaries of the black 'homelands' which now formed an essential part of the apartheid mosaic. To do this, it went back to the original 'native reserves' established in 1922, and expanded them as it saw fit. The Hereros succeeded in having their old reserves consolidated into a new, 368,750-square-mile homeland. This now stretched from the Waterberg – the starting point of von Trotha's war of extermination against them in 1904 – east across the Omaheke to the Bechuanaland border. Farther north, the Kavango reserve, originally concentrated along the banks of the Okavango River, was extended a long way south. Sandwiched and squeezed between these two was the 112,500-square-mile Kung Bushman homeland. Gordon describes the carve-up which resulted from this 'apartheid poker game' as the 'de facto greatest theft of Bushman land in the history of Namibia'. What happened in Etosha was equally disastrous from the Bushman's point of view. The Odendaal commission decreed that a large portion of the park should be transferred to Ovamboland; ironically, it turned out to be exactly the same area as Schoeman's interim report had suggested should be set aside for the Haikom.

Part Three

Dawid Kruiper

CHAPTER TEN

Dancing with Death

'That farmer's wife beats. If her husband says he is finished, then she will force him and then he will go and beat somebody. If her husband doesn't want to, then she will force him and say, "Are you licking his shit? Are you licking a black person's arsehole?"'

Bushman woman, Gobabis, 1998

In 1950 an American millionaire, Laurence Marshall, the founder and owner of the Raytheon Corporation, which specialised in radar and other secret defence work for the United States government throughout the Second World War, decided to retire. As his wife, Lorna, was to explain later, Laurence, a civil engineer by training, had worked long hours during the war. He did not have time even for a long weekend, let alone a family holiday. 'He wanted to be with us,' Lorna wrote, 'and, now that he was free to do so, he wanted us to undertake some interesting project together. First of all, however, he wanted to take a trip to Africa with his son.' Although not anthropologists, Laurence and his son, John, consulted their anthropologist friends about where they might go, and what research they might do. As their holiday plans developed, they became especially interested in two African deserts – the Kaokoveld in north-west Namibia, as it now is, and the Kalahari, the largest desert in southern Africa.

The two Marshalls, father and son, spent most of the summer of 1950 travelling in the Kaokoveld. They then went to Xai-Xai in north-west Botswana, and were told that over the border Bushmen were still leading a traditional hunter-gatherer way of life. The area they lived in, Nyae Nyae, was a wilderness which had effectively isolated them from outsiders, black and white. The Marshalls decided this was the family project they had been looking for, and determined to return the following year with

Lorna and John's elder sister Elizabeth. Because of the difficulties of travel, they would need to mount a full-scale expedition, complete with large stocks of fuel, food and water, and four-wheel drive vehicles.

In 1951 the whole family set out on their Kalahari adventure, and had the good fortune, as Lorna explains, to meet an 'uncommonly intelligent, able man, much esteemed by his people' named Toma, the leader of a Bushman family group, which she named Band 1. As they got to know one another it became clear, Lorna wrote, that 'no white people had ever before wanted to understand the customs of the Nyae Nyae Kung,* and that the Nyae Nyae Kung were not averse to having a little attention paid them. . . . He [Toma] just gave us his approval and agreed to let us live with him.' Toma also gave his visitors Bushman names, the names of his own family, which acted as an introduction to the whole Nyae Nyae area, and 'no time was lost in overcoming shyness and suspicion on the part of the Kung in other bands'.

Thus was forged one of the most extraordinary and productive relationships ever to exist between free, independent Bushmen and philanthropic, liberal whites. Lorna, who had studied English literature at Berkeley and Radcliffe, went on to write her Bushman classic, *The !Kung of Nyae Nyae*, and to become the doyenne of American anthropology – she celebrated her 100th birthday in 1998. Her daughter, under the name Elizabeth Marshall Thomas, wrote a best-seller, *The Harmless People*, about her experiences with the Bushmen; and John filmed the Kung of Nyae Nyae for most of the second half of the twentieth century, compiling in the process a unique film record of virtually the last of the hunter-gatherers.

Circumstances had undoubtedly favoured the Kung's independence. With few permanent water holes and no permanent surface water, the Nyae Nyae area, as Professor Schoeman discovered, was unsuited to white farming and colonisation, and so the Kung avoided the fate of so many Bushmen in other parts of southern Africa – the loss of their land and often of their lives

---

* The Kung are usually known today as Juwa.

as well. When the Marshalls arrived, the Kung were protected not only by their environment, but also by law. As Crown land, Nyae Nyae was closed to white farmers and to black pastoralists, either from South-West Africa (Namibia), or from across the border in Bechuanaland (Botswana). Nor was there any government presence; no administrative post, no mission, no school.

I visited Lorna Marshall in New Hampshire in 1999. She was 101, but still had vivid memories of her visits to the Kalahari: 'It was a wonderful experience to sleep under the stars in flat country like that, with no trees overhead ... I loved it, I just loved it.'

Lorna recalled making camp late at night in the open, 'and a lioness came and walked among us, and she stood beside our interpreter and leaned over him like this – you could see her claws going in, like that – and we thought it was because he smelled so bad that he saved our lives, because she moved away.' Lorna chuckled at the memory, but her daughter, Elizabeth, remembered the incident rather differently, recalling that it was not one but three lions which had visited their camp that night. 'They'd come and check us out,' she said. Being cats, they were curious. The Marshalls were not afraid to sleep on the ground in the open at Nyae Nyae, because the behaviour of the lion population was 'very different' then. 'The lions left the people alone for excellent reasons,' Elizabeth said, 'and the people left the lions alone for excellent reasons.' If Bushmen who had wounded a wildebeest and were tracking it caught up with a pride of lions – perhaps as many as 30 – which had taken possession of the kill, the Bushmen would walk up to the lions and tell them the meat belonged to them. 'They talked to them respectfully, but kept advancing on them and the lions grumbled and grumbled but they did back off.' Bushmen were able to do this 'because as fellow-predators over thousands of years, Bushmen and lions had evolved a *modus vivendi*'.

One day, however, Elizabeth had tried to use the same technique in Etosha National Park: 'I thought this is how you handle lions, because this is what the Bushmen did ... I got out of the vehicle and advanced on this lion, speaking politely ...' and the lion charged. 'I was standing next to the vehicle, so I jumped in and slammed the door and here I am.' Elizabeth said many people had been killed by lions in Etosha, and she herself had been hunted by lions there. 'It's unsafe, you can't get out of your vehicle, you can't walk.' She attributed the change in lion behaviour in Etosha to the time when Bushmen were 'cleared out'. 'After the Bushmen were gone you had a couple of generations of lions without any Bushmen to show them how it was done.'

In Nyae Nyae, on the other hand, where there were a lot of Bushmen, encounters with lions were commonplace. 'We never had any trouble. We always slept on the ground, often without tents. . . . The same night that the lions came – the night mother was talking about – the lions went to the Bushman village and looked over the tops of the little huts, and the Bushmen said, "You have to go," and they said it firmly. Each knew the other. It's an old, old thing, this lion–Bushman relationship. The Bushman archaeological past goes back 35,000 years, probably more. . . . Lions have been living here [in the Kalahari] for over 700,000 years.'

As a student of lions, Elizabeth spoke of the many parallels between predator and hunter. 'Bushman and lion hunting practices are very much the same, interestingly enough. They're both water-dependent, unlike antelopes. They both need to live within walking distance of water. Lions used water at night and Bushmen used it in the day; you never saw a lion drinking in the daytime. The Bushmen used the hunting lands by day, the lions by night. I saw lions all over the place in Etosha, but never in Nyae Nyae, except when they came to us. We never stumbled on one. They hunted the same game, their striking distance was the same.' Five or six lions would hunt together in a pride, whereas the normal size of a Bushman band was 25. But the weight of the two groups was much the same and their caloric needs were 'pretty close', Elizabeth said. In Nyae Nyae, they both respected water holes. 'I never saw a lion scat near the water, nor did the people. . . . In Etosha, the lions go and crap all over the water hole.'

Elizabeth then talked about Bushman society as she came to know it in Nyae Nyae in the 1950s, when she was nineteen, and how impressed she had been by their knowledge of the natural world, talking about arrow poison as an example. 'It comes from a grub, it makes the poison in its pupa stage, the pupa is three feet underground, under a certain type of tree, and the cocoon, or pupa casing is made from grains of sand. . . . So it's exactly the same as the sand around it – invisible. Nevertheless, somebody knew the environment well enough to find it, and then to find its qualities and then to apply them and then to have the arrows to fit.' Bushman arrows were so light, that without poison 'they could barely kill a bird.' 'People think that just because they're hunter-gatherers, Bushmen are ignorant. They're not. The tremendous knowledge . . . and the tremendous abilities they had knocks my socks off. Unbelievable.'

Of the many memorable portraits she draws in *The Harmless People*, one of the most appealing is that of a young girl nicknamed Beautiful Ungka. 'She was probably the most beautiful girl in all Nyae Nyae, and even though she was only sixteen years old she already had a flaming past,' Elizabeth wrote. She was married for the first time when she was ten, but hated her husband (who was older) so much that she managed to have the marriage dissolved. Another man, although already married and also much older, became so inflamed by her beauty that, having failed to persuade her to marry him, he kidnapped her in the middle of the night. Reaching his hut 'he flung Beautiful Ungka down in the back of his *scherm* on the far side of his wife "to show," said the Bushmen, "that he wasn't afraid of his wife or anybody," and Beautiful Ungka lay still, as if subdued, until she heard that her captor and his wife were asleep. Then she got up, stepped over them, and walked home. That was the end of that episode.'

She was finally married again, aged fourteen, against her will but at her parents' insistence, to a presentable young man in his twenties who was quite well off. But although she was now old enough for intercourse, she refused to sleep with him 'and he was driven to despair . . . once he walked forty miles, from Gam, where he was living, to Gautscha, where we were, to ask us for medicines that would relieve headaches that Beautiful Ungka had, then forty miles back again to bring her what we gave him.'

In vain. Ungka spurned the medicines, and continued to reject him. Eventually, poor young man, he was kidnapped in one of the first raids on the Nyae Nyae Bushmen by local white farmers, and not seen again.

So even in the 1950s, the outside world was beginning to impinge on what had been the impenetrable fastness of Nyae Nyae, and to their dismay the Marshalls discovered that they had been the unwitting cause of the first raid. The farmers had simply followed the Marshalls' vehicle tracks in the sand, had found the little Juwa villages, had rounded up the men, and had driven them off to their farms as forced labour. This happened three times, according to Elizabeth. 'They came all the way to Gam, where they had found the Bushmen, no longer shy of Europeans, and had offered to take them "for a ride" on their trucks but had promised to bring them back.' The Bushmen had believed them, had gone for the ride, and of course were never seen again. One group of farmers had taken some young Bushman children who had been playing in the veld. When the mothers had called their children, and received no answer, they had walked in the tracks the trucks had left and had followed their children to the farms. Neither the mothers nor the children had ever returned. The second time the farmers came, they kidnapped Toma, who had been seriously hurt in a hunting accident, and was unable to run away.

Toma had shot a big bull buffalo with a poisoned arrow at Gautscha Pan, and after waiting for a day and a half for the poison to work – longer than usual because buffalo are so dangerous – set off with another hunter, Lazy Kwi, to track the wounded animal. They tracked it for three days, and finally found it on the morning of the fourth day, lying sprawled on the ground, apparently dead. Even then, Toma, a highly experienced hunter, watched it for most of the day, and only when it had neither moved nor shown any other sign of life, did he creep up to it, and raise his spear to give it a final thrust. Suddenly, the buffalo struggled to its feet, and charged, tossing Toma in the air and goring him. One horn pierced his body, the point emerging from his back. Toma was unconscious when Lazy Kwi picked him up and carried him back to Gautscha where, despite all the

Bushman cures they tried, he seemed to be dying. So Toma asked Lazy Kwi and another man to carry him home to his own people in Gam, and it was there, helpless, that 'blackbirding' farmers found him and took him away.

As it happened, the raid saved Toma's life. When the farmer who had kidnapped him saw how ill Toma was, he fed him, gave him drugs and dressed his wounds. Toma began to recover and, as the weeks and months went by, slowly regained his strength. One night, when the veld was quiet and dark, Toma had 'thanked the farmer in his heart', gathered together all the Bushmen on the farm, and led them across the desert, all the way back to Nyae Nyae. It had been a long walk, but Toma had managed. Although the wound where the buffalo had gored him still ached on cold days, and sometimes his vision was 'blurry', Toma was pleased to be back in his own country. Lazy Kwi told Elizabeth this story one night, when they were camping in the Kalahari and searching for Toma, who had disappeared again. Next morning they saw some bush fires in the distance and went to investigate, since Lazy Kwi was convinced that Toma was nearby. As they approached the smoke of the first fire, they saw a man running towards them with long swinging strides. It was Toma. He had heard the sound of the jeep but had hidden and watched carefully until he recognised them. Climbing into the jeep, Toma and his companion, Gao Big Feet, embraced Elizabeth and Lazy Kwi in joyful reunion.

In the late 1950s, change overwhelmed Nyae Nyae, prompting Elizabeth Marshall Thomas to add an epilogue to *The Harmless People*, in which she described the fate of the Bushmen she had known. Her main purpose, she says, was to explain that Bushmen no longer lived as hunter-gatherers. 'The concept of Bushmen in a far-away Eden, pleasant as we may find it, is simply and perniciously untrue.' That way of life was no more. 'It is gone from the face of the earth at enormous cost to the people who once lived it.'

In 1959 Claude McIntyre, who as a young man had worked as a clerk on the Schoeman commission, became the first Bushman Affairs Commissioner in Tshumkwe, where he built an office, a house and a borehole. The Dutch Reformed Church founded a mission. A road and airstrip were added. 'The Kung', as Lorna Marshall noted, 'were no longer remote.' Foreseeing that the Bushmen would lose their land, McIntyre suggested they learn subsistence farming by growing millet and maize, and raising goats. He went to consult the people, including Toma, who later told John Marshall and Claire Ritchie, also a film maker and an anthropologist: 'At first we didn't want to go, but we talked about it and decided it was a better life for us and we would learn to live like other people. So we came to Tshumkwe in the hot season, before the rains.'

Tshumkwe was founded on Christmas Day, 1959. Working on building the settlement were nine Bushmen, two of whom were taught to drive a tractor. Others planted vegetables and herded goats. The old kinship rules of sharing everything died hard. People with vegetable gardens and livestock found that their envious relatives would arrive from the bush, expecting to share the fruits of their labours, including the goats. Some families abandoned the struggle and went back to the desert. But Toma made a success of it, probably because he and his family all came together, as a band, and sharing did not present the same problem.

In 1970, as McIntyre had predicted, the Bushmen lost most of their land in a carve-up dictated by the iron laws of apartheid. The result, as Elizabeth Marshall Thomas succinctly put it, was that: 'The land available for a hunting and gathering economy was gone.' It shrank, in fact, from about 27,000 square miles (70,000 square kilometres) to 2,400 square miles (6,300 square kilometres), a loss of almost 90 per cent.

When Claude McIntyre's health forced him to retire, his successor abandoned his policy of helping Bushmen to help themselves. The number of Bushmen employed in low-paid jobs for the administration jumped from 9 in 1967 to 85 by 1972, with disastrous effects on the community. Previously, able-bodied men had been the mainstay of the old economy, responsible as hunter-gatherers for feeding a large number of relatives, including the young, the old and the sick. Now standards of living declined alarmingly. The miserable wages were barely enough to feed one person, let alone an extended family. Deprived of the old healthy diet, the Bushman began to suffer from malnutrition and disease.

In 1978 the South African army arrived in Tshumkwe to expand its operations against SWAPO, the South-West Africa People's Organisation, which was waging its war of independence from bases in Angola. The South Africans recruited both Kung and Khwe Bushmen from Angola, professional soldiers who had fought in the past with the Portuguese, but had not been hunter-gatherers for generations, and young Juwa Bushmen from Tshumkwe. The latter were neither experienced soldiers, nor were many of them brought up to hunt in the bush, but that did not deter the South African army from propagating the myth of Bushman invincibility and 'legendary' tracking skills. As Colonel Delville Linford, a South African who commanded Bushmen troops, wrote in his foreword to Ian Uys's *Bushman Soldiers*: 'The Bushman soldier is unique in many respects. Born to use a bow and arrow, he learnt to use modern weapons with surprising efficiency, and his incredibly keen senses and thorough knowledge of the bush made him a soldier feared by all that crossed his path.'

Claire Ritchie dismissed this as 'bullshit', yet another example of the Bushman myth, pointing out that the Bushmen themselves told a very different story, quoted in *Shaken Roots: The Bushmen of Namibia* by Megan Biesele, an American anthropologist and Bushman rights' activist, and Paul Weinberg, a South African photographer. One young Bushman, Kaece Kunta, who served with the South African army in Angola, described his experiences: 'We saw the villages of the dead, those who had been killed and their dead children ... When you walked through these villages, you were stepping on death, the corpses of dead people. It was horrible. You had to step on them and they just crumbled to dust. If hunger gripped your middle while you were on these "ops" and you hadn't seen food for three days, and then you had a chance to eat, you couldn't eat the food because it all tasted like death.' He spoke of how Bushmen had to be drugged before going into battle or being forced to cross minefields. 'If you were too weak to work, they'd prick your one shoulder with a needle, then prick your other shoulder, so you'd have strength to work well.'

The lure of army wages, however, proved irresistible, and young Bushmen flocked to join up. As a result, according to Elizabeth Marshall Thomas, the community was soon divided into haves – 'soldiers with good clothes and food and money to buy candy for their children, and ghetto blasters for themselves – and the have-nots – people with no jobs at all, people dressed in rags, people who stole and whored to keep from starving, a new underclass.' Ready access to alcohol accelerated the decline. 'There were murders, killings, people would kill other people, and not know in the morning what had happened. They wouldn't remember anything about it, people would kill their own family members.' Her brother, John, and Claire Ritchie witnessed a terrible fight, Bushmen threatening one another with knives and making accusations of whoring, selfishness and stealing. 'It was so upsetting that one weeping woman ripped open the buttons of her dress to bare her breast, hysterically calling on her adversaries to stab her.'

After McIntyre left, a non-Bushman opened a shop in Tshumkwe which, among other things, sold sugar. Non-Bushmen used it to brew home-made beer, which Bushmen began to buy, although they could ill afford it and were unused to alcohol. It was to prove the thin end of the wedge. In 1981 the same shopkeeper obtained a licence to sell alcohol, and a government loan to start an off-licence. For him, it was an extremely profitable investment, but it was disastrous for the Bushmen, as Claire Ritchie discovered when she made a study of just how much money Bushmen soldiers and their families spent buying alcohol on pay-day: a staggering 760 rand (about £600), and double that over the weekend.

The Dutch Reformed Church lamented the depravity, the whoring for food, the stealing, drunkenness, and the fighting, but they did not make many converts. The Bushmen were aware that Tshumkwe, like some Kalahari Sodom and Gomorrah, was destroying them, but seemed powerless to stop it. They called it 'Face of Sickness', 'Face of Fighting' and 'Where the Fight

Follows You'. One woman, Nai, whom the Marshalls had known as a little girl, said 'Death is dancing with me.' Her father, Gao Big Feet, who had come running with Toma to meet Elizabeth and Lazy Kwi, died of tuberculosis. One of Nai's sons was in the army, another died of malnutrition and diarrhoea at the age of ten. Nai's youngest brother, once known as Little Dabe, became a soldier, and one day when very drunk smashed Toma's head with a stone. A girl went mad after her husband, a heavy drinker, attacked her violently and bit off one of her ears. Lazy Kwi's son, Gao, died of tuberculosis in his twenties. Several young girls, including Beautiful Ungka, died of malnutrition and tuberculosis. One woman died in a coma after being kicked by her son, Qui, who came home blind drunk one day to find his wife had fallen asleep after a drinking bout, rolled on their baby and killed it. In his intoxicated state, he thought his mother was to blame. Two years later in another drunken rage he killed his second wife, Ungka Norna, Toma's daughter and named after Lorna Marshall.

Throughout this period, from 1960 until 1978, John Marshall was unable to visit Nyae Nyae, having been banned by the South African government. After repeated requests he was finally allowed back in 1978 and made a film about the disasters that had befallen his friends seen through the eyes of Nai, and named after her.

He also resolved to do something practical to help, not as a personal crusade 'to save the Bushmen', but as a member of Toma's family, the bond between the old Bushman and the young American being exceptionally strong. By 1980, when Marshall returned to Nyae Nyae with Claire Ritchie, things were even worse. There were twenty-three illegal shebeens (bars) in Tshumkwe, one of them run by a local official's family. Both Marshall and Toma agreed on the urgent need to move people away from Tshumkwe, back to their *nores* – their home territories in the Kalahari where, in the words of another Bushman leader, Kaece Kxao, 'the trees are ours, and the elephants are ours. This is our land. Our things we make and wear come from it – our ostrich beads, our bows and arrows.'

Toma, with what remained of his family and friends, went

back to Gautscha, the place where he had shot the buffalo that nearly killed him. John Marshall used his own money – he had been left a farm by his father, who died in 1980 – to start a cattle fund, and eventually about 80 Bushmen settled at Gautscha, owning between them about 100 head of cattle. With cattle as their mainstay, some hunting and gathering, and some casual labour at Tshumkwe, they were able to subsist. Two more settlements were founded, and by the time John Marshall and Claire Ritchie left in 1982 the Nyae Nyae experiment had been legally established. Over the next few years, Marshall and Ritchie were busy fund-raising, lobbying for support in South Africa, the United States and Europe, and promoting the farming project in the face of official hostility and 'constant threats of permit withdrawal', according to Claire Ritchie. The novice Bushman farmers, meanwhile, had to contend with a seven-year drought, made worse by elephants destroying water points and lions killing their cattle. So crass were the game laws that a Bushman farmer who killed a marauding lion was liable to a long prison sentence – even the man who, in desperation, speared a lion that was clinging to the belly of his bull.

In 1984 a government report recommended a game reserve should be established in Bushmanland, which Marshall and Ritchie strongly opposed on the grounds that the Bushmen would lose what little land they had left. The government's response to this and other pressing problems was to spend no money directly on the Bushmen, but instead to build a new jail, a bigger police station, more white housing and a tourist camp in Tshumkwe. There were successes, however. Toma's son, Tsamko, and John Marshall travelled the country, addressing groups of Bushmen. In Claire Ritchie's words: 'Political consciousness is blooming, and the seeds of the Farmers' Union – self-representation – are being sown.' Five more settlements were started; the Farmers' Union took over cattle distribution, and elected a management committee – the latter a difficult concept for some of the older people, used to a 'culture where everyone is a chief and no one must be seen to "touch his head against the sky".' The Nyae Nyae Development Foundation started to compile a *nore* map as a basis for a potential lands right claim, although continuing to face police harassment, and pressure from the Hereros for grazing in Bushmanland. The well-known aggressiveness of the Hereros was epitomised by their Chief Ruruaiku whose attitude was: 'Wherever my cattle throw their shadow, the land belongs to me.' Between 30,000 and 40,000 Herero refugees living just across the Botswana border were given permission to vote in the forthcoming elections, and to return to Namibia after independence.

John Marshall's plan of 'holding on to the land' was fully endorsed by the Nyae Nyae Bushmen, who realised its urgency: 'We must pull ourselves up, or die out.' This was no exaggeration, as Megan Biesele, who joined the team as project director in 1988, was quick to grasp: 'Today 33,000 people classified as "Bushman" in Namibia have no land on which to hunt, gather or produce food and are increasingly without work,' she wrote. 'Without land they have resorted to employment in the army or to ill-paid work for white and black farmers. The vast majority who have been unable to get employment squat near places of work, dependent on the wage earners.' Those who had joined the South African army now found themselves on the wrong side in the independence struggle; the SWAPO nationalists they had been fighting would soon become the new government.

Forced to withdraw first from Angola, and then, after prolonged pressure by the United Nations, from South-West Africa in 1988, South Africa left its Bushman soldiers with the agonising choice of either staying behind, unwelcome in the new Namibia, or resettling far to the south, in alien territory. In both cases, stay or leave, they faced an uncertain future, in which the old truths had disappeared and new demons awaited.

The period leading up to Namibia's first free elections in 1989 was one of increasingly hectic change. The old apartheid homelands system was dismantled, so Bushmanland ceased to exist, putting the very existence of Nyae Nyae at stake. The United Nations arrived in force to prepare for the elections, and Nyae Nyae was deluged by outsiders of all nationalities, including a battalion of Finns who arrived at Gautscha 'lost and speaking no known language'. Nevertheless, there was a remarkable improvement in relations with SWAPO, due in no small measure to Paul Weinberg, famous for his Bushman photographs, who arranged a meeting in Windhoek between a delegation from Nyae Nyae, including Toma's elder son Tsamko, and SWAPO leaders newly returned from exile. SWAPO was anxious to wean the Bushman vote away from its main opposition, the pro-South African Democratic Turnhalle Alliance, inviting Nyae Nyae leaders to one of its public rallies, where Tsamko met Sam Nujoma, the head of SWAPO, and a self-declared 'friend to all Bushmen'. The elections took place in November, with the Bushmen, like so many others, voting for the first time in their lives – the polling booth had to be airlifted into Bushmanland by helicopter. SWAPO won a decisive if not absolute majority, and on 21 March 1990 Namibia became independent, with Sam Nujoma as its first President.

Before the elections, John Marshall and the Juwa lobbied hard for legal recognition of Bushman land rights, and in 1991 their persistence seemed to have been rewarded. A national land conference held in Windhoek resolved that 'disadvantaged communities' including the Bushmen 'should receive special protection of their land rights', and the *nore* system was officially recognised. However, in practice little was to change, as was soon demonstrated by what happened on a farm near Gobabis called Skoonheid, which means beauty in Afrikaans. The farm was bought by the Namibian government specifically for local Bushmen, but unfortunately for them, the handover coincided with the onset of the great drought of 1990. As a result, Herero tribesmen were given 'temporary' permission to graze their cattle on the farm, but nine years later they were still there, having by then occupied most of the farm, and pushed the 200 or so Bushmen into one corner. 'Life is not worth living here,' one Bushman said. 'The Hereros have taken all the places, and most of the land . . . We thought it [Skoonheid] was for the Bushmen, but the Hereros also moved in, so we find today we're being forced out.'

Frederic Langman, the Bushman chief designate for Omaheke

North, told me he had spent many hours travelling backwards and forwards to Windhoek and Gobabis, trying to establish his people's rights to Skoonheid, but was continually fobbed off. Officials in the capital, Windhoek, would tell him that the farm was for the Bushmen, while other officials in Gobabis – many of whom were Herero – said it was 'for everyone'. There was no water in the Bushman village, except at the nearby farmhouse, which was now occupied by the farm manager, a Herero woman in her thirties who, Langman said, was 'not helpful' to the Bushmen. In desperation, with practically no money to run their pathetically small farming operations – only three families owned livestock – and not enough water to grow crops, he and the rest of the Bushmen at Skoonheid talked of having to go back to work for Afrikaner farmers. To Langman, who had spent twenty years on white farms, it was the end of a cherished dream. But he saw no alternative. 'We do at least make some money, even if we are treated badly.' 'How badly?' I asked. 'It's still the same treatment,' he said. 'It's as if the government had empowered the black and white farmers to treat the Bushmen badly.'

Given their poverty, it is small wonder that Bushmen will grasp at any straw. On my last evening at Skoonheid, I came across an old storyteller and healer, Engnau, lying drunk or asleep on the bare concrete porch of his little house. Next morning, I found him again, this time sharing an early morning pipe with his tiny and equally wrinkled wife, Uia. He had been brought up at Skoonheid, before it was an Afrikaner farm. 'There was a lot of game here, then,' he said, 'eland, kudu, gemsbok . . . we'd all like to hunt, but we are not allowed to.' One day he was approached by an Afrikaner farmer, Nick van der Merwe who, in return for 'all the meat you can eat', offered to drive Engnau, his wife, brother, sister and three other Bushmen from Skoonheid to his game lodge, called 'Lion Farm', at Harnas, where they would be employed playing the part of 'traditional' Bushmen in front of tourists. They had to sing and dance all the time, Engnau said, but received no pay, not even for the bows and arrows and other handicrafts they made for the tourists; and after the first meal of gemsbok, there was no more meat. After a couple of years, deeply upset to discover that the farmer had not been putting aside their pay, Engnau told him: '*Baas*, we don't like it here, you must take us back,' to which the farmer replied: 'If you want to leave, you must walk.' Engnau had only one leg, having lost his foot in a borehole accident some years before, and it took them three days to reach a Bushman village 25 miles away, from where they got a lift home.

When I asked him if he liked being back in Skoonheid, he said he used to like it, but not any longer because of 'the bad words . . . I'd like to take my daughter and go,' he said. 'There is too much fighting, too much drunkenness.'

Sadly, the Bushmen of Skoonheid, like so many farm Bushmen in Namibia, have lost their culture as well as their land, and the young men can no longer perform the trance dance, the very heart of Bushman culture. If Skoonheid has been a failure as far as the Bushmen are concerned, a happier state of affairs exists on two farms, Donkerbos and Sonneblom, near Tallismanus, farther east towards the Botswana border. Here the western fringe of the Kalahari stretches to the horizon, an endless, burning plain of sand, now red, now yellow shading to grey, and covered in thick bush and small trees. I drove past heavily over-grazed Mbandero or Herero cattle posts, the cattle listless from too little food. Unlike Skoonheid, which was purchased from its Afrikaner owner by the Namibian government, Donkerbos and Sonneblom were given to the Bushmen – extraordinary as that may seem – by a chief of the Mbandero, an offshoot of the Herero, against the wishes of his own people. Although they had been in possession for several years, the Bushmen had done little with their new property, and were still in the early stages of fencing it, making roads and starting cultivation. Funding, provided by a German NGO, terre des hommes, had been erratic, the Bushmen said, and the Namibian government's contribution seemed to be limited to basic food stuffs.

To a Western mind, there was a lack of drive and initiative. Each farm had an official donkey cart, for example, but neither was serviceable, because of a shortage of inner tubes. Fritz, the Sonneblom chairman, told us he was waiting for a local Swiss pastor to provide new ones. He had been waiting for some time.

As we prepared to return to Donkerbos in our privately-hired donkey cart – which did work – we had to wait for Willem, my interpreter, who was having an animated conversation with the assembled men of the village. When I questioned him afterwards, it emerged that he had spent a month in the past at Sonneblom, persuading the villagers to join the Pentecostal Church, which among other things, bans alcohol. Now, none of them drank, Willem, himself a teetotaller, said proudly. He had been born and brought up on a white farm, where his father still worked. The farmer, he said, was 'a very cruel man' who used to punish his brother and himself with a whip, when they were boys of ten or eleven, for any minor transgression: not the short, rhinoceros-hide *sjambok*, Willem said, but a long, thin, cattle whip. It had been an unhappy childhood, but at least he had been able to attend a Dutch Reformed Church primary school, and at sixteen was lucky, or enterprising, enough to obtain a place at a government secondary school in Gobabis.

In 1993, aged seventeen, when he and his brother were visiting their father, the farmer saw them and reported them to the local policeman, his son-in-law, who arrested them. They were both found guilty of trespass, and sentenced to three months in prison, but soon afterwards the farmer appeared and asked for their release to work on his farm. Willem was paid N$48 [£5.30] a month, plus food. 'I was so poor,' he said, 'I couldn't buy anything for myself, my wife or my child.' It was about this time that Willem, who had been a heavy drinker, joined the Pentecostal Church, gave up drinking, and later became a minister. He also became a trainee with WIMSA (Working Group of Indigenous Minorities in Southern Africa), a regional network which, under its co-ordinator, Axel Thoma, a German landscape architect turned aid worker, is probably the most effective of the various organisations which support Bushman rights. Thoma, a dedicated supporter of the Bushman cause, was at one time co-ordinator of the Nyae Nyae Foundation, but left after a series of arguments and personal clashes over development policy. Even John Marshall, the inspiration behind the original Nyae Nyae concept, was on one occasion unceremoniously ejected from a meeting.

Into this muddle finally stepped the Namibian government at the head of a number of other agencies including LIFE (Living in a Finite Environment), a joint venture between the Namibian government, USAID (United States Agency for International Development) and the WWF (World Wildlife Fund). The upshot was a radical departure from the original concept of subsistence farming in favour of conservation and tourism, changes which were reinforced in 1998 when the Nyae Nyae Conservancy came into existence, the first to be created in Namibia.

Today, in the view of both Marshall and Ritchie, the emphasis on tourism and hunting, at the expense of food production, has led Nyae Nyae into a blind alley. Axel Thoma, on the other hand, thinks the Conservancy is a 'fine concept, it just needs to be implemented by the community.' Polly Wiessner, an American anthropologist who worked in Nyae Nyae in 1999, said Baraka, the headquarters village, seemed to be 'collapsing'. She also spoke of 'a growing culture of dependency', a judgement which seems to be supported by James Suzman's recent (2000) study, *The San of Southern Africa*, in which he stated that even in as well-established a project as Nyae Nyae, 'the majority of participants depend on food aid from the central Government'.

The Juwa Bushmen of Nyae Nyae, however, have been more fortunate than their fellow Bushmen, the Khwe of the Caprivi Strip. In late 1998, 1700 of them – many of the men had fought for the South Africans against SWAPO – fled south into Botswana after heavy-handed threats by the Namibian army. Although the Khwe 'chief', Kipi George, was among the refugees, his deputy, Thadeus, who stayed behind told me that Namibian soldiers had come to their villages at night to question them about a secessionist group with tribal links to Zambia. When the Bushmen denied all knowledge of the secessionists or their bases, they were prodded in the chest with rifle muzzles, and told that if they did not produce an answer soon, they would be shot. Many of those who took flight with their women and children that night, were still refugees in Botswana in late 2000.

But perhaps worst-off of all in Namibia today, after more than ten years of independence, are the 6,500 Bushmen who work on white farms in the Omaheke, the Namibian Gulag, trapped in lives of serfdom and often brutality. James Suzman, a young South African anthropologist who knows the area well, says, 'They are the most depressed, demoralised, beaten-up, drunken and bedraggled people I have come across.' The Afrikaner farmers of the Omaheke, he told the *Sunday Times* in 1998, were 'renowned for their ferocity, and the Omaheke is the most racist place left in Southern Africa.' Beating was always the Afrikaner way of 'civilising' the Bushmen, Suzman said, adding: 'Bushmen were perceived as intrinsically wild. You couldn't civilise them, but you could beat the wildness out of them. Since independence, the beatings are less, but I don't know of any adult Bushman who hasn't experienced the fists of a farmer.'

Driving back to Skoonheid one day I passed a farm owned by an Afrikaner farmer, who was alleged to have the habit when drunk of chaining up his Bushman labourers and beating them insensible. Beatings, fuelled by alcohol, were said to be frequent, and administered while his wife stood by and egged him on. Such cases hardly ever come to court because the victims are usually too frightened to report their employers to the police, having little confidence in the law; or sometimes, as with the woman quoted below, they are too loyal to old or sick relatives to leave. Recently, a courageous researcher interviewed a number of men and women on the farm and took statements under oath. To protect the witnesses, I have not used their names, nor those of their interlocutors. These are voices crying in the wilderness, crying to be heard.

Woman: If you say you want to leave, then you will be beaten half-dead and he [the farmer] will take you here [to the garage], and then you will be wearing a chain. He will put a chain around your neck and put a padlock on your neck. Your head also [goes] 'hoa', 'hoa', 'pow', 'pow'. You must [pretend to] be very weak, do not stand up. And you must lie there and you will get water thrown over you – bagahh! He will start from your legs.
Interviewer: Has he beaten you like this?
Woman: Me? In the beginning, it's why I don't have teeth any

more. With his fist. . . . And my arm isn't right now. He hurts me on my arm, and if I'm working too much, it's not good.

Interviewer: Does he still do this now, in these days, since independence?

Woman: He's still doing it. . . .

Interviewer: [What about] the farmer's wife?

Woman: She also beats and there are some walking sticks . . . for men and for women. If his wife says, 'Come and do this,' and if you say, 'Wait, I must do this,' then she will say 'Waar is my kierie?' [Where is my walking stick?] And if she runs in and takes that walking stick then you must look out. Then she will beat you. That farmer's wife beats. If her husband says he is finished, then she will force him and then he will go and beat somebody. If her husband doesn't want to, then she will force him and say, 'Are you licking his shit? Are you licking a black person's arsehole?'

When asked why she did not bring charges against the farmer, she replied, 'To where will you go to charge? Because . . . if you try to go and charge him, [and] hitch a ride [to Gobabis], he will go and bring you back . . . and beat you . . .' She also said she could not leave without her old mother. She was asked about her mother's pension – often the only money a Bushman family has to live on. She replied that the farmer always handled the money, buying mealie meal, sugar and tea for her mother, and keeping the change.

Interviewer: How does the farmer get the pension money?

Woman: The old woman is pressing her thumb on the cheque for him. . . . She doesn't want to press her thumb . . . but they force her so that she can have food to eat.

Interviewer: They take her ID [identity card]?

Woman: They have her ID.

Interviewer: How long has she been on this farm?

Woman: She gets old here.

Several other Bushmen who worked on the farm made similar allegations, also under oath, describing how it was routine for the farmer physically to assault them. The questioner asked one man if they visited their relatives on other farms?

Man: Sometimes we go to visit nearby farms. Not me, only the children [young men]. The next morning, he [the farmer] will beat the children and say that they are not allowed to go to visit other farms. He puts a chain around their necks.

Another farm worker, who volunteered to make a statement about a beating, was asked to give details.

Man: I was tied up.
Interviewer: When did this beating happen to you?
Man: Last Saturday, [no] it was Sunday.
Interviewer: What happened, did he beat you or hang you up?
Man: I and another man were fighting, and then he [the farmer] came up and brought me here.
Interviewer: How did it begin? Did he say anything?
Man: Yes, he said something. We were in the house and then he came and grabbed me like this [grasps his throat].
Interviewer: And what did he say? Did he beat you?
Man: Yes, when I got up there, he beat me.
Interviewer: With what did he beat you?
Man: With his fist.
Interviewer: Did he hang you up?
Man: Yes, he grabbed me and tied me up.
Interviewer: Were you very hurt?
Man: Yes. He tied me up.
Interviewer: Why did you not report it to the police?
Man: No, my legs were sore.
Interviewer: With what did he hang you up?
Man: A chain.

The foreman, who was said to have suffered the most brutal treatment of all, also made a sworn statement. Human rights officials in Windhoek wanted him to testify in court against his employer, but before charges could be brought, he left the farm and disappeared. He told the interviewer he was often beaten for no good reason.

Foreman: If a thing is wrong, or if a thing [animal] is sick, or if the car's oil is not right, then I'm in trouble. . . . If he comes out of the house and sees a thing wrong, then he swears at me and fights, even if it is another man's fault.

Interviewer: How many times has he beaten you?

Foreman: Many times. I cannot remember, but it was many times.

Interviewer: How did he beat you?

Foreman: Before, he hit me [with his fist], but this last time he did not. He beat me with a stick.

Interviewer: Were you very hurt?

Foreman: Yes, I could not see and my vision was closed. One day he went to Gobabis, and when he came back his son said to him that I am drunk. And he came back from there [his house] to here [the foreman's house] and takes me and beats me half dead.

Interviewer: Why did you not go to the police to complain?

Foreman: How can I go there?

Interviewer: When did it happen?

Foreman: The time when he beat me was last year. And when he beat me last time was at Christmas . . . I was down there with him. He said I must go back because I am drunk. Then I came back to my house, and then he came and picked me up and took me to the post and there he tied me up in the garage. I lay there until the evening. Only in the evening he went there and untied me and brought me back.

Interviewer: With what did he beat you?

Foreman: With his hands, and then with a stick. Maybe he broke my rib. I am still not right, because of my rib. Maybe it's bent.

CHAPTER ELEVEN

People without a Voice

'We have come to ask you a question. You are the son of the N/oakhwe [Red People] so perhaps you can answer this question. Whose land is this?'

Khomtsa Khomtsa, 1992

When George Silberbauer first went to the Central Kalahari to start his Bushman Survey in the late 1950s, the Gwi and Gana inhabitants (roughly 6000 of them) were still living the traditional life of hunter-gatherers, much as their ancestors had done for thousands of years. Outside the Central Kalahari, however, the future of the Bushmen in Botswana was already precarious. In many parts of the country, above all in the ranching belt round Ghanzi to the west, they had long been drawn into, or forced to work in, the white farm economy as herdsmen or labourers. Although indispensable to the viability of such farms, they were treated little better than serfs, paid next to nothing, and liable to harsh punishments. Farmers had the legal right to administer corporal punishment to their workers, acting as both judge and jury, and were seldom slow to exercise their rights. A typical punishment involved tying the miscreant to a wagon wheel and flogging him with a *sjambok* while reading aloud, presumably during breaks in the punishment, from the Bible, selecting passages which the chastiser thought appropriate.

In the 1890s, however, the initial contact between the Bushmen and the first trekboers to arrive in Ghanzi was very different, and on the whole friendly. Since the Bushmen did not feel threatened by the newcomers' relatively small numbers, they showed the trekboers where to find water for themselves and their cattle, and in return obtained protection against the Tswana tribesmen and other enemies. Gradually, a quasi-feudal relationship developed

163

between Boer and Bushman, which in some ways was similar to the master-servant relationship, known as *mafisa*, which existed between the Bushmen and the Tswana long before the arrival of the white men. On the whole, these early Boer farmers treated their Bushman workers humanely, if paternalistically. Members of the same Bushman family or band would often remain with the same Boer family for generations, the children playing together, and learning to speak one another's language – the Bushmen children being especially good linguists. One considerate employer, a seventy-year-old Afrikaner widow who farmed near Ghanzi, made a point of giving her Bushman workers a hot meal every morning. You could not expect a man to put in a good day's work if he did not have a decent breakfast, she maintained, and to prove it there is a photograph of her standing, soup ladle in hand, surrounded by her Bushman staff in the middle of the veld.

By the time the anthropologist Mathias Guenther arrrived in Ghanzi at the end of the 1960s, however, the old paternalistic relationship between Boer and Bushman was beginning to change. 'Inside the velvet glove of paternalism was a hard fist,' he observed, 'and throughout the middle decades of the present (twentieth) century the glove was shed by many European farmers.' With it went the more benign aspects of European paternalism, 'rendering blatant its inherent inequity, deprivation, exploitation and oppression'. The Nharo Bushmen of Ghanzi had a word for the powerlessness and despair of their lives; it was *sheta*, probably derived from the English word 'shit' which, along with '*fok*' was then common parlance in Ghanzi.

Guenther draws a striking contrast between the deplorable condition of the Ghanzi Bushmen in the 1960s, and what it had been more than 100 years before. Then, early travellers described them as being of 'manly independence' or 'very superior, in physical respect, to those in Great Namaqualand' on the Orange River, and showing 'no timidity or distrust or want of confidence' towards strangers. Livingstone, who 'discovered' Lake Ngami, north-east of Ghanzi, in 1849, spoke admiringly of the courage of Bushmen who hunted lions with bows and arrows, and described them as 'independent gentlemen'. The British explorers, James Chapman and Thomas Baines, who travelled extensively in the area in the 1850s and 1860s were eloquent in their admiration, above all of the Nharo of the Ghanzi area, and the Juwa-speaking Augei Bushmen farther north, finding their self-confidence so great as to border on arrogance. Chapman considered them a 'much finer race of Bushmen than we had generally met with' and 'more independent and fearless than any I have seen'. Baines, 'the artist with an eye for beauty', in Guenther's words, with strong leanings towards the ideas of Jean-Jacques Rousseau, 'could not help but admire' the deportment and dress of these 'manly fellows', who decked themselves out in feathers and beads. He even broke into verse in his account of the journey, quoting approvingly from Pringle who saw the Bushmen as 'lords of the desert land' and the embodiment of the 'noble savage'. In Baines's eyes, in 1861, they were still 'lords of the desert', living 'in a country where neither Hottentot nor Bechuana dare permanently settle'. Some of the early travellers claimed even to have found evidence that the Bushmen were 'politically and militaristically organised by powerful chiefs' including the famous Augei named Dukuri, a Bushman warrior king who conquered the Nharo and kept black and Hottentot invaders at bay.

By the end of the nineteenth century, however, much of the game on which the Bushmen depended for survival had been slaughtered; in the north-west, they had been largely subjugated by the Tawana, one of the eight Tswana tribes which had migrated south from Central Africa; and European-borne diseases, such as smallpox, were exacting a heavy toll.

During his fieldwork in Ghanzi, Guenther was told many tales of the days – probably around the turn of the century – when the Bushmen, if no longer 'lords of the desert', were still strong enough to fight back bravely against Tawana encroachment. One old man told him the story of his uncle, a 'headman' called Tsabu, who led his band in battle against Tawana marauders, and drove them off, killing one of them, despite the Bushmen being armed only with bows and arrows against the enemy's rifles. The Tawana, however, launched a second attack, this time successfully, and captured Tsabu. 'He was tied to a tree and tortured and, after refusing to allow himself to be taken away into servitude, he was shot.' The Tawana then departed, taking with them into captivity the rest of the band.

By the middle of the twentieth century, as if subjugation and dispossession were not enough, the Bushmen, who had been forced to adapt to being a race of menial farm labourers, suddenly found themselves the victims of unemployment, dispossessed anew by an influx of blacks who were considered better workers. Part of the problem was the arrival of a fresh wave of settlers from South Africa, this time English-speaking, who in the process of 'rationalisation' either did not employ Bushmen if they were hiring new labour, or sacked them if they had inherited them. 'From the 1950s onwards, more and more farm Bushmen lost their jobs and began to wander from farm to farm in small family groups akin to the traditional bands, with their belongings packed on the family donkey's back,' reports Guenther.

As the downward spiral gathered pace, poverty, hunger and malnutrition took their inexorable course; diseases such as tuberculosis became rampant, and the infant mortality rate soared. The once self-confident, even arrogant 'lords of the desert' now saw themselves as *k'amka kweni*, literally 'mouthless people' or 'people without a voice'. Guenther recalls a Bushman using an even more damning expression to him one day. Pointing at some other Bushmen who were scavenging on the farm's rubbish heap, hoping to find a few scraps of food or something they could use, he observed bitterly that the once proud 'lords of the desert' had become 'rubbish people'.*

Moved by the plight of the Bushmen, the British colonial administration of Bechuanaland felt obliged to provide them with an opportunity to preserve their old way of life. George Silberbauer was therefore given the task of seeing how this could be done, and spent the best part of five years preparing for and executing his formidable task, learning a Bushman language,

---

* Quoted in 'From "Lords of the Desert" to "Rubbish People" ', an article by Mathias Guenther in *Miscast*, the catalogue of an exhibition at the South African National Gallery, Cape Town, 1996.

Gwi, as well as spending months travelling and living in the Central Kalahari. In *Hunter and habitat in the central Kalahari Desert*, Silberbauer gives a fascinating account of the Gwi way of life as he witnessed it in the late 1950s. Their communities, or bands, varied in size from 25 to 85, adults and children. Membership of a band was voluntary, and although they were mainly formed on the basis of kinship, non-family were also eligible. Depending on the season and the availability of food, bands came together when there was plenty, and split up when food was scarce. They had no chiefs (in contrast to what the early explorers reported), leadership emanating from the most experienced and respected members of the band. All major decisions, however, were arrived at through discussion in which all adult and near-adult members of the band could take part. Consensus having been reached, all members of the band were expected to abide by the decision. Such a system made for a genuinely democratic society.

Living in small, self-sufficient units was essential for survival in a place like the Kalahari Desert, although game and bush foods were generally plentiful. It also encouraged what Silberbauer calls the opportunistic freedom or initiative hunter-gatherers need to stay alive. But it had its drawbacks, too: 'Opportunism in the band, although an effective adaptation to the circumstances of isolated hunter-gatherers, is a highly specialised trait. Depending on a close-knit network of intimate relationships, it makes the Gwi social order singularly vulnerable to dislocation when a more forceful people intrudes,' says Silberbauer. 'The narrowness of the specialisation and its vulnerability are shown by the shocking rapidity and the tragic extent of the collapse of the social organisation of the Gwi and other Bushmen when they are overrun by ranchers or cattle-post owners and are reduced to empty, aimless demoralization.' If that was true in Silberbauer's day, in the late 1950s and early 1960s, how much more so is it in Botswana and Namibia today.

Among his recommendations for the establishment of the Central Kalahari Game Reserve was one key stipulation: Bushmen leading the traditional hunter-gatherer way of life should be allowed to continue to live in the Reserve, and to hunt and to gather bush foods and materials freely. Silberbauer was well aware that the idea of giving the Bushmen exclusive rights to the Reserve would be open to criticism, and had his answer ready. 'The retention of the Bushmen in the Reserve would appear to be a reversal of the policy of economic advancement advocated for the rest of the Bushmen of Bechuanaland. The resolution of this paradox is that it is not intended to preserve the Bushmen of the Reserve as museum curiosities and pristine primitives, but to allow them the right of choice of the life they wish to follow.' Such a view was accepted by the British administration of the day as being in the best traditions of enlightened colonial rule. It also fitted well with the Constitution of Botswana which came into effect five years later at independence, in 1966. Under Section 14 it guarantees 'protection of freedom of movement', giving citizens 'the right to move freely throughout Botswana' and 'the right to reside in any part of Botswana'.

At independence, Seretse Khama, famous for marrying an Englishwoman, Ruth Williams, and causing a major crisis in the powerful Bamangwato tribe, became Botswana's first President. Educated in Britain, Sir Seretse as he now was, well understood the Westminster model of parliamentary democracy. In 1968, two years into his presidency, he defined Botswana's position on human rights in a statement worthy of the Mother of Parliaments herself. 'Our guiding principle in international affairs,' he said, 'is that every national group has a right to self-determination, that the essence of democracy is that minorities and ethnic groups comprising a nation should not be subjected to any form of discrimination, and should happily accept the authority of the national government in the knowledge that they form no insignificant part of the national community.'

He went on to rule wisely and well, although it is doubtful if the Botswana government ever treated its minorities in quite the way Seretse described. As every politician knows, ideals are easier to aspire to than to achieve. Seretse died in 1980. Six years later, in 1986, after a fact-finding mission to the Central Kalahari Game Reserve, the Ministry of Commerce and Industry served notice that, Seretse Khama's pledge notwithstanding, the Bush-men would have to move out. In Circular No. 1, of 15 July 1986 it ruled that the social and economic development of the various settlements in the Reserve, including the largest village, Xade, should be 'frozen' because they had 'no prospect of becoming economically viable'. This seems perverse if not downright discriminatory, since the Reserve was not created with economic viability in mind but, as we have seen, to enable Bushmen to lead the life of their choice in the place of their choice – their ancestral homelands. The Ministry further ruled that 'viable sites for economic and social development should be identified outside the Reserve and the residents of the Reserve encouraged – but not forced – to relocate at those sites.' Those four words, 'encouraged – but not forced', have caused endless argument. Imposing a 'freeze' on all development in the reserve sounded like 'forced' rather than 'encouraged', unless it was the kind of encouragement Voltaire satirises in *Candide*.*

Later, there would be reports of government threats and bullying, several allegations of torture, and even one of possible murder. In short, the original, liberal British policy of guarantee-ing the Bushmen the right to live their lives on their ancestral lands in the central Kalahari in their own way, was cancelled by the stroke of a pen. The same stroke of a pen also nullified Seretse Khama's famous pledge to the minorities of Botswana – 'minorities and ethnic groups comprising a nation should not be subjected to any form of discrimination'. Pushing the Bushmen out of the Reserve was a decision that seems to have been born of cynicism and greed: cynicism in its total disregard for previous commitments; and greed on the part of the Tswana ruling class who saw the chance of turning the vast empty spaces of the Central Kalahari Game Reserve into highly lucrative mining or tourist concessions.

Diamonds may be a girl's best friend, as Marilyn Monroe so evocatively sang, and there can be no dispute that in the space of

---

* Alluding to the execution of Admiral Byng for failing to relieve Minorca, Candide says, 'In this country [England] it is a good idea to kill an admiral from time to time to encourage the others.' (*Dans ce pays-ci il est bon de tuer de temps en temps un amiral pour encourager les autres.*)

a few years they have transformed Botswana, with a population of only 1.5 million, from a dirt-poor British Protectorate into one of Africa's richest countries, a net lender to the International Monetary Fund, and with the strongest currency in Africa, the pula. Botswana's Diamond Rush reads like a fairy story.

In 1967, a year after independence, the second biggest diamond pipe in the world was discovered at Orapa, about 70 miles east of the Reserve near Makgadikgadi Pans, by a geologist working for De Beers, the South African diamond giant. Six years later De Beers, founded by Cecil Rhodes in 1888, and which controls two-thirds of the world's rough diamond sales, struck even richer. At Jwaneng, about 80 miles south of the Reserve, they came across the world's largest known deposit of diamonds, although their geologist nearly missed the discovery of a lifetime because the diamond-bearing kimberlite pipe was hidden under 150 feet of Kalahari sand. It was only when he had 'another look' that he found that various trace elements – ilmenites, zircon, garnets and chrome diopside – had been brought to the surface by a colony of termites. These tiny but inexhaustible miner ants excavate great caverns and tunnels underground, and erect above them pillars of red earth which dot the African bush like so many phallic symbols. By tunnelling down through the sand to the kimberlite, and bringing up the trace elements, the termites in effect confirmed the existence of what turned out to be the richest diamond mine in the world, producing in 1999 11 million carats of gemstones, more than the production of all De Beers's South African mines put together.

Diamonds were also discovered inside the Reserve, near a Bushman village called Gope, in the 1970s by Falconbridge, a Canadian company which formed a joint venture with De Beers in 1997. At the time of writing the mine is ready to start full production, but no decision to do so has yet been taken. Whether this is for political reasons – mining is opposed by the local Bushmen, and by First People of the Kalahari, and might have international repercussions – or for economic reasons, or a combination of both, is not clear. What is incontrovertible, however, is that however rich Botswana and De Beers have grown from the Kalahari's diamonds, the one community which

PEOPLE WITHOUT A VOICE

has not benefited at all is the Bushmen, although the Gope mine is very clearly in the Central Kalahari Game Reserve, and on their ancestral territory. This did not deter the government from deciding to move the Bushmen out of the Reserve. On the contrary, one of the reasons it gave for its resettlement policy was that the Reserve contained 'resources of national importance', mainly diamonds, but including gold and other minerals as well. More recently, in 1999, De Beers discovered 'substantial' diamond deposits near another Bushman village in the Reserve, Kukama.

The immense wealth which has accrued to Botswana from its diamonds since the late 1960s, and the infinitesimal amount allowed to trickle down to its Bushman minority, was one of the most telling criticisms of the regime made by John Hardbattle, the driving force of First People. On a tour of Canada in 1994, he gave an eloquent account of the plight of the Bushmen. Independence in 1966 had given them hope, he said, that perhaps finally they would be accepted as equals by the other races in Botswana, blacks and whites. They had taken as the truth the words of Sir Seretse Khama when he said, 'We are all equal; black, white and red [meaning Bushmen].' The constitution of the new multi-racial, multi-party democracy guaranteed that there would be no discrimination on the basis of colour, race or creed. It also guaranteed that Bushmen were full citizens of the new country, and would 'stand equal with all others and eat from the same bowl'. But twenty-eight years later Bushmen were worse off than at the time of independence, or at any time in the past.

'We know now,' John Hardbattle told his Canadian audience, 'that not all men are equal in Botswana. Some races have lost where others have gained. Some have got fat whilst others are crying in the dust from hunger. Those who got fat are the blacks and whites. Those with the empty stomachs are the Noakhwe [Bushmen]. How and why is that after twenty-eight years of independence?' Since then, Botswana had prospered from its diamonds and cattle, 'yet our people are said to be the poorest of the poor.' They lived mostly on government settlements, and commercial farms owned by others. Some lived by begging, some from drought relief, others existed simply as slave labour. 'What happened to the equality and the promised integration? These are the questions we are asking, and why is it that only the Noakhwe lost their territories whilst others gained?'

He went on to draw a damning picture of how the ruling tribal elite kept power in its own hands. 'If we look in the House of the Chiefs, we see only the eight tribes of the Bechuana are represented there. If we look at the districts, we see those eight tribes are the only tribal and land authorities.' This then was the power base of the Tswana people. The Chieftainship Act guaranteed that the Tswana were 'the only authority and power in the land'. As the House of Chiefs did not recognise the existence of the Bushmen as a people, it was easy to see why 'the people of the Sandface no longer have a life. For without land you have no life.'

Born in Bechuanaland in 1945, John Hardbattle was the elder son of a half-Bushman mother, Khwa, and an English father, Tom Hardbattle, who served in the South African police at the end of the Boer War before moving to Bechuanaland where he became a wealthy farmer. Tom was born in the South Yorkshire village of Nafferton on 6 February 1879, raised in the village of Roos, east of Hull, and was in many ways typical of the men who served the British Empire in its Victorian heyday. He came from honest, God-fearing yeoman stock, and after attending the local Methodist Church school, started work on the family farm at the age of twelve. Wages were low and hours extremely long. 'I think I was getting £6 a year working all hours of the day and sometimes at night,' he wrote to his niece Marie Neale more than fifty years later.

In March 1899, by now twenty and a strapping 5 feet 10¾ inches, Tom joined the City of London Police as a constable, at the pay of 25 shillings a week. As a new recruit, he had to find his way around the congested square mile in the heart of London which constitutes the City, and learn how to control a horse on ceremonial occasions such as state visits and the Lord Mayor's show. He enjoyed the challenge of his new life, he was to tell his children, except for walking the beat at night in winter, when the temperature was below freezing. On very cold nights, he admitted, he would sneak into a cemetery out of the wind, and revive himself with a nip of whisky from a well-concealed flask. No doubt the cold made him think of sunnier climes, and the outbreak of the Boer War in October 1899 offered a means of escape. He resigned to join the South African Constabulary, sailing for Cape Town as one of a batch of recruits in March 1902. He travelled steerage, sleeping in 'a little box' with his feet sticking out of the door, but without his boots and trousers on, 'otherwise they'd have been pinched in the night,' he explained to a friend, Ted Flattery. He was just twenty-three.

The Boer War ground on until 31 May 1902, when the dazed and defeated Boer leaders and a victorious Kitchener signed the surrender terms in Pretoria. Tom Hardbattle spent most of the next three years in Matabeleland, before being demobilised at the end of his service in 1905. What happened to him after that is not clear. Did he board a train in Bulawayo, the capital of Matabeleland, with the intention of travelling south to Cape Town from where he was due to sail for England? We do not know. But years later his son John would tell the *Okavango Observer* that his father was on a train which stopped at a tiny village called Ramotswa, just south of Gaborone, the present Botswana capital, on the main line to the South African border. What happened next is part of Hardbattle family lore. 'Getting out to stretch his legs on the platform,' the story goes, 'he fell into conversation with the local policeman, another Englishman, who confessed to being desperately homesick. Being in two minds about going home, Tom Hardbattle offered to change places with him. "You can have my ticket back to England," he said, "and I'll do your job here."' They shook hands on it, and while the homesick policeman departed for Cape Town, Tom moved into the police station at Ramotswa. Apart from his duties there, which included travelling up and down the line as a railway detective, he was also expected to help to develop the embryo Bechuanaland police service. 'My father was often given five pounds,' John told the *Okavango Observer*, 'and told to go and build a police station.'

It did not take very long for Tom Hardbattle to realise how profitable buying and selling cattle could be. As a policeman, he was not supposed to engage in trade, but his superiors turned a blind eye, since most of them were similarly involved, and before long he was able to buy a farm in the Mafeking area. Transferred to Tsau in Ngamiland, some 350 miles to the north-west, he continued to buy and sell cattle, and to keep the peace with a firm hand – too firm for one resident, H.F. Kirkham, whose middle name was Faithful. In 1911 Kirkham, a local farmer and trader, complained to the Anti-Slavery Society in London that Corporal Hardbattle had 'unmercifully flogged' local tribesmen on two occasions, once on the orders of the local magistrate, and once when his Bushman herders 'lost' two or three of his own cattle. The British resident commissioner made enquiries but both the magistrate and Corporal Hardbattle denied any knowledge of the incidents, and the matter was dropped. Ted Flattery, who had known Tom Hardbattle well, told me that flogging was 'commonplace' then. 'The local chief had the right to flog . . . it was standard,' he added.

Well before the outbreak of the First World War, Tom Hardbattle resigned from the Bechuanaland Police, bought his first farm in the Ghanzi area, south-west of Tsau, and started cattle dealing in earnest. One night, early in the war, a German patrol crossed the border at Rietfontein, heading in the direction of Ghanzi. Dick Eaton was told the story by Tom Hardbattle himself: 'One night the Germans at Fort Rietfontein decided to come in here. Tom Hardbattle, George Burton, one of his neighbours, and half a dozen more of them got wind of it somehow and decided they'd have to try and stop them. . . . So they took their rifles and a lot of ammunition – it was at night – and they'd fire a shot and run along, fire a shot and run along, and the Germans thought it was an army. . . . So without coming any further they turned around and went back and they never came here again.' Eaton laughed. 'They stopped the Germans coming in.'

Eaton remembers Tom Hardbattle as 'one of the most honest people I've ever met. He was a hard man, very straight.' He did not believe in contracts. 'If you said to him I'm buying the cattle for so much, that was his word, it didn't matter if the price went up fifty per cent tomorrow, that was an agreement.' He was a shrewd speculator who hated parting with his money. 'If I've got to give someone a tickey* it's like pulling one of my teeth!' Eaton recalled him saying. Ted Flattery agreed. 'He was unbelievably mingy, although now and again he had a flash of generosity.' One of his cannier habits still makes his children laugh. When Tom Hardbattle bought his first vehicle, a four-wheel drive, he always carried a stout chain in the back. Dick Eaton recalled going to see him one day with George Burton, and finding Tom sitting in his favourite home-made chair, with his new vehicle chained to a camel thorn tree, 'just in case somebody tries to steal it. We had a good laugh about it,' said Eaton. 'So did he himself!' Perhaps the oddest thing about Tom Hardbattle, according to Dick Eaton, was the spartan way in which he chose to live. 'He didn't have a house. He didn't want to spend money so he never built a house. He had a long hut . . . and big, tin trunks. He kept all his stuff in tin trunks.' Equally eccentric was his method of making tea. 'The fire was outside, with the black pot with the water in, and you just threw in the tea . . . when he'd made the tea, he got the bucket of milk – it was covered black with flies on top – so he blew *whoooo!* the flies and the cream off the top, and poured it into the tea.'

In his early days as a struggling rancher, Hardbattle would drive his cattle right across the Kalahari desert to market in Lobatse, a distance of more than 400 miles. It was a formidable journey, with ranchers and their drovers facing extraordinary hardships and dangers during the long, thirsty trek across the desert, which the Bushmen call the Sandface. Dick Eaton described the pioneer days vividly: 'They speculated, they bought cattle in Ngamiland, brought them here and trekked them through the Kalahari. They trekked on the *tsammas* [wild melons] and pans, because there was no water in between. When it had rained well here, they'd take out the cattle, but as you know it doesn't always rain well on the other side. Burton once took his cattle and started trekking, and on the other side there

* Then a South African threepenny piece.

was a drought, and before he got to the other side all his cattle died. In those days you had a Scotch cart pulled by oxen, the oxen started dying, and they only just got to the other side alive themselves. Tom would have gone on horseback, the Scotch cart was just to take the supplies. It took 28 days to Lobatse.'

Laurens van der Post, who visited Ghanzi on a number of occasions while making his film *The Lost World of the Kalahari* in the 1950s, met Tom Hardbattle, and the two men, so different in many ways, became friends. In *The Heart of the Hunter*, van der Post states that Hardbattle had a terrible struggle to make a living, but he was never tempted to give up and return to England. '"I found all I wanted here, and here I'll stay until the end," he told me in one of his last letters. But what had he wanted? ... A personal challenge and call to individual battle . . .?' Van der Post went on: 'As if battle with the physical desert were not enough, Tom was soon in battle of another kind. He began to live openly with Bushman women.' This horrified Hardbattle's Calvinist Afrikaner neighbours, of course. To cohabit with a Bushman woman was bad enough, even if done on the sly, 'but done openly was unforgivable'. Tom Hardbattle, however, refused to let himself be shamed by something that appeared perfectly natural to him. People waited in vain for his nerve to be broken but, says van der Post, he continued to enjoy his hard life, and his success, and the 'exuberance of his spirits seemed to his neighbours the product of an almost treasonable collaboration on the part of Providence.'

Van der Post tells a story of a convivial evening in Ghanzi at which almost everyone drank too much brandy and talk turned, 'drearily', he writes, to sex. 'One man asked Tom: "Is it true that once you have slept with a Bushman woman, it spoils white women for you for ever?" "I can't say," Tom answered blandly. "I've never slept with a white woman."' Van der Post then pays Tom Hardbattle what both men would have considered a supreme compliment. 'Finally, he alone in that part of the world openly championed the Bushman and fought the rules and regulations which seemed to him unjust to them.* Old and in

* This is unfair to men like George Silberbauer who spent much of his working life trying to improve the Bushman's lot.

ill-health, he remained unbroken in spirit, a staunch ally in the battle for recognition of the Bushman's claim to a life of his own.'

Some contemporaries took a less rosy view of Tom Hardbattle than van der Post, alleging that he treated his Bushman workers just as harshly as the other Ghanzi farmers. That may have changed, however, because at the age of sixty-three the life-long bachelor took a half-Bushman girl of sixteen, named Khwa, as his wife.

Khwa lived with her Nharo Bushman mother on one of his farms, where her father, Isak Kotze, an Afrikaner, was a manager. Their story is typical of its time and place. Kotze already had a white Afrikaner wife and family and when Khwa was born he ignored her, both then and later, making no contribution to her upbringing or schooling. In fact she never went to school. 'My mother grew up on my father's milk and food – that's the way the Bushmen put it,' says Andrea, their elder daughter.

When Khwa was sixteen, her mother went to Tom Hardbattle and, in Andrea's words, said, '"Isn't it time you got yourself a wife? You've got all these cattle and farms but you've got no children." My father said, "I'm too old." So she said, "What's wrong with my daughter?" "She's too young," replied Tom. My grandmother replied, "She's old enough now." When Khwa was consulted, her answer was forthright. "He's an old man. If I'm going to have a husband, I want a nice young man." My grandmother said, "There is no other young man who's going to take care of you like this old man."' Eventually, Khwa agreed, although she was 'a bit afraid of this old man, because my father used to shout quite a lot at the Bushmen. . . . But my grand-mother wouldn't give up, she kept on at the two of them and eventually they agreed. And here I am.'

Andrea was born in 1943, and John two years later, followed by another boy who died in infancy, then Polly, and finally young Tom. They all grew up at Buitsivango where – thanks to the famous Ghanzi limestone ridge – there was enough water to support tall trees and thick bush, then well-stocked with game. The two older children spoke Nharo with their mother and

English with their father, who taught the boys how to hunt and shoot. It was an adventurous and happy childhood on the farm, but beyond its boundaries there lay the colour-conscious world of white settler Africa. Despite being a British Protectorate, Bechuanaland was in many ways an extension of South Africa. The great majority of Ghanzi farmers were South Africans and Afrikaners, who automatically considered all non-whites second-class citizens. Tom Hardbattle was a prominent citizen. But his children were officially classified as Coloureds, and thus not eligible to attend the local white school, although their father had given it a large amount of money.

When Tom Hardbattle died of cancer in December 1960 aged eighty-one the family split up, the girls, Andrea and Polly, flying to Britain to stay with their cousin, Marie, in Liverpool. The boys, John and Tom, went back to school in Plumtree, just across the border in Southern Rhodesia. Tom, only seven, was deeply unhappy there, according to his sister Polly. A few months later both boys followed their sisters to England, Tom joining them in Liverpool, but John going to Hull, in Yorkshire, to stay with his Aunt Ada, not far from the old family home at Roos. After their carefree, barefoot lives in the Kalahari, playing with Bushman children of their own age, learning the secrets of the bush and its inhabitants, life in a post-war industrial England only just recovering from rationing and other privations, must have seemed cold, drab and strange. Andrea and Polly, however, were pretty teenagers, and were soon enjoying at least some aspects of life in Liverpool, where the Beatles were beginning to make a name for themselves.

On the other side of the country John, now sixteen, although he found his aunt rather old-fashioned and strict – she forbade him to read in bed, but he bought a torch and hid his book under the blankets – was doing well as an apprentice diesel mechanic. He worked hard, winning the Apprentice of the Year award and attending evening classes at the technical college. Gregarious and adventurous, he joined the British Army in 1972 at the age of twenty-seven, the oldest recruit of his intake and the first from independent Botswana. Enlisting in the Royal Electrical and Mechanical Engineers, better known as REME, he was posted to the British Army of the Rhine. In the 1960s and 1970s, the bulk of the British Army was stationed in north Germany, as part of NATO's deterrent against a possible Soviet invasion of Western Europe. John Hardbattle loved army life, he was to tell friends later, cutting a dash in his uniform on the parade ground, and less glamorously but more importantly, employing his now considerable mechanical skills servicing and repairing British tanks.

In 1973 he used his army leave to return to Botswana for the first time since his father's death in 1960; he had one overriding purpose in his mind – to find his mother, with whom he and the rest of the family had had virtually no contact for thirteen years. His efforts to track down Khwa were frustrating and unsuccessful. Each time he discovered her whereabouts, he would arrive to find she had just left on a visit to one or other of the numerous members of her extended family. On one occasion he was driven by friends to a farm where she had been staying, only to find that she had just left by donkey cart. By the time Khwa heard John was in the country and looking for her, he had flown back to London, disappointed but determined to return the following year. He was already thinking of settling in Botswana for good.

John flew back to England just as his younger sister, Polly, flew out to Botswana with her husband, who had been offered a job in Gaborone. Polly then took over the task of trying to find their mother, travelling from Gaborone to Ghanzi, a journey of 400 miles. 'I had a hell of a job,' she said later. 'We seemed to be running around here, there and everywhere ... We eventually found her near some relatives of hers, the Afrikaner side of the family ...' John, who by now had decided to buy himself out of the army, made two more trips to Botswana in 1974, taking young Tom with him on the second.

Then, partly because Polly and her husband were already living in Botswana, the whole family decided to move to Buitsivango, their childhood home. It held poignant memories for all of them, especially the ridge where the original house had stood, near their father's grave, shaded by tall trees. But what was intended to be a happy reunion in the old, familiar surroundings, turned into an acrimonious family quarrel.

Because of lack of accommodation, they were all obliged to live in one house, which was too small, and there was clearly little, if any, community of purpose. 'We started having arguments . . .' Polly recalled. 'So Tom and I left.' The failure left a deep scar. The ensuing estrangement took years to heal.*

John stayed on at Buitsivango, although he later moved to another of the Hardbattle farms, Jakkalspits, which was nearer Ghanzi, but things were no easier there. The family estate, comprising nine and a half farms, was bankrupt, he discovered. There were compensations, however. He was able to do the things which he enjoyed most: hunting and visiting his friends – and he had many friends. Charming, good-looking, apparently without a care in the world, John Hardbattle's personality was epitomised by his wonderful laugh.

Clare Flattery, the wife of Ted Flattery's nephew Martin, recalled how when he stayed with them, 'the house would just ring with his laughter. . . . He enjoyed life, even if things weren't very good.' He was unusually attractive to women, his Bushman genes giving him a 'Latin' look. If someone asked him where he came from he would smile and say Portugal or Spain. A Danish friend, Birthe, who met him in the 1980s when she was working for Ghanzicraft,† which sold Bushman handicrafts, remembers him as 'very charming, very attractive, very striking . . . he had this exotic look, . . . he was kind of white, but with dark looks.' Clare Flattery, in whom he seems to have confided most, says he always joked about his name, and how fitting it was: 'the name of Hardbattle was exactly how his life was. It was just a battle, a constant battle.' Apart from the struggle to make the farms viable, and to support his mother's huge, extended family, there was John's busy private life. 'Of course we went through all his love life, his ups and downs with Anne Mette [Hybertsen],' a good-looking Norwegian engineer, who was working in Ghanzi on an aid project. They had a tempestuous affair, as a result of

---

* Ironically, the Hardbattles found themselves in a situation which traditional Bushman society was so skilful at avoiding. Everyone knew that once they started fighting with poison arrows, someone would be killed. When things became too tense, they simply moved away.

† Of which John was later chairman.

which Anne Mette had a son, whom they called Thomas, after his grandfather and uncle. They never married – John seems not to have been the marrying kind – and when the relationship later collapsed, Anne Mette returned to Norway. 'I think that,' says Clare Flattery, 'created a lot of stress.'

Clare recalled one weekend when John invited some friends to Buitsivango. 'He'd got the best Bushman musicians together, we had a wonderful evening sitting round the fire. They were all playing their musical instruments and telling stories.' His Easter parties became famous, with hundreds of people, many of them Bushmen, coming from far and wide. The farming, the hunting, the parties, the intense private life would have been enough to occupy most men. Perhaps they would have been for John too, if one Sunday afternoon in March 1992, a distant relative of his mother's, an elderly Bushman called Khomtsa Khomtsa, had not arrived with a question that was troubling him. As John was to say later:

'"John," Khomtsa Khomtsa began. "I have come to ask you a question. You are the son of the Noakhwe [Red People] so perhaps you can answer this question. Whose land is this?"

'I replied. "This land is the land of the Noakhwe." And then he asked me, "And Ghanzi, whose land is that?"

'And I replied, "Ghanzi belongs to the Dingkhwe Nharo, for they have never sold it. Just as the deep sand places belong to the Gokhwe, for they too have never sold it."'

'"That is what we wanted to hear," Khomtsa Khomsta said, adding. "You are a man of two worlds. You can sit at the fire of your mother's people, and you can get up and sit at the table of your father's people. Will you show us the path, will you open the doors for us, so our voices can be heard?"'

'I said "Yes".'

Although he could hardly have dreamt where that simple affirmation would lead him, John Hardbattle had just embarked on a crusade which, in the space of a few hectic years, was to take him all over Botswana, and to Europe, Canada and the United States, even to Balmoral, the royal family's estate in Scotland, to meet Prince Charles. It was a crusade not only to right ancient wrongs but to fight, as he said himself, for the very survival of the Bushmen.

CHAPTER TWELVE

The Blanket of Fear

'You think that these outsiders [foreign donor agencies] will always help you, well, one of these days they will be gone and there will only be us, and we own you, and will own you till the end of time, and you will not achieve what you want.'

Geoffrey Oteng, Assistant Minister of Local Government, Lands
and Housing, Gaborone, 1993

After the meeting with Khomtsa Khomtsa John Hardbattle received an invitation to attend a conference. The invitation came from the Botswana Society, and the theme of the conference, to be held in Gaborone, was sustainable rural development. From this dry as dust debate was to emerge a trumpet call for the liberation of the Bushmen, calling forth in reply a furious hymn of hate from the Botswana government. Apart from Khomtsa Khomtsa, John recruited, to go with him, Roy Sesana, a Gana Bushman from Molapo in the Central Kalahari Game Reserve, and two young men from one of the Bushmen settlements. 'We did not expect much,' he was to say later, 'since in the past the voices of the Noakhwe had not been listened to in meetings.' Nor had the organisers any idea of the stir John Hardbattle would cause when he eloquently translated Khomtsa Khomtsa's moving words about the 'sense of injustice and grief' felt by the Bushmen of Botswana. John's delegation raised a whole string of issues: forced resettlement from the Central Kalahari Game Reserve; loss of land and natural resources; bullying and beating.

There was 'stunned silence' for a month, and then 'the wheels immediately turned to kill the voice.' A letter arrived from the Minister of Local Government, Lands and Housing, Chapman Butale, inviting John and a delegation to a meeting to discuss the issues raised at the Botswana Society conference. It turned out to be a trap. Instead of meeting the minister and the permanent secretary, they were taken to a conference room in police headquarters, where they were confronted by 'a line-up' of two assistant ministers, the Ghanzi district commissioner, the chief secretary, three councillors, the MP for Ghanzi and others.

'It all went sadly wrong,' John Hardbattle wrote later. The government side insisted on speaking in Setswana, despite English being the official language. Since neither John nor any of the others were fluent in Setswana, he asked for the meeting to be conducted in English, so that he could translate for his Bushman colleagues. His appeal was refused. Since it was now clear, he said, that this was not a meeting but 'an interrogation', he called for a recess, and tried to hand over a letter to the minister, stating their position. This was also rejected on the curious grounds that 'we do not know who wrote it'. It seemed, John Hardbattle concluded, that all they wanted to find out was which foreign agencies had put 'these wild ideas' into the heads of the Bushmen. Then, 'to show the tone' of the meeting, John quoted a violent diatribe delivered by Geoffrey Oteng, one of the two assistant ministers: 'You think that these outsiders [foreign donor agencies] will always help you, well, one of these days they will be gone and there will only be us, and we own you, and will own you till the end of time, and you will not achieve what you want.'

Each member of the delegation was then asked to make a statement, even if it was in poor Setswana. This caused the Bushmen 'great duress and stress', with questions being fired at them by 'the up to ten powerful figures opposite', and after four hours the meeting ended in deadlock. The letter, drafted the previous evening, was sent off to the minister, but – in what was to become the rule rather than the exception – never answered. Its first sentence put the problem in a nutshell. 'Twenty-six years of independence have brought Botswana forwards and us, the First People of the Kalahari, backwards.' It went on to say the Bushmen had been 'consistently marginalised', and demanded the government should acknowledge them as one people, and recognise their 'diversity in terms of language and territorial ownership'. That, of course, was the sticking point. The Botswana government has always refused, and still refuses, to recognise Bushman land rights.

The letter then proceeded to explain how Bushman society functioned. 'When we had control of our territories there was a network, a constant interaction and contact amongst us. Territorial rights were recognised, whilst sharing resources with neighbouring groups.' The letter proposed the formation of a Bushman 'national council' to be recognised as a 'legitimate negotiating partner'. It also asked – a forlorn hope in the circumstances – for a grant to cover the costs of setting up the council. Finally, it strongly urged that 'ongoing or further alienation of land, either through resettlement or fencing' should be halted until the council was established, and asked for a meeting to discuss the requests before a forthcoming conference in Namibia.*

The letter was the first official statement issued by Kgeikani Kweni, or First People of the Kalahari, which officially came into being sixteen days later, on 2 June. After that first disastrous meeting with government officials in Gaborone, John Hardbattle's attitude changed dramatically, according to Emy Koen, an attractive, Turkish-born doctor from Germany, who was doing medical research at Maun hospital, and by whom he later had a daughter. 'Inside, John said I will never meet this government again unless I have the power . . . I think at that meeting he felt so humiliated, both on his own behalf, and on behalf of his people that he really decided – I will go for it.' Rather than arguing with hostile Tswana officials who insisted on conducting meetings in Setswana, he would address a much wider audience, first by way of the media, and later by personal visits to Britain, Canada and the United States. The world at large was to prove much more receptive and influential, and

---

* The minister's response was not only to ban John Hardbattle and the rest of the delegation from the Namibian conference, but to insist on making all the arrangements himself, including choosing the members of the delegation, and briefing them 'to praise Botswana, because Botswana is better than other countries'.

before long his tactics of bringing pressure to bear on the government from abroad began to pay off.

But first, John Hardbattle had to build up, virtually from scratch, some sort of organisation at home. He began an ambitious programme to spread the word to scattered Bushman communities up and down the country. He had few resources, apart from enthusiasm, a staff of two, and a couple of old vehicles. Government settlements, which were little more than dumping grounds for Bushmen forced out of the Central Kalahari Game Reserve or evicted from European farms, were an obvious target. The roads to the settlements were some of the worst in the country; their vehicles broke down constantly, and they had no radios to enable them to keep in touch with the office in Ghanzi. John never lost his sense of humour. The workshops, he told an audience on one of his fund-raising trips, were 'gaining in power'. One was 'so strong that a child of First People was born' during the proceedings. Despite these and other successes, however, the picture would be incomplete, he added, if no mention was made of 'our fears and harassment of the past two years'. Much of 1993 was spent in raising funds from abroad – largely from Denmark – and it was not until 1 March 1994 that First People, having taken eighteen months to obtain registration, opened an office in Ghanzi.

A local newspaper, *Mmegi/The Reporter*, published a full-page feature on the new organisation under the headline 'Kgeikani Kweni Finally Gets Recognised', and reprinted Geoffrey Oteng's by then notorious remark: '. . . we own you and we will own you until the end of time. . . .' *Mmegi* commented that such a statement might easily have come from the 'rulers of South Africa's apartheid era of yester-year when rebuking the blacks for demanding basic rights. Or any repressive, authoritarian regime anywhere in the world.' The surprise was, it pointed out, that the remark was made by an 'assistant minister in a government that claims to cherish democratic ideals of freedom of association, freedom of expression, and all other associated freedoms.' In the space of a few short months, John Hardbattle had made the Bushman story front-page news in the domestic press, and in the months ahead he would, to the mounting displeasure of the Botswana government, make it an inter-national issue as well. What had begun as a Sunday afternoon meeting with friends on his farm had developed into a personal crusade.

John Hardbattle knew, however, that the remark by Geoffrey Oteng, although intemperate, was by no means the ranting of some extremist crank. On the contrary, it reflected solid, middle-of-the-road Tswana opinion. The Tswana had always had Bushman serfs, and they still had them, although it was no longer politically correct to say so. The assistant minister was guilty of no more than an indiscretion. Irritation that John Hardbattle and his First People colleagues should dare to challenge the old owner-serf relationship had made Oteng let the cat out of the bag. The concept of 'ownership' of Bushmen is deeply embedded in Tswana history. In the 1890s, Lieutenant Fuller reported that the Bushmen he encountered on his reconnaissance to Ghanzi stuck to his party like leeches because they feared Tswana raiders, who were in the habit of stealing their women, and killing the men or taking them as slaves. In 1935 the London Missionary Society, which had despatched Livingstone to Africa almost 100 years before, sent a delegation to Bechuanaland to investigate reports of Bushmen being kept as slaves by the Bamangwato, the biggest of the eight Tswana tribes. Their brief was to investigate the charges and to confer with the Bamang-wato chief, Tshekedi Khama, as to how the Bushmen might be given 'full liberty in the disposal of their labour and in the control of their persons'. The wily Tshekedi naturally denied that the relationship was a form of slavery, or serfdom, although one of his senior councillors, Serogola, was franker. 'I have nine Basarwa [Bushmen] who were owned by my father,' he told the missionaries. Tshekedi did, however, give the missionaries a pledge that the Bushmen would be brought into the tribal system of the Bamangwato on an equal footing with the Bamangwato themselves, and would 'enjoy the full privileges of tribesmen in the body politic' – including the ownership of land. Since no Tswana government had or has ever conceded the Bushman right to land, Tshekedi was either fooling the missionaries, or his successors, including the present government of Botswana, have torn up the pledge. Certainly Tshekedi's nephew and successor, Seretse Khama, does not appear to have felt bound by any such aim, as the following anecdote suggests.

One day in the 1950s in the Bamangwato capital, Serowe, two Bushmen who had been arrested by police were brought in front of a British district commissioner on a charge of poaching a giraffe. Giraffes were classed as royal game, so this was a particularly serious case. Being a humane man, the DC did not want to send the Bushmen to prison, so he imposed a fine instead. 'That will be £5,' he told them, a very large sum of money in those days, especially for a Bushman. 'Can you pay?' 'Our owner will pay,' they replied. 'And who is your owner?' asked the DC. 'Seretse Khama,' came the answer, and the very next day a farm manager appeared with the money to pay the fine, Seretse himself, the heir to the chieftaincy, being then in England in exile because of his controversial marriage to Ruth Williams. History does not relate whether he continued to 'own' Bushmen after he became President in 1966. It is rumoured that his mother had Bushman blood. Given the quasi-family, feudal kind of relationship between Bamangwato and Bushmen described by Tshekedi, it would not be altogether surprising if he did, and she had.

Forty years later, John Hardbattle was under no illusions about the relationship between Bushmen and Tswana. 'Many among the elite today still consider them no more than serfs since they "inherited" them from their forebears. The Setswana word for serf is used even today, being *malata*,' he told an international conference in Denmark in 1993. In a powerful critique of the Botswana government's settlement policy, he went on to describe the obstacles facing any Bushman trying to integrate himself in Tswana society. 'He is expected to overcome the destruction of his own culture and in less than two decades to integrate into a society which has always discriminated against him.' The Bushman had to compete on level terms with all the other Batswana, despite the lack of respect for his inheritance, language, land rights, social standing, education, economic base and political power. 'The image that emerges of the present-day Noakhwe, then, is of a shadow people who raise their hands at election time to vote for a councillor and for a member of parliament.' Quite often those elected, instead of representing their constituents, ruthlessly exploited them in the name of business. 'In this way he becomes rich and powerful in the settlement and dominates the will of the people.'

In his speeches to foreign donors and human rights groups, John Hardbattle spoke with growing concern about the Central Kalahari Game Reserve which was already becoming the focus of his campaign for Bushman rights. Since the beginning of the 1980s 'a very subtle but effective programme of intimidation' had begun to force the inhabitants out of the Reserve. There had been threats to cut off all services, including water and the mobile health clinic, and to use physical violence if the inhabitants did not move to Xade, the largest village, which was then to be degazetted from the Reserve. 'It must be obvious to anybody how the people living in Molapo, Metsiamanong and Gope [other Bushman villages in the Reserve] feel about being told to leave their ancient lands, as well as the severe stress it will add to the people already living in Xade.' Worse still, none of these people had been consulted, nor given any compensation.

The constitution declared that all Botswana citizens were to have enough land according to their needs. 'And yet the Noakhwe have been completely stripped of all their lands and territories. . . . Why is it that my people have been moved off lands they protected since the beginning of time to create a game reserve?'* The past twelve years of drought had been hard on the people there. 'Water has been the carrot, and torture by the wildlife authorities the stick. But still the people say no to resettlement outside of their ancestral lands.' Government spokesmen, he went on, continually flouted the constitution, giving the example of a district attorney-general who told the Southern African San (Bushman) Conference – of all people – in October, 1993: 'It would be unconstitutional to give land to the Basarwa [Bushmen].'

In 1978, when Seretse Khama was still President, Denzil Will,

---

* John Hardbattle did not mean the Central Kalahari Game Reserve as it was when established in 1961, but since 1986 when the resettlement policy began.

a British civil servant and the attorney-general's litigation consultant was asked by the land development committee what the 'rights of Basarwa [Bushman] occupants of tribal land' were. His illiberal and ungrammatical reply: 'The Basarwa has [*sic*] no right except that of hunting.' That opinion had never been revoked, John Hardbattle said. 'There is then no right to land. The rights to hunting are being severely limited and torture, at the hands of wildlife authorities, so common that you fear to pick up a spear to follow the tracks of the gemsbok.' Despite wide coverage in the press of cases of 'torture, death and castration' at the hands of the authorities, no one had been brought to court. 'Is there equality before the law?' he asked.

The constitution also guaranteed that there should be no land dispossession without compensation. But, since hunting and gathering were not recognised as a land use, and the people themselves were not recognised, the Noakhwe were the only ones who were not compensated when dispossessed. Was this not discrimination? He quoted the words of a fellow Bushman, Abaki. 'We have lifted our arms up so many times they are parting from our ribs so we will lift them no more. For this year is the year of voting and we will vote no more to empower those who oppress us.' The United Nations declared 1993 as the Year of Indigenous Peoples, but the Botswana government refused to observe it, because 'as far as we are concerned, all Batswana are indigenous to Botswana.' In words both poetic and tragic, John Hardbattle said that when his people heard the words 'There are no Basarwa only Batswana' they recognised 'their own doom. . . . For all around them they saw the tears of their parents, and the hunger as their children cried themselves to sleep; they saw the exploitation and the torture, and they asked themselves: "What is this road that we are on. And who can help us . . .?"'

It was soon after he returned from Canada that John Hardbattle met Emy Koen in Maun. Emy was looking for a house to rent, and was given the name of Andrea, John's sister, who offered her either her own house, or John's cottage. Emy not only fell in love with the cottage and its position in a secluded valley outside

Maun, she also fell in love with John, although their first meeting, in Andrea's hairdressing salon, was hardly calculated to encourage romance. For Emy, however, it was love at first sight. She found John 'very good-looking, black hair, tanned skin . . . more like a South American or Mongolian . . . a very very gentle person, very loving, very non-aggressive.' These are all, or can be, Bushman characteristics, and John Hardbattle, by some accounts, never relished political or any other kind of confrontation, although one anthropologist who knew him well disagrees, saying 'he never, in my experience, shied away from a fight.' Whatever the truth, John Hardbattle seems to have been able to steel himself to challenge the government – he was, after all, half Yorkshireman.

In May 1995 a party of high-powered American women, led by Rebecca Adamson, the president of First Nations, a charity which supports indigenous groups in America and elsewhere, flew to Botswana to meet John Hardbattle. The group, which included Gloria Steinem, the feminist writer, and Anne Roberts, a daughter of Nelson Rockefeller, the millionaire former Vice-President of the United States, and Governor of New York State, spent three days in the Central Kalahari Game Reserve with John as their guide. The visitors were deeply impressed. Seven months later, in December, John Hardbattle arrived in America on a return trip.

Rebecca Adamson, herself half Cherokee Indian, recalls being in Gloria Steinem's apartment in New York when a fax arrived from Roy Sesana in Botswana, announcing government threats to begin a mass removal of Bushmen from the Central Kalahari Game Reserve. The dramatic message appealed for help and said 'they [the Botswana authorities] have told us we have to leave our homes. They are coming to get us in the trucks.' John Hardbattle then telephoned Roy Sesana in Botswana who confirmed the news and told him: 'Everybody in the Reserve has been told they have to move.' Rebecca Adamson said her immediate response was to say to John Hardbattle, 'They can't do this to you. That day is over.'

She immediately began to organise a two-part strategy: an intensive media campaign to stop the removals, and take the case before world forums such as the United Nations; and a longer-term plan to raise funds with the ultimate aim of making a land claim on behalf of the Bushmen of the Central Kalahari Game Reserve. First Nations had its office in Fredericksburg, Virginia, and on 5 December the local paper, the *Times-Dispatch*, gave the crisis prominent coverage: 'John Hardbattle says the indigenous people of Botswana are being stripped of their lands and ancient nomadic way of life by government policies aimed at promoting economic growth,' the report, by Christine Neuberger, began. 'Thousands of people, known world-wide as the Bushmen of southern Africa, have been herded into settlements to make room for a thriving cattle industry, according to Hardbattle. . . . "Land is everything to my people," Hardbattle said yesterday. "Without land, we can't survive. We are beggars in our own country. . . ." Feminist Gloria Steinem has scheduled a briefing Thursday in New York to gain publicity for Hardbattle's cause. "It's a human rights issue because a whole culture is being wiped out," Steinem said last night. "This culture is so valuable, it would be suicidal on our part not to pay attention. They have so much knowledge, whether it's medical, whether it's a view that violence is not a usual way of solving conflict, whether it's their stewardship of the land without its destruction."'

The paper quoted Rebecca Adamson, whose charity had raised more than $8 million in 15 years to help indigenous groups in America, as saying the persecution of Botswana's indigenous people illustrated that 'the colonial process of exploiting native people is alive and well. . . . The survival of anybody should be a fact of life. But under the guise of civilisation, people are being destroyed.'

The *Washington Post* of 20 December 1995 published its own interview in which John Hardbattle blamed the European Union's beef policy for accelerating the dispossession of the Bushmen. 'After Botswana gained independence from Britain in 1966, there was a proliferation of cattle farmers, white and black. . . . An agreement with the European Union in 1972, known as the beef protocol, allowed Botswana to sell cattle at the highest world prices.* Livestock ownership became not only lucrative but a status symbol and the cattle population grew to several million.'

John Hardbattle went on, according to the *Washington Post*: 'To make room for cattle and huge fenced areas for their protection, the Noakhwe have been forced into settlements where they have been provided with little except schools and the odd water tap, one for each 500 people. . . . In a state that calls itself democratic and is among Africa's richest, these foragers have been cast adrift into an unfamiliar wilderness where nothing grows for miles.' The report ended with John Hardbattle asking: 'What has happened to our viable culture? Now they can give them food, and when they take it away, our people have nothing. What else can they do to our people? Just put a gun to their heads. . . . This is my mission, my whole life. It is all that I have known, all that I believe in. If I have any ambition, it is that my people should live.'

On 1 April 1996 John Hardbattle addressed the 52nd session of the United Nations Commission on Human Rights in Geneva. It was strong stuff. He began by saying that although Botswana had ratified the International Convention on the Elimination of All Forms of Racial Discrimination, it had lied to the United Nations about its treatment of the Bushmen. It had told the United Nations that they could live wherever they chose; that the government had an adequate programme to meet their basic needs; and that they had never complained about their situation.

'This is not the truth. The Commission has been lied to,' John Hardbattle declared. 'Since the 1970s Khwe [Bushman] people have been systematically driven from their traditional territories. Even as we sit here, the last traditional Khwe community is being

---

* Since it wanted to sell beef to the EU, which insisted it must be disease-free, the Botswana government erected hundreds of miles of fencing, thereby causing the deaths of hundreds of thousands of wild animals in the 1980s, as they tried to follow the traditional migration routes, now blocked, in the desperate search for water. Some wildlife experts, however, maintain the game would almost certainly have died in any case because of the drought, since the Boteti river and Lake Xau, their goals, were dried up and overgrazed.

forcibly removed from the Central Kalahari Game Reserve, their last remaining ancestral lands.' He quoted the words of the Botswana Minister of Local Government, Lands and Housing, Patrick Balopi, speaking at a *kgotla* (meeting) in Xade, in the Reserve, on 7 February that year: '"You Khwe will have to leave the Central Kalahari Game Reserve in the interest of wildlife. I have not come to discuss any other subject, except that you must move! You can harvest your crops, and then you must be out by June." Our people ask: is this what is called democracy?' Even the lions of the Kalahari had more security than the Khwe. 'Why is it, today, that the lion is to be given rights and we the Khwe are not given any? Mr Chairman, we ask the Commission on Human Rights to safeguard our human rights – to stop the forced removal of Khwe people from the Central Kalahari Game Reserve.' Why was it, he asked, that in one of Africa's wealthiest countries the Khwe were classed as destitutes by the state? 'Why must we give up our language and go to government schools where our children are abused, discriminated against, beaten and raped? Why are our people fenced in government-controlled settlements, where life there means our hands are cut off and put into our pockets? Where dependence, apathy, exploitation, alcoholism become our future? The government does not see the tears, nor do they hear the cries of our people.' Contrary to government claims, he went on, there was overwhelming evidence that the *kgotla* was rigged. Not only did the chairman prevent opponents of resettlement speaking, but known yes-men were given the floor, including one who said at the end of the meeting that Bushmen were nomadic anyway, so one more move would make no difference. Ministers then knew they had won the day, and closed the proceedings despite loud shouts of disapproval.

Botswana had reported to the Commission, John Hardbattle said, that the Khwe had no complaints. He gave the lie to that, too. 'Roy Sesana and myself, John Hardbattle, can tell you that fear is a blanket worn by our people. The fear of torture, detention, and intimidation can silence a people.' He spoke of the case of Roy's nephew, Gaolikwe Kilo, 'who died after being tortured by the game wardens, for merely possessing a strip of cured eland hide. He was accused of poaching – beaten as he stood in the centre of the village, dragged to the game department compound, suspended by his feet and tortured. Upon his release he crawled to his wife and told her, "They have killed me." Kilo died shortly thereafter. No one has ever been prosecuted for his death.' Hardbattle's allegations of torture were nothing new. In 1992, the Botswana Christian Council commissioned a report on human rights among Bushmen in the Central Kalahari from Alice Mogwe, the director of Ditshwanelo, the Botswana Centre for Human Rights. In her report, entitled *Who Was [T]Here First?*, she stated that Bushmen in the Central Kalahari Game Reserve suspected of poaching were tortured to 'encourage them to provide the [Department of Wildlife] officials with information.'

The most common form of torture, the Mogwe report said, 'comprised the use of a "rubber ring" placed tightly around the testicles and a plastic bag placed over the face of the person . . .' One Bushman described what it felt like: 'You are castrated, you are throttled so that you excrete all which you have eaten and is in your stomach.' In addition, the report went on, the person would then be beaten. 'This torture tends to occur in the bush where the "poacher" has been arrested. The weapon and horse used for "poaching" are confiscated. The Mosarwa [Bushman] is then placed in lengthy custody, at times for a period of approximately two weeks,' before the case was heard, although such detention was illegal under the Constitution. In court, Bushmen often pleaded poverty or hunger as the reason for 'poaching', but government officials rejected such pleas, stressing 'the need for the law to be enforced stringently, regardless of the role of hunger and poverty'. The report recommended that 'thorough investigations' should be made into allegations of torture and illegal detentions by Wildlife officials and police. Yet, eight years later, in 2000, the author of the report says no action was ever taken.

John Hardbattle reminded the Commission that in 1992 – the year of the report – an assistant minister, Geoffrey Oteng, told the Bushmen '"You belong to us. Don't think the donors will be here forever. They will leave, and when they do, it will be just you and us. And we own you. And we will own you till the day you die." Mr Chairman, I ask you. Can a government own a people? If the answer is no, then this Commission can no longer accept the lies from our government. If need be you must send in a delegation of U.N. observers to stop the forced removal of Khwe out of the Central Kalahari Game Reserve, and to assure compliance with Articles 2–5 and 14 of this Convention. We ask you and the distinguished members of this Commission not only to protect our rights as minorities, but to protect our very survival as a people . . .'

From Geneva, John Hardbattle and Roy Sesana flew to London where, at a press conference, Hardbattle said he was optimistic the Botswana government could be persuaded to change its mind by the strength of public opinion. 'We have the support of the US Senate, the Danish government is sending a delegation to Botswana, and the South African government is looking seriously at what is happening there.' He went on: 'It is time for our people to speak and for others to listen, for we too are a people. We have a right to land, to culture and to a life as all others do.' He was also interviewed on television, and talked to Laurens van der Post who, as an ardent campaigner for Bushman rights and an old friend of the family, had become one of his most influential supporters. Although nearly 90, the indefatigable van der Post arranged for Hardbattle and Sesana to fly to Balmoral to meet Prince Charles. They got on well. Prince Charles already knew a good deal about the Bushmen, since he had travelled to the Kalahari with van der Post and knew of his fascination with Tsodilo. Prince Charles ended their conversation by offering to help in any way he could and, since First People were always short of vehicles, gave them a new Land Rover.

Royal patronage, even at an informal level, would have meant a great deal to John Hardbattle in his increasingly bitter struggle with the Botswana government. Prince Charles's very real interest and sympathy must have raised his spirits. Emy Koen says of the meeting: 'it was the highlight of his [John's] life. He was very proud about it. I think he was very touched because when he was ill he [Prince Charles] wrote to him and when John died I got a condolence card with a couple of words.' Emy believed that if John had lived Prince Charles would have helped 'in one or the other way'.

There was an amusing side to the visit. As John Hardbattle and Roy Sesana were walking in the park beside the castle, Sesana, who urgently needed to answer a call of nature, was about to seek relief behind a tree. John Hardbattle stopped him with the words, 'Hold on Roy! Can't you see all the photographers behind the bushes?'

In May the House of Lords in London discussed the issue of Bushmen being expelled from the Kalahari in what the Botswana weekly, *Mmegi*, called an impassioned debate. During the course of it, Baroness Chalker, the Minister for Overseas Development, said Britain had been assured by the Botswana government on 29 April that no Bushmen had been moved [against their will from the Reserve], that none would be forced to leave, and that those who preferred to stay would be allowed to do so. In view of the concern expressed by several peers, however, Baroness Chalker instructed the British High Commissioner, David Beaumont, to visit the Central Kalahari Game Reserve as soon as possible to assess the situation there.

Mmegi said that the 'government stand on the CKGR [Central Kalahari Game Reserve] was not only unpopular with the affected residents', but also with the entire Bushman community in the neighbouring areas of Kgalagadi and Ghanzi. Even the local MP, Johnny Swartz, a member of the ruling party, was against the idea. *Mmegi* compared Beaumont's visit to that of George Silberbauer, who it said 'was also assigned by the British parliament to investigate human rights abuses' against the Bushmen. Silberbauer's mission, as we have seen, culminated in the establishment in 1961 of the Central Kalahari Game Reserve as a permanent home for both Bushmen and wildlife. David Beaumont's mission, although a fleeting visit and in no way comparable to Silberbauer's detailed study, was to have the opposite effect. It seemed to endorse the Botswana government's claim that 'it was not using force or the threat of force to remove the Bushmen from their ancestral lands.' Just how bogus their claim was would be demonstrated by the Botswana authorities themselves, but not for another year, and much was to happen in the interval.

Early in June, John Hardbattle, Roy Sesana and two other Bushman delegates flew to the United States to confront President Masire of Botswana in Washington on the resettlement issue.

The journey started badly. Despite being invited by members of the United States Senate, and having valid passports and visas, the delegation was barred from boarding the Lufthansa flight in Johannesburg. At first, Emy believed that the officials concerned had been put up to it by the Botswana authorities, but she now wonders whether 'it was a racist thing.' They were able to fly the next day, but were a day late.

The encounter with Masire was a piece of inspired showmanship by Rebecca Adamson, the president of First Nations, who used her considerable political clout, including her contacts in the Senate, to persuade the President of Botswana to attend. In fact, there were two meetings, one in public, and one in private, both on 13 June 1996 in Washington. The private meeting was held 'behind closed doors' at the Botswana Embassy, Masire being accompanied by the Botswana ambassador and various officials, including two from the Ministry of Local Government, Lands and Housing who were flown over specially.

Rebecca Adamson, who had organised the meeting on behalf of First People, said Masire was 'upset at what we'd done in Geneva' – a reference to John Hardbattle's blistering attack on the Botswana government before the United Nations Commission on Human Rights. Masire's attitude was 'a mixture of politeness, and not'. She was struck by the incongruity of being served tea in 'little china cups' while being asked what she was doing consorting with 'these people' whom the ambassador described as 'savages that ran around in animal skins'. When proceedings started Masire went straight into the attack, 'bawling out' John Hardbattle and the rest of his delegation, which included Roy Sesana and Aaron Johannes.

'He was mad at them,' Rebecca recalled. 'He chastened them like little children. Why did you do this in America? Why do you want to make Botswana look bad? Why did you not come to talk to me in Botswana?' The answer, Rebecca added, was that John could either not reach Masire in Botswana or Masire would not listen. 'We were all a bit nervous, and when I'm nervous I feel like giggling,' she confessed, but she managed to restrain herself, and tried to bring the discussion back to a more rational plane. 'John and I discussed our strategy before the meeting and agreed that John should push the idea for co-management of the Reserve.' When Masire had calmed down 'John pushed very hard to get the co-management idea discussed,' Rebecca Adamson remembered. 'We hoped they would sit down and negotiate, but they wouldn't.' Roy Sesana spoke 'very beautifully' of the Bushman's affinity with the wildlife of the Reserve, saying 'the eland used to take care of us, and now we take care of the eland.' But Masire refused to address the subject of co-management. 'He shut the discussion down, basically, and just bawled them out.' John Hardbattle and Aaron Johannes endured the tirade without losing their tempers, Rebecca recalled: 'They were so dignified.'

If there was no meeting of minds at the Botswana Embassy, the 'public briefing' which President Masire gave at the World Wildlife Fund's offices in Washington, proved equally hardline and unproductive. Rebecca Adamson said, 'My take on that meeting – everyone has a different take – but my take was the way they [Masire and his officials] were so used to being able to treat the Bushmen any way they wanted, as if no one else was watching. Roy Sesana stood up to ask a question, and the President started to talk right over him, he started to talk to someone else, they talked among themselves.'

Masire's speech was predictable. It made no concessions and treated criticism from the floor with contempt. He repeated the well-worn party line that Botswana was trying to persuade the Bushmen to leave the Reserve and resettle elsewhere 'for their own good', and reiterated the equally stale pledge that 'no one would be forcibly removed' from the Reserve. He then presented two options, according to a report in the *Okavango Observer*: 'For people to remain where they are with no new developments,

[or] to relocate to settlements which the Khwe [Bushmen] call "places of death"'. Rebecca Adamson presented a third option in which the Bushmen and the government would find mutually agreeable ways of managing the Reserve. This option was not discussed.

Roy Sesana ended the meeting with 'an eloquent spiritual and cultural explanation as to why the land was so important' to the Bushmen. Masire's response was that 'such beliefs were outdated'.

It is hard to believe that Masire would have agreed to the Washington meetings at all had it not been for considerable pressure from the United States Senate, and in particular from Senator Patrick Leahy of Vermont. Senator Leahy had taken up the cudgels on behalf of First People of the Kalahari in a strong letter addressed to Patrick Balopi, then Minister of Local Government, Lands and Housing, the previous March. It would be a 'tragic mistake' the Senator wrote, if the Botswana government carried out its 'plans to displace the several thousand Bushmen inhabitants of the Central Kalahari Game Reserve to other locations, to make way for tourism'. If Botswana was to avoid repeating the costly mistakes of other governments, 'the Bushmen need to have a meaningful role in decisions which affect them,' the senator added. This was particularly so when the decisions involved the status of land where the Bushmen had lived for centuries. 'For this reason we strongly urge you to reconsider any action that would result in their displacement.' The letter, which carried the full weight of the Appropriations and Foreign Relations Committees of the Senate, and was signed by eight other senators, pointed out that American aid to Botswana since 1962 had 'exceeded $335 million [£209 million]', a vast sum given Botswana's tiny population of less than 1.5 million for most of that period.

The Botswana minister replied at the end of April, and after expressing his 'sincerest appreciation' of Senator Leahy's letter, which he considered 'a reflection of the spirit of true friendship', wrote: 'It is unfortunate that over the years some misinformation about the treatment of the Basarwa [Bushmen] has been allowed to grow unabated. I believe the time has come to put the record

(*Above*) The great rocky outcrop of Tsodilo in north-west Botswana. It was sacred to the Bushmen who believed their gods resided there.

(*Below*) The ridge on Female Hill which contains most of the more than 4000 rock paintings at Tsodilo, including the famous Laurens van der Post panel.

(*Above and left*)
The Laurens van der Post panel. 'Although a good 30 or 40 yards away, the red eland bull stood out clearly and proudly, lord of all he surveyed, as he had done for hundreds, possibly thousands, of years.'

(*Facing page*)
'On another smooth, honey-coloured slab, stained pale mauve by age and weather, two magnificent rhinoceros with enormously long horns, a male above and a female with a small calf below. "Look how they are painted with their heads right next to the crack in the rock," Andy said. "As if they are talking to the spirits in the hills"'

'A brilliantly realistic solitary lion.'

'An unusual painting of a giraffe lying down.'

Kagga Kamma.
Khomani Bushmen
wearing 'skins' make
ostrich-shell beads and
other handicrafts,
as a tourist attraction.

Cait Andrews.
After visiting Kagga
Kamma, she became a
dedicated campaigner
for the rights of
Bushmen to live in their
traditional way, on their
own lands.

Tom Hardbattle with his half sister, Christina, at New Xade.

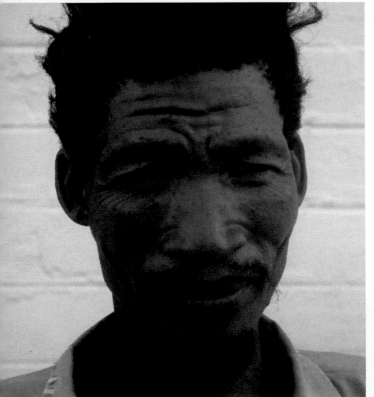

Frederic Langman, the Chief Designate of Omaheke North. He worked for twenty years on white-owned farms before moving to Skoonheid, bought by the Namibian government ostensibly for the Bushmen, but later virtually taken over by Hereros.

Roy Sesana taking part in a trance dance. After John Hardbattle's death, Roy took over as chairman of First People.

Mathambo Sesana, Roy's brother and headman of Molapo. He said: 'We are made the same as the sand. So this is our land, because we were born here.' He died of a heart attack in 2000, after allegedly being beaten up by police and wildlife officials.

(*Above*) Representation of the death of Regopstaan, whose family was several times evicted from their traditional lands in the Kalahari Gemsbok National Park.

(*Below*) Dawid Kruiper, campaigner and son of Regopstaan, talking to Cait Andrews. In March 1999, Thabo Mbeki, now President of South Africa, stood beside David Kruiper at the edge of the Kalahari, and signed a document giving back their land to the Khomani Bushmen.

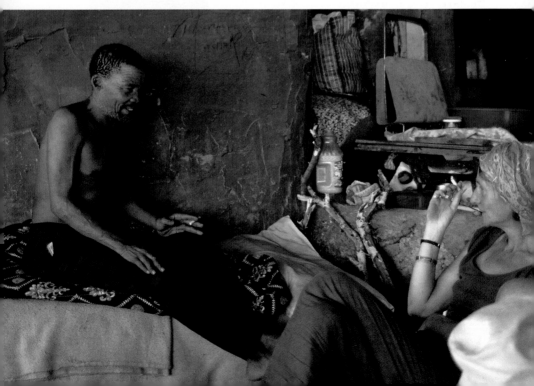

straight . . . I therefore refute allegations that we plan "to displace the several thousand Bushman inhabitants of the Central Kalahari Game Reserve to other locations . . ." ' The population of Botswana was increasing by 3.5 per cent a year, he added, and the Central Kalahari was no exception.* While the human population was growing so fast because of improved living conditions, the wildlife population was diminishing.[†] 'In recognition of this, consultations with residents of CKGR [Central Kalahari Game Reserve] are on going [sic] to persuade those who are willing to relocate but continue to have free access to the Game Reserve.' Some wanted to leave, he went on, but 'others have indicated that they would opt to remain in the Reserve. They are free to do so and were so informed during consultation meetings. Mr Senator, may I reaffirm our commitment to the ideals of Democracy. The corner stone to our democracy is upholding human rights and encouraging freedom of choice.'

Either Patrick Balopi was living in cloud-cuckoo-land, or he was a glib and cynical politician. Bushmen had never enjoyed anything approaching human rights in Botswana since independence, as any student of the politics of the area was well aware.

Whatever he may have thought privately of Balopi's protestations, Senator Leahy wrote back on 18 July saying he was 'pleased' the Botswana government did not plan to displace the Bushmen from the Reserve. 'From your letter it would appear that the goal of sustainable coexistence between the Bushmen and the native wildlife is one that we share. However, less clear is how to ensure that the Bushmen in the CKGR have access to adequate and reliable sources of water, as well as other basic services. I am informed by my embassy that USAID and the Botswana Government agree that the Bushmen need to be included as full partners in decisions concerning the conservation of the area.' There was also the situation of Bushmen living outside the Reserve, Senator Leahy added. 'While I am aware that in principle they are entitled to the same rights as other

---

* This was incorrect. The human population of the Reserve was diminishing more or less of its own accord.
[†] This was also incorrect. See footnote on p. 203.

Botswana citizens, the reality, as I understand it, has been that they have suffered much of the same types of discrimination and hardships as indigenous people in other countries. I am encouraged,' he went on, 'that your government, USAID, the UN Development Program, the World Bank, and others are interested in working with the Bushmen to address these problems.' Senator Leahy ended by saying he looked forward to hearing what progress was being made on these issues. 'Please stay in touch,' were his final words.

There seems to have been no answer, and the senator's staff say they have 'no record of a reply' from Mr Balopi.

A month before, on 17 June, Senator Leahy had written to the American ambassador in Botswana, Howard F. Jeter, welcoming President Masire's statement that his government did not intend 'to forcibly remove the Bushmen from the Central Kalahari Game Reserve'. However, he told the ambassador, there were 'real concerns that unless the government permits the Bushmen to have access to adequate and reliable sources of water, as well as other basic services, they will have no choice but to abandon their homes for settlements outside. . . . Past experience has shown that this often leads to dependency, deforestation, unemployment, apathy and exploitation.' There was an opportunity here, the senator urged, to 'protect the natural resources of the Kalahari in accordance with the traditional practices of an extraordinary and unique culture. This is a central goal of the Convention on Biological Diversity, to which Botswana is a signatory. It is important to note that it is in the CKGR and other areas where the Bushmen still practice their traditional way of life, that the natural environment and wildlife have been preserved.'

The ambassador responded promptly, saying that in late May he had been on a fact-finding trip to Xade in the Central Kalahari Game Reserve with the British High Commissioner, the ambassadors of Sweden and Norway, and the European Union representative. One of the important results of the mission had been to 'elicit a firm public commitment' that the Bushmen of the Central Kalahari Game Reserve 'would not be forcibly resettled . . . I personally do not believe,' the ambassador went on, 'that the Government of Botswana would have "forcibly" evicted the Basarwa [Bushmen] from the Reserve,' firstly because it would be 'out of character', and secondly because of the 'strong local and international reaction' that would have followed.

The ambassador was right on the second point, but woefully wrong on the first. Far from forcible eviction being 'out of character', it is now thought likely that both the minister, Patrick Balopi, and the Ghanzi District Commissioner were determined to get every single Bushman out of the Reserve – not just out of Xade – 'whether they liked it or not'. It also seems indisputable that the Botswana government 'backed off' because of the outcry, both domestic and international, after the Xade removals.

Mary Robinson, the former President of Ireland who was then United Nations Commissioner for Human Rights, is reliably reported to have urged the Botswana government – successfully – to halt further removals from the Reserve. How long the Botswana government would stay its hand was, however, another matter. Like the French, it might think: *'reculer, c'est pour mieux sauter'* – to withdraw is the best way to advance.

In his letter, the American ambassador went on to repeat the statement so assiduously peddled by government spokesmen about the decline in wildlife numbers. 'Wildlife populations have fallen dramatically in the CKGR over the past fifteen years.'* This had been caused partly by pressure on migration routes, but it had also been 'exacerbated' in the areas round the largest Bushman villages by Bushmen using 'modern hunting methods rather than traditional techniques'. The ambassador, however, agreed wholeheartedly with Senator Leahy that the Bushmen must be made 'full partners in the wildlife conservation of the area'. That meant they must obtain 'tangible benefits, in particular jobs'. Community-based wildlife conservation was a central tenet of USAID policy and the responsible minister 'seemed favourably disposed to extend this concept' to the Bushmen. To that end, he had urged the Botswana government

---

* The Wildlife Department itself nailed this myth in 1999 when it announced that game numbers had doubled in the ten years from 1986 to 1996.

'to fully engage' John Hardbattle on new approaches to ensure the well-being of the Bushmen.

John Hardbattle's campaigning abroad angered the Tswana establishment at home. 'They would freak out,' Emy Koen recalls. 'Why does he challenge Masire in the United States? Why is he not trying to negotiate?' The explanation, she says, was that 'he was still acting from this 1993 perspective.' In other words, John Hardbattle had not forgotten the deep humiliation of that first meeting in Gaborone, when the Bushman delegation were treated like so many serfs. Yet, surprisingly, Emy says, when they were in Washington, one of Masire's ministers, whom John knew, said, 'When we are back in Botswana you must come and we must talk.' That was about the time, Emy added, that there was a split in the ruling party between the conservative wing and the 'little bit more liberal' wing of younger members. Samora Gaborone, a rebel member of an influential Tswana family, offered to act as a go-between to arrange the meeting. 'So everything', according to Emy, 'was moving in a very good direction.'

The first night after his return from Washington, on 19 or 20 June, John Hardbattle felt ill. 'He thought it was just a viral thing,' Emy Koen said later, 'and he was hospitalised with this high fever for two weeks.' In July Emy, with whom John had somehow found time to conduct a passionate love affair, gave birth to a daughter, Zoe. While she was in the maternity wing of a hospital in Heidelberg, however, John was in the surgical ward being operated on for cancer. They remained in Germany with baby Zoe until mid-September when they flew to Botswana, where John spent a month convalescing on the farm.

One day, Emy recalled, John said, 'Look, I have lumps here.' Emy recognised them as lymph nodes, and immediately concluded 'there was no medical chance for him.' John decided to undergo a course of radiation treatment in Johannesburg. Emy was convinced it would be of no use, but said nothing to John; 'You cannot say, if someone says I want to go for it, don't go for it.' They stayed with Reg Vize in his large house in Houghton, one of Johannesburg's oldest and most expensive suburbs, not far from Nelson Mandela's house. There, in the spacious garden, far from the rush and racket of the city, John spent his last days sitting in the garden, watching the birds. He died on 12 November 1996.

By a curious set of coincidences, Emy says, Khomtsa Khomtsa, the elder who first asked John to help the Bushmen, died a week before, and Laurens van der Post died a month later, on 15 December.

John's body was flown from Johannesburg to Botswana, and the funeral took place two days later in Ghanzi. Despite the comparatively short interval between his death and burial – which caused friction between John's sister, Andrea, and Emy – Bushmen came from all over Botswana and Namibia to pay their last respects. Emy remembers the speed with which the news spread. 'It was amazing. People from Namibia had come already. You know telephones don't work, there are no faxes . . . [but] their communication and information thing is amazing.' President Masire came, although he had neither met nor spoken to John since the confrontation in Washington. John was buried at Buitsivango where he was born, next to his father, old Tom Hardbattle. Simple boulders from the river serve as the headstones of their graves, on land the Bushmen had hunted over for thousands of years. 'His heart was Africa,' as Emy said.

John's mother, Khwa, was heartbroken, convinced that John died as a result of witchcraft, the victim of a spell laid on him by enemies – possibly other Bushmen, although Bushmen are not normally given to the practice of witchcraft. Before the funeral tears were dry, however, there were ominous reports of deportations in the Kalahari. They had started again, according to Emy, while John was still abroad. 'At exactly the time John met Masire in the United States, and exactly during the time of his illness and operation, the Botswana government started to go to people and say – they were very organised about it – "we will pay you 40,000 Pula [£5,700] if you move out." This is like me saying I will pay you £4 million if you move out. . . . They were systematically recruiting younger people . . . They went so far as to threaten people . . . they really got forceful.'

At that point, Emy says, she and John were having 'loads of

discussions' – which would appear to be a euphemism for arguments – in which she urged him to scale down his international campaigning and concentrate more on what was happening at home. 'If the people don't know there is someone backing them up, they will become insecure and they will move out [of the Reserve]. We need more contact,' she urged him. 'But he never had the chance.' Their disagreement on policy may well have been intensified, if not indeed caused, by what a close friend called John's 'infatuation' with Rebecca Adamson. Arthur Krasilnikoff, the Danish writer, who had helped John Hardbattle with advice on policy and funding in the early days of First People, says he was in the embarrassing position of being caught in the middle, having to pass messages from Emy to John and back again. In the end, John's illness and death cut short the argument. Emy, however, was determined that something must be done to bolster morale in the Reserve. Not long after the funeral, she organised a three-day workshop at Xade. It had two purposes: to inform the local Bushmen of their legal rights, particularly on resettlement; and to document what was happening on that front. It was attended by Glyn Williams, First People's South African lawyer, and Samora Gaborone, as well as Emy's five-month-old baby.

'This was something I organised,' says Emy, 'because I was very well in the picture of what was happening.' She succeeded in obtaining funding for the three-year period 1997–2000 from IWGIA, the Danish NGO which already supported First People. Her proposal concentrated on organising workshops in the Reserve, supporting the people, and paying lawyers to prepare a land claim. 'That was the next step, that was John's wish.' Emy's drive and efficiency put a lot of backs up. 'I was hated in Botswana at that time, I was hated at Kuru [the Dutch Reformed Church's Bushman project at D'kar], they tried to exclude us; I was hated by all of them . . . because suddenly they had this paranoia that I wanted to take over and [that] I had a personal interest. I didn't at all. I just wanted to finish my duty, because it hurt me so much that [after] all he had done . . . there was nobody. I just took it to the point where they [First People] got the funding and went on with my life.'

John's death, followed three months later by Emy's departure, paralysed the organisation to which he had given his life. Deprived of his dynamism, First People of the Kalahari virtually collapsed. In the short term John Hardbattle has proved irreplaceable, although Roy Sesana, despite his lack of English, has shown great courage and tenacity in the face of heavy odds. There are, in addition, some young Bushmen who may prove worthy successors in the future.

John Hardbattle's death was an unexpected stroke of good fortune for the Botswana government. Just when their human rights record was coming under serious scrutiny – especially by the Senate in Washington – their only critic with international standing was suddenly removed by a cruel destiny. Or, as the Bushmen themselves might have seen it, their old gods *were* dead. In March 1997, Patrick Balopi revealed his real intentions. To finance the planned resettlement, he asked for a budget of 6 million pula [£857,142], to be spent mainly on establishing two new settlements, one at New Xade, west of the Reserve, the other at Kauduane, to the south.

On 14 March the *Okavango Observer* reported that the mood among the residents 'remains anxious as the Botswana government allegedly steps up a house to house campaign to persuade people to leave . . . with verbal promises of hard cash.' Roy Sesana told the paper: 'We are hearing through the grapevine that people are being promised enough money to buy two cars and still be able to build a house with the rest.' It went on: '. . . villagers allege that the government's latest attempt to get them off their ancestral land involves bribes and subtle threats. . . . Residents point out that none of this is being done through the proper channels, for example through the Chief, the *kgotla* [tribal council], or Village Development Committees. In addition, people are reportedly being offered different amounts, some saying they have been promised houses, others several thousand pula in cash.'

On 28 March, under the front page headline 'We are tired of being moved', the newspaper* quoted the headman of Xade,

* As a consistently critical watchdog, the *Okavango Observer* came under

Tuelo Sekalabue as saying: 'I believe the resettlement is totally illegal and unrightful [*sic*] . . . They don't consult me. They just do whatever they want and still say I am the headman. Those who move will move but I remain here.' Villagers' feelings, the *Okavango Observer* added, echoed earlier reports from First People that 'the majority of the residents have no intention of going.' One of the reasons they gave was that they had not yet been paid compensation for the original move to Xade, when it became a permanent settlement in 1992. '"When we were moved from Molapo the government promised us cattle and goats. Up to now we are still asking about the livestock and getting no answer," says Nyatsang Dira.' Many other residents made the same complaint.

On 23 April the *Midweek Sun* reported that the Bushman community wanted to meet President Masire to 'discuss issues of concern to them in relation to their imminent move from the Central Kalahari Game Reserve'. Their request was turned down. Two days later, the permanent secretary to the Ministry of Local Government, Lands and Housing, Elridge Mhlauli, reiterated in the *Okavango Observer* that government policy on resettlement 'has always and will always be that people are encouraged but not forced to relocate to settlements outside CKGR [the Central Kalahari Game Reserve]'.

The print was hardly dry when, at the begining of May, the axe fell. The long-threatened but much-denied eviction of the Bushmen of the Central Kalahari Game Reserve, especially those living in Xade, had finally begun. The stealth and duplicity of the exercise would have done credit to a much more totalitarian regime than the government of Botswana. Many people, including local newspapers, were taken by surprise. 'Just when we thought', editorialised the *Botswana Guardian* of 23 May, 'that the Government was working on an acceptable solution to all

---

increasing government pressure. The editor, Caitlin Davies, was threatened over the telephone in her office in Maun and was arrested by police and charged with 'causing fear and alarm'. The newspaper's owner, Peter Sandenbergh, a successful businessman with profitable interests in tourism, eventually closed down the newspaper, pleading financial losses. The case against Miss Davies was finally dropped.

stakeholders on the removal of Basarwa [Bushmen] from Xade . . . the official media announced last Sunday the removal was well underway.' It urged President Masire, even at that late date, to intervene 'to find a lasting and acceptable solution' to what it described as a 'forced removal'.

On 13 June the *Okavango Observer* reported that 183 adults and 242 children had been resettled in New Xade. The village headman, Tuelo Sekalabue, who a few weeks before had been so positive about remaining, told the paper: 'They have just packed their belongings in trucks and left. So as you can see I have no alternative but to follow them. If it wasn't for this position [as headman] I would remain here because I am not happy to be leaving. [But] I cannot remain a headman for trees.' He complained that people had not been given a chance to build new houses before being moved. 'They just dump you there with your materials. Some are still living in the open.' The paper said he 'hotly denied' reports in the *Midweek Sun* that he had been involved in 'forcibly registering people through intrigues and manipulation'.

A former Bushman councillor for Xade said that school children, some teachers and a nurse had been moved early to New Xade, thus forcing the children's parents to follow. He was asked if he too was moving: '"I don't think anyone will remain here as more and more are being trucked every day, as you can see," he said as a council truck roared past with a family on the back.' As for compensation: 'We are told that compensation is determined by the number of your huts and kraals, rumours say it ranges from 300 to 2400 pula [£43 to £343].' In other words, and contrary to international legal practice, no specific amount of compensation had been agreed to in advance of relocation. The questions of how much, and when the money would be paid, seem to have been left to the whim of individual, and often junior, officials. In a separate report, the paper quoted Aaron Johannes of First People as saying that he and his colleagues were always in the Reserve 'because sometimes if we are not people are told bad things. They are told the BDF [Botswana Defence Force] will shoot them if they don't move. Now people are afraid.'

Similar allegations of threats to use the Botswana army to evict people were reported in September by *The Times* of London. In a dispatch from its Africa correspondent, Sam Kiley, *The Times* said that Botswana government officials were involved in 'apartheid-style forced removals' of Bushmen from the Reserve, 'cutting off water supplies and threatening the hunter-gatherers with attack by the army'. Several residents, the report said, had told First People that they had agreed to move 'after they were threatened with deployment of the Botswana Defence Force and had been told that soldiers would force them into lorries at gunpoint. . . . The forced removal of Bushmen from Xade and Gope,' the *Times* report said, 'flies in the face of calls for a moratorium on the movements until an international fact-finding mission has visited the area and been able to produce a report.' Chris Erni, a spokesman for First People, which was due to take part in the fact-finding mission later in the month, said the government seemed bent on moving out as many Bushmen as possible before anyone visited the Central Kalahari.

The mission did eventually go to New Xade, under the chairmanship of the British High Commissioner, David Beaumont, accompanied by the American, German and French ambassadors. He found conditions grim. 'There's a water tower, and that's all. The school is in a tent and there's very rudimentary accommodation. There was an air of disappointment and I think it was justified.' As to the crucial question of force being used, Beaumont said: 'I'm not saying I'm 100 per cent satisfied, but there was no physical force used. I hesitate to use the term bribe, but people were enticed with offers they couldn't refuse.' One man told him he had received 18,000 pula [£2571] 'and it certainly looked like he had it.' Beaumont said he had raised allegations of harassment and 'nasty stories' about the army and the department of wildlife with the Commerce Minister, George Kgoroba, who told him to produce evidence and they would be investigated. 'Of course I don't have the evidence, but I have no doubt harassment did occur.'*

---

* From an interview in the *Okavango Observer*, 1 August, 1997.

Harassment, or force? Harassed to leave, or forced to leave? The distinction is fine. After centuries of persecution, few Bushmen are able to stand up for themselves against more dominant groups – whether black or white – especially those in some sort of authority.

By the end of the year, no one was left in Xade, except for a handful of Wildlife Department staff.

CHAPTER THIRTEEN

The Graves of the Ancestors

'How can you have a Stone Age creature continue to exist in the age of computers? If the Bushmen want to survive, they must change or otherwise, like the dodo, they will perish.'

Festus Mogae, Vice-President of Botswana, 1996

The Bushmen call New Xade a 'place of death'. It has none of the three pillars of Bushman life: game for hunting, bush food for gathering, and the graves of their ancestors for healing. Nor is it, at the other extreme, a modern, custom-built new town. As the British High Commissioner, David Beaumont, said when he first saw it in 1997, 'I'd rather live in Wormwood Scrubs.'

One foreign observer told me that the Botswana government had 'thrown money at New Xade, to try to make the place work and show the outside world that it has done its best'. When I visited New Xade in January 1999, twenty months after the move, I found it difficult to see where the money had been spent. New Xade does not begin to compare, for example, with the lavish Beduin resettlement scheme at Mughshin in Oman on the edge of the Empty Quarter, another huge desert. Oman is rich, but no richer than Botswana. Mughshin was designed by an architect and includes a mosque, an administrative building including the office of the *wali*, or governor, guest quarters, and a string of neat, semi-detached houses. New Xade looks like a squatter camp. Christina, a half-sister of the late John Hardbattle, who had been in New Xade for a year, said, 'No one wants to stay here. They say there's nothing to eat, they were eating ants. . . . People are going back [to the Reserve], not coming out.' When Ivan Baehr, the Danish adviser to First People, and Roy Sesana visited New Xade in 1998, people came running to meet them and begged: 'Help us to go back to the Reserve. If you move our possessions [by lorry], we'll walk.'

Why does the Botswana government always seem to resort to bully-boy tactics? When the minister, Daniel Kwelagobe, who finally succeeded in moving the inhabitants of old Xade to New Xade in 1997, returned to the scene in November 1998 he immediately issued a new threat: 'I am going to stop all services [water and food] to those who stay [in the Reserve],' he declared. 'They won't get anything inside.' His next announcement, he added, would merely be to give the cut-off date. Some residents said they thought that he would not carry out his threat; he was simply trying to 'frighten the people'. But there is little reason to think that the Botswana government will abandon its frequently stated intention of emptying the whole Reserve of its Bushmen inhabitants. International pressure has had a deterrent effect in the past, for a time at least. Perhaps the only tactic that would persuade the government to rethink what have been called its apartheid-style policies would be a tourist boycott. Although difficult to organise, a boycott would hit Botswana where it hurts most, in its pocket.

Almost the first person I met in New Xade was an old man, Tshekelo, who lost no time in telling me what he thought of his new home: 'We call it a wasteland. The government said it would develop the people and the area, but it hasn't,' he explained. 'We call this place *gkwesa kani*, seeking for life. We were told there would be life here, and there isn't any life. It looks barren, there are no tall trees, no wood for good houses; this place is not good.' Tshekelo said he wanted to go back to Xade, but, without help, he did not see how he could. It needed 'great people' like the late John Hardbattle to help them to return to their old village. He spoke forcefully and with conviction, as if he did not care who was listening. 'The government has taken away our culture and made us throw away our traditional way of life.'

When he lived in the Reserve, the men hunted and the women gathered bush food. Now at New Xade, 'there is nothing to dig up, and we are not allowed to hunt unless we're very old!' He laughed at what he clearly considered an idiotic restriction. 'My wife has a licence. The government gives drought relief [money] to old people, but only my wife gets it, so she gets the [hunting] licence.' In any case, Tshekelo said, the hunting licence system was bad: 'The government doesn't allow me to hunt eland, gemsbok, kudu, wildebeest or giraffe – only smaller animals.' Like many Bushmen I spoke to both inside and outside the Central Kalahari Game Reserve, he had strong views on his rights, and what was rightfully his. God had given them the land where they lived among the animals, he said, but the government had 'cheated' them by making them leave the Reserve and the animals on which they depended for food. It had also not consulted them about the possibilities of tourism in the Reserve. 'They are selling the animals to the tourists [park fees in Botswana are among the highest in Africa], so we're waiting for the government to give us the money. Yes, we'd like the tourists' money to go to us. It's our land, and the money should be ours.' I asked Tshekelo how much compensation the government had paid. 'They didn't pay us nicely,' he said. People with grass huts were given 200–500 pula (£28.60–£71.40). (One official told me the average was considerably higher.) 'Some are still waiting. Some were given five cattle, some are still waiting.' People were not happy with the amount of compensation they received, and no sum was mentioned in advance. Less than half received compensation, and about half were given cattle, he estimated. Some were not paid at all because they pulled down their houses before they had been measured by Ghanzi Council staff.

He then voiced another frequent complaint. The government, he said, doesn't listen. 'If individuals go to government offices for food, they tell them to wait [while they] check their names. If their names are not on the list, they are told to go away; many people are not on the list, so they get nothing.'

Half a mile away across the deep Kalahari sand we came to a group of three large huts, set in a wired compound covering perhaps half an acre. This was the home of Monyaku, a brother of Roy Sesana, the head of First People. Monyaku was sitting outside one of his huts with several members of his family, including his wife, a large, plump, very dark lady who looked Kgalagadi, a Bantu-speaking tribe which settled in the Central Kalahari centuries ago and intermarried with the Bushmen. Monyaku said he had decided to move to New Xade from

Molapo eighteen months ago because there had been a shortage of water and his cattle were starving. He did not like New Xade. There were no jobs, only 'drought relief' in the form of building work, but that was limited because only a few houses were being built. They did get free food but less than they needed; one kilo of mealie meal, flour, sugar and one packet of tea per month, which lasted only a day or two. As the owner of several huts and fences, which he had brought with him, he was paid 10,000 pula (£1428) compensation, and five cattle. 'Now I have ten.' When I suggested that was a lot of money, he said: 'One man got 24,000 pula [£3428] which is the maximum, but he had an extended family, and many huts and fields.'

Sitting in the half-circle round Monyaku, and silent throughout our conversation, was a well-built young man, his half brother, Phodiso. When I asked him if he wanted to stay in New Xade, he said the young people would prefer to go back to Molapo to be with their grandparents. Monyaku interjected: 'We have schools and clinics but no jobs.' Phodiso wanted to be a teacher, he could write and speak English, but could not get a job because he had failed grade 7. He had no money. His father had been paid 7000 pula (£1000) compensation, and given five cattle, a field and seeds.

I asked Monyaku why, for a man who had done relatively well out of his move, he did not appear very happy. He replied: 'I'm not sure the cattle are ours. I don't trust the government.' He, and other Bushmen I talked to, seemed to think the government was using them merely as herdsmen, and would one day remove the cattle they had been given. He also felt, like many other Bushmen, that the government had failed to keep its promises. 'Our ancestors lived in old Xade. The government removed us to New Xade for "development" but the government has not developed the lives of the people, only the village.' Confused and anxious as he seemed to be about the future, he was very sure about one thing: 'We know it is our own land. We feel the land is ours. But we can't go there because the government is more powerful than we are.'

Later that afternoon, as I was sitting in the Land Rover under a big acacia tree, two old men approached, one leading the other, who was blind, by a stick held between them. They turned out to be brothers. The first brother, who could see, said: 'We didn't want to come to New Xade but we were forced to leave. My [blind] brother was paid 2240 pula [£320] for his hut. They told him if he came here he would get five cattle, but he's still waiting. His horses were all killed by lions, but he's still not got compensation. He doesn't want to go back because all [the rest of] his animals will be eaten. He's happy here because his donkeys at least are alive.' The blind brother had six donkeys and two horses. He, on the other hand, received only 1500 pula [£214] for his hut, and no cattle. 'When the government allows me to go back, I will. I can't stay here for the rest of my life.'

The blind brother took a step forward. He also had something to say. 'I'd prefer to stay here because of my animals. Some people have gone back. If they were going to Xade, I'd go with them. But they're going farther, to Metsiamonong.'

I heard that evening that Christina's husband, Sixpence, who drove the ambulance, had been called out to rescue an injured hunter. Four Bushmen from New Xade had been out hunting gemsbok and, as one man went in for the kill with his spear, the gemsbok, which has long, very sharp horns, had gored him in the stomach.

We left New Xade next morning, Tom Hardbattle at the wheel, following the sand road to old Xade, now deserted, a ghost village with here and there the sagging remains of old huts. Being made of poles and grass thatching these huts soon return to the bush whence they came, leaving hardly a trace. The only humans I saw were some Department of Wildlife officials manning the Xade Gate where we paid our hefty entrance and camping fees. The journey to Molapo took several hours, as the Land Rover yawed and slid through the deep sand like a boat in a choppy sea. It was heavily loaded with all our gear, food, water and fuel for a week, and five passengers: Tom Hardbattle; Michaela my youngest daughter, the expedition photographer, artist and researcher; myself; and two Bushmen, an interpreter and a guide. Confusingly, both the Bushmen were named Karnels, so they were known as Number One and Number Two.

The thick bush grew monotonous in its uniformity, but, for the wilderness lover, the Kalahari is a paradise, and this was its centre. Black korhaan sprang up from the desert floor, rising almost perpendicularly with a clatter, the males showing off their striking black and white markings. Gemsbok, or oryx, are stunningly beautiful big antelopes, with black and white faces, and spear-sharp horns which sweep straight back. Number One, who was riding on the roof of the Land Rover, spotted four gemsbok, five kudu, seven or eight wildebeest, and a herd of springbok. The bush here was so thick that without our lookout, the rest of us would have seen little or nothing. We arrived at Molapo, the most northerly of the six Bushmen villages in the Reserve, at about noon. After inspecting the designated camp site, Tom declared it unsafe, there being too much cover for snakes and other undesirable creatures.

We camped under some trees near a big hut belonging to Mathambo, the headman, whom I had met almost a year before. He still wore the dirty old red ski hat he had been wearing then – somebody, somewhere, must have a corner in ski hats, every Bushman seems to have one, even the women and children. He looked, I thought, down at mouth. I asked him how many people had left since my previous visit. 'Only three,' he said, meaning the three families who were being moved out then. 'No more?' I asked, surprised. 'No,' he replied. We hurried to set up camp before the sun went down – it looked as if it might rain. The rainy season should have been over, but large cumulus clouds, heavy with moisture, floated in the southern sky.

The springbok which had been so much in evidence the previous year, grazing along the dry bed of the Okwa, were nowhere to be seen, but only a few hundred yards from the village a flock of several hundred European white storks were massed on another stretch of grassland which we had used then as an airstrip. Although we passed close to them they ignored us, all-absorbed in their own private air show. On some agreed signal, about a quarter of the flock would take off in small groups of 10 or 20 birds, one following the other in succession, until about 100 were airborne. Necks outstretched, pinions beating in unison, they rose to a height of several hundred feet before wheeling and gliding, wings stiff as they planed high above the bush, dazzling white against the blue of the Kalahari sky. While they were still in the air, another section of the flock would go through the same manoeuvre, so that half the flock was always aloft, and the other half on the ground, feeding or resting. It reminded me of my national service in the RAF, when trainee aircrew used to practise take-offs and landings, known in the trade as circuits and bumps.

Leaving the storks in possession of the field, we walked back to the village to find, waiting in the shade of the trees by our camp, most of the village elders. Molapo is the most important village in the Reserve, not least because it is the home village of Roy Sesana, whose senior wife still lives there. As headman and Roy Sesana's brother, Mathambo – very tall for a Bushman – is an important figure in the community. Calm and dignified, he began to tell us what had been happening in Molapo in the ten months since I was last there. Most importantly, he said, First People had been telling the residents to stay put. All the villages were still receiving monthly supplies of water, brought from the borehole at Mothomelo by a council water tanker, and free handouts of maize meal. But the Bushmen were 'angry' that the Minister (Kwelagobe) had said that in future he would cut off all water and food to the Reserve. The Minister was stopping 'white men', by which Mathambo meant tourists, 'helping us to improve our lives'. The year before, wildlife officials had accused the Bushmen of being interested only in 'visitors' tea', meaning money.

More seriously, the mobile clinic which used to visit all the villages had – as threatened – been suspended. Now they had to treat themselves, which was becoming increasingly difficult because most of the old Bushman doctors – the shamans, or traditional healers – were dead. Sick children had to go for treatment as far as D'kar. Mathambo continued to speak slowly and calmly, never raising his voice, in spite of his anticipation of the worst. 'Even if they [the government] cut off the water, we can stay and use traditional methods. I and my family will stay, others will leave. With wells [underground sipwells], and good fruits, and *tsamma* [melons] . . . we won't leave.' There was also another, age-old method of obtaining liquid – by squeezing out the stomach juices of the animals they killed.

Then came his *cri de coeur*. 'The government is crazy about animals. If we touch a gemsbok we get sent to jail. Some of our people are in jail. Some people killed a gemsbok, were arrested and sent to court, but the magistrate refused to hear the case. He said, "These people are dependent on animals for survival." '* His voice still measured, Mathambo ended by saying people in the Reserve were very poor: he himself, like everyone else, was dressed in tatters. 'There is no drought relief anywhere in the Reserve. We get food – $12\frac{1}{2}$ kilos of mealie meal, 1 kilo of flour, 1 kilo of samp [millet], 1 kilo of sugar, 1 packet of tea, 1 bar of soap, a box of matches, and 1 bottle of cooking oil per month. But no drought relief, no work, no money.'

However grim the circumstances, the remaining residents were adamant about one thing. They would not, indeed, they said they could not, leave the graves of their ancestors. Ganema, the wife of the medicine man whom I had met on my previous visit, said: 'We stay here because the skulls of the forefathers are buried here, and we want to die here.' Mathambo felt so strongly about the physical necessity of the bond that he would only consider leaving if the government exhumed the bodies of the dead for reburial at the new settlement. 'If it wants to move us it must take our ancestors from the ground.' The graves were 'uncountable, youngsters, women, old men.'

Mathambo explained why being near the graves was all-important: 'If we are sick we have to go to the graves to be healed'; and described the healing process. First of all, the patient was taken to the ancestor's grave. 'We go to the grave, wash our hands, using special herbs, sprinkle water on the grave, and pray to the spirits over the grave, until the person gets better.' If someone died unexpectedly, a different method was used. 'They [the spirits of the ancestors] can help. . . . If someone just passes away, without being ill, we take a coal from the fire, place it on the neck, because God gave us the light through fire, take the

---

* They were lucky. Most Bushmen arrested for alleged hunting offences receive stiff prison sentences.

body to the grave, and lay it beside the ancestors, and the person will live again. . . . We believe that a person who dies without being ill will live again, if the coal is placed on the neck. This stops the spirit going to heaven.'

The friendly healer, Ngwagaosele Ketheetswele, and his attractive wife, Ganema, also seemed depressed, she in particular showing no sign of her old flirtatious manner. When I asked him what his plans were, he answered: 'Rain comes only through God. I stay here only because there's nowhere I can go. I only throw the bones – it's the only way to make some money.' Then, rather unconvincingly, he added: 'I'm staying here, we are both happy here.' Ganema, who had been so full of joy and laughter when we drove into Molapo the previous year, now looked sulky and dissatisfied. 'I am not happy here . . . God is making me suffer too much. I was making some money helping women to have babies and by dancing, but no one [tourists] is coming to make us dance.' She corrected herself. Some tourists did visit the Reserve, 'but even if we dance, they don't give us any money.' In spite of her financial difficulties, however, Ganema insisted she was going to remain in Molapo, 'even if they cut off the water'. Would the young people not leave? I asked. No, she said, the young children would stay, too. 'We'll teach them how to find water. Everyone will stay.'

I reminded Ngwagaosele that a year before, on my previous visit, when I questioned him about the government's resettlement policy, he told me: '[President] Masire is killing us.' I asked him what he thought of the political situation now. His answer was magnificently quixotic: 'Masire has run away. We've chased him away. We're waiting to see how this one [Festus Mogae, Masire's successor as President] will progress. We don't like Masire. He ran away because we will not leave [the Reserve] and he's frightened to stay. . . . He ran away, because we're complaining so much he didn't want to have to appear in court.' Mahensie, another elder who now joined the discussion, seemed to be living in an equally surreal world. 'Masire was the one who tried to force us out of here, and he was chased away. [President Festus] Mogae is trying to do the same, and he'll also be chased away, and next Ian Khama* will be elected, and he will change the policy. He will be better because he is the son of the greatest chief. Ian Khama is the grandson of a Bushman, because Seretse Khama's mother was a Bushman, from Kweneng, a Gana, like Speed.'

Speed, whom I interviewed the following day, was First People's representative in Molapo. He took a predictably firm line against resettlement, and introduced what was to become a familiar theme. 'If the government wants to move us, they'll have to use force and bring the army in to do it.' He seemed convinced this was not only a possibility, but a certainty. 'The government is going to do that,' he said, 'because they have already done it in Xade.' The Botswana government always routinely denies that its officials intimidate the Bushmen. Yet, in every village I visited I was told repeatedly, often without prompting, that threats to use force were commonplace. Ganema said: 'The government always comes and threatens us. They say they will pour petrol over us and burn us.' One old man, Molatlhwe, known as 'The Chief', agreed with her, but was stoical. 'So if the soldiers come with their guns and kill us, it will be better, because they'll bury us here with our ancestors.'

Speed took a similarly uncompromising stand on education. Like virtually every other Bushman I talked to, he felt let down by the system which, they say, victimises their children. Nevertheless, I suggested, Bushman children still needed to go to school. 'We don't want schools,' he said. 'They go to school, and then they [school authorities] say they've failed and bring them back again to the village. When the children come back, they want to eat the things they had in school. Therefore we don't want them to go to school. Even if they go to school, there are no jobs. My younger brother completed form 5, but the government says he has failed. I also sent my only daughter to school. She had a child, and dropped out.'

That night we had a thunderstorm, and the impromptu awning we had rigged from the roof of the Land Rover to give us some shelter collapsed under the weight of the rain water,

---

* Former head of the Botswana Defence Force, and currently vice-president.

putting out our fire and ruining our supper. Next morning I happened to come across Kaingote Kanyo, an independent-looking man of about forty. I remembered meeting him the year before and admiring his horses. I asked him how they were. 'All dead,' he said. 'All poisoned by this little plant,' and he started searching the ground beneath our feet. It was a small plant with a white flower, he said, very poisonous to horses. He told me he needed help, adding cryptically: 'Those who can defeat the government will help us. The government doesn't want to help us.'

The previous night's rain was a godsend to every living thing in the desert, ourselves included, making the soft, deep sand of the track harder and easier. We made good progress, averaging possibly five miles an hour, and arrived in Metsiamonong at about noon. Like all villages in the Reserve, it is spread out over a large area, so it is difficult to get an accurate idea of the number of inhabitants. The first person we met was a thirty-year-old farmer, Sethiwanare Mothomelo, who was born in the village and made a living growing maize, melons and water melons, some of which, he said, he sold. 'I want to stay,' he said, 'although the government tells us to leave.' We drove into the centre of the village, and sat down in the shade of a hut to talk to the First People representative, Mongwegelwa, whose large extended family, including numbers of small children, crowded round to observe us politely and listen to the conversation. 'We're being told to leave,' he began, 'but we refuse because this is our ancestral place. . . . The minister [Kwelagobe] from Gaborone . . . told us: "You people who are refusing to leave will not benefit in any way from the government, neither by cattle, water, goats, nor any other livestock." But as a representative of First People, I ask the minister: "Am I not a resident of Botswana to be supported by the government in all sorts of ways?" The reason is that the minister is stealing something valuable. At Gope there is a mine. There are also many animals. It is very important that this Central [Kalahari Game Reserve] is available to us because it contains diamonds, mineral resources, that is why he is scratching his head.'

I then asked Mongwegelwa if he thought that the government would send in the army. 'It is the Bushmen who are people who can be killed easily. They'll come with their guns.' Would the Bushmen resist? 'No, we'll just raise our hands, and they'll shoot us.'

Many Bushmen in the Reserve, men and women, were highly independent and outspoken. One such resident of Metsiamonong, Kadiwela, a middle-aged married woman with three children, was clearly a well-known character; people started to laugh as soon as she took the floor. 'I went to the council office in Ghanzi and told them I can't leave my ancestral place. They measured my hut without consulting me, gave me money, and asked me what I'm going to do with that money. I told them I'll spend it on what I like . . .' I told them I didn't ask them to measure my hut and give me money. But they pulled down my hut and gave me 1700 pula [£242]. I do what I like. No person can force me.'

The audience laughed knowingly.

'They loaded me with my hut on the lorry to New Xade. After they unloaded the hut I returned to my old place [at Metsiamonong.] The government was angry. How can the government be angry? How can it come and destroy my hut and follow me everywhere I go?' There was more laughter. They had probably heard the story before, but that did not make it any the less enjoyable. 'I didn't ask them to give me any money. I just used it to build a new hut. I have been to New Xade. I waited there in 1997, and didn't do anything. [There is] no life there. So I came back at Christmas 1998. I left my children at New Xade, but I want to bring them back here. They're not attending school. One works for [the] Wildlife [Department]. He often comes visiting. The others don't work. They'll come here.'

Another man, also a representative of First People, explained that the importance of ancestral graves was not restricted only to healing. 'We normally go to the graves when we have a problem, when we pray asking God to help us to solve our problem. That is why we can't leave the place where the spirits of our ancestors are. Recently I went to my grandparents' graves and asked for rain because of the drought on our fields, and the next day it rained.' Were his prayers always answered? 'Always. It happens sometimes that I'm hungry and I ask God for berries, and the rain falls ... there are lots of berries now.' He was also very positive about the efficacy of the healing process. 'I can just take the sick person with me to the grave and they will be healed. It always works. When someone is very ill, he or she gets much better. ... For four months the government has not appeared here with medical treatment. But we are always going to the graveyards with anyone who's sick, and it works. ... We use some existing herbalists to help us. ... It will be difficult, but we can stay. Nobody wants to leave.'

A young Bushman, Mosodi Phillox Gakelekgolae*, told me that in Ghanzi only five out of 500 pupils at the school were Bushman. 'I feel I failed my exams because of discrimination. Since then I have failed to get a job [although he speaks English]. Tswana who are less well educated get jobs. I have no contacts and nowhere to stay [outside the Reserve].' He then broke into English. 'If wishes were horses, beggars would ride.' After we had congratulated him, he went on: 'I applied to Wildlife for a job when I was doing National Service [on roads and administration] but never got a reply ... I felt I was treated badly.'

We camped that night at Bape, near a small pan, surrounded by tall acacias. It was utterly peaceful.

That evening I watched a sunset so splendid it would have taken Turner himself to do it justice. On the great canvas of the sky unrolled before us, a bank of massed cumulus reared up orange and blood red on a ground of palest duck-egg blue. From behind the cloud mass, the dying sun cast effulgent rays across the heavens in great shafts of light, like some huge Renaissance painting. Half an hour later the spectacle was over, darkness stole over the pan, and I walked back to camp, where Numbers One and Two were preparing supper over a crackling camp fire.

Next day we drove south to Mothomelo to ask directions to Gope, the remotest village of all, on the eastern boundary of the Reserve, where the De Beers diamond mine has provoked so

---

* Mosodi now works in Ghanzi for First People.

much suspicion among the Bushmen. In Mothomelo, where we were confused by a maze of tracks, we had difficulty finding the road to Gope, until an obliging horseman brandishing a spear showed us the way, galloping in front of us for a couple of miles. Two hours later, as we approached the mine, we came to a barely legible sign which read: No Admittance Without Prior Permission from General Manager and Site Geologist. Report to Site Geologist, it added, but when we tried to do so we were told he was in Lobatse. The Bushman village was only a short distance away, the various households scattered through the bush. We drove to the nearest, consisting of four huts in a compound surrounded by a brush fence, inside which roamed a collection of scrawny goats, dogs and chickens.

The only occupants, sitting on the sand in the shade of one of the huts, were an imposing, middle-aged lady in a blue dress, her silent son-in-law and a grandson. Ketlhalefang told us she was born in Gope and had 4 children; 2 sons and 2 daughters. Only five families were left in Gope, numbering 20 to 25 people. She described how one day lorries belonging to Kweneng District Council, which administers the southern half of the Reserve, arrived to remove the inhabitants to the resettlement village of Kauduane, to the south. Ten families left – about 50 people – but she had refused to go. She said she had never been told about the move, and in any case her children were at school in Ghanzi. If she had moved to Kauduane, they would never have found her. Ketlhalefang was articulate and politically aware, but she said she knew nothing about 'the Xade meeting'. 'Roy [Sesana] has never been here. John Hardbattle came here three times.' Ketlhalefang said she had been to some of John Hardbattle's meetings in Gaborone, and she supported First People. 'Government will never force us to move. Government is ready to surrender;* it has told people they can come back from Kauduane, because they are suffering there.'

Ketlhalefang explained the wider concept of 'place' and 'territory' for which each Bushman language group has its own

---

* This was a prescient remark because, little more than a year later, about 200 people were moved from Kauduane back into the Reserve, some of them in council lorries. The government would seem to have 'surrendered' at least in that instance.

name. 'This is our place, that's why we want to stay here. . . . When I feel ill, I can go to my father's and mother's graves. I gather sand there, and use it in the way I have been taught. When I'm sick, I dream of my parents, so that's why I can't leave my ancestors behind. I go before dawn to collect sand from the graves. Then I put it in water and wash in it. I also put the grave sand on the fields if they are not doing well. Sand is very important, it's got all the ingredients. When we die, we are buried in the sand. We find food under the sand.' Mathambo's words about the sand of the Kalahari were equally poetic: 'We are made the same as the sand. So this is our land, because we were born here.'

We could hear the roar of the machinery in the backround as Ketlhalefang talked about the diamond mine. She was opposed to it on several counts. 'Why can't they remove this mine and these mine people? If this place is for animals why do they have these prospectors here? No animals can dig out diamonds. We were created with the animals. Some [people] were created with cattle [the Tswana], we [the Bushmen] were created by God to live with the animals. If diamonds are found in one place, they also belong to us. They are our property. If we don't know [how] to dig them up, why can't they send our children to school and teach them how to run the mine? The government wants to move us from our own place of origin. Why do they bring in people from other places to dig up diamonds and work in the mine? Only one boy from Gope works in the mine. He is the driver of one of the crushers and also does maintenance. . . . The noise from the mine has driven the animals far away. They've said that in the future they'll be bringing more vehicles and machines; the mine will grow.'

She then raised the subject of HIV/AIDS, which is widespread in Botswana – some put the figure of those infected as high as 30 per cent in the worst areas. Although HIV/AIDS is less common among Bushmen, it is said to be on the increase. Ketlhalefang claimed that some of the people in Kauduane were found to have AIDS. 'Because of that they wanted to bring them back home to Gope, but the villagers are refusing. . . . If Bushmen were listened to, they'd remove this mine because it is bringing in people we don't know. . . . Some [Gope] girls slept with people from the mine, so I can't say if they got AIDS here or in Kauduane.'

As we packed up camp next morning, Number One caught a black scorpion under Tom's tent. Trapping it neatly under the heel of his trainer, he broke off its sting and then released it to run off with its stingless tail held high.

Mothomelo was the fourth village on our route. Of the three families which appeared to be still there, we visited one which, I estimated after a rough count, comprised about 17 adults and 20 children – a total of about 37 persons, young and old. There must have been four generations present, I guessed; one very old lady who was carried to the edge of the circle on a home-made stretcher to watch the proceedings certainly looked like a great-grandmother. One man wore an old knitted ski hat bearing the legend New York. Xhawa, in a red shirt, who seemed to be the head of this extended family, told the now familiar story of the departure of six families from Mothomelo to Kauduane. As Xhawa was telling me that a number of people had come back because they could not find any bush food in Kauduane, a sturdy-looking matron strode into the middle of the circle and tossed on to the hot sand a wild cucumber (small, green and prickly), what looked like an outsize radish, another large white root and a piece of melon, to show us what they were talking about.

The conversation turned to education and a girl in her teens, Thabo Seganaphofu, was encouraged to tell us what it was like to be a Bushman pupil in a Tswana-run school. Both she and her sister were bullied at school. 'Some of the other children beat us up and the teachers, too . . . They said I came from a faraway place and was different to the others . . . [because] I was depending on wild foods. They picked on me because I am Bushman.' Both girls 'dropped out because we were beaten and discriminated against and threatened, so I could not go to classes. Even teachers and older boys threatened to beat me if I went to lessons. I was trying hard, but there was no progress, because . . . I was always being picked on. I left when I was thirteen.'

A fine-looking old hunter, wearing a headdress made of antelope skin, possibly a steenbok, who had been sitting quietly at the back of the group, now cleared his throat. His name was Thogoya Phuduhudu, and he looked about seventy. He spoke courteously – I found most Bushmen extremely well-behaved, always waiting their turn to speak, and hardly ever interrupting – but his message was anything but polite. 'I won't go to that shithole*,' he announced. 'I won't run away, I'll just stay here. I'll let the government load me in its trucks, but when it unloads me [in Kauduane], I'll just come back because I didn't agree to go there.'

I asked if the government had explained its reasons for wanting to remove the Bushmen from the Reserve? 'They always come and explain,' he replied, 'but I can't leave my [wild] animals behind. I depend on them for meat. From the beginning I was dependent on the animals to feed my children, to use the skins for clothes, and to make the land beautiful.' The old hunter said he was still hunting; his last trophy was a spring hare. Did they still initiate the young men into the hunt? I asked. Yes, he said with a smile of great happiness.

Tired of all this talk, the young men and women said they would like to dance for us – the girls had been itching to do so since our arrival, wriggling and twisting their bodies, laughing and giggling. They made two lines against the tall fence which surrounded one of the huts, the boys in front, the girls behind, and the girls started clapping with that insistent beat which is so characteristic of a Bushman dance. The boys began to sway, picking up their feet and stamping them in the sand. There is nothing quite like Bushman dancing for sheer natural rhythm – they were, after all, among the world's first dancers. One boy was exceptionally good, stamping his foot so hard in the sand it might have been an enemy, twisting and turning as easily in the loose soft sand in time to the girls' clapping as if he had been on a dance floor, never once missing the beat.

Several people spoke of John Hardbattle that day.

---

* He used the Setswana word *masepa*, which means 'shit'.

Our next stop was Kikau, 30 miles south of Mothomelo, half-hidden beneath large, shady trees. As soon as the Land Rover came to a halt, a stocky, smiling man of about fifty came forward to introduce himself. Mooketsi Rabaoikanyo, the headman of Kikau, had worked in the mines in South Africa, and spoke some English. As we walked towards a large, umbrella-shaped acacia, the intense noonday glare bouncing off the hot sand, Mooketsi asked me in the friendliest possible way for a beer. Knowing the Bushman weakness for alcohol, I sorrowfully shook my head. Unabashed, he gestured to me to sit at the foot of the big tree while he sat opposite on the sand, as amiable and talkative as Ulysses, with all around him the waves of the Kalahari.

Mooketsi said six families had been moved out of Kikau, representing about 40 people in all. Five families – about 30 to 35 people – had stayed. One of his sons, Moepi, had just come back from Kauduane, where he had gone with his fiancée when she moved there with her parents. Now they had come back, and were going to stay in Kikau. They were not happy in Kauduane, Mooketsi said, because they had been told there would be 'developments' and there were none. They had been given nothing, he added, so they were forced to come back. He then gave a detailed account of a visit by a government resettlement team.

'The sub-chief of Ghanzi administrative area, Botselo [a Tswana], he came. The Ghanzi DC [District Commissioner], the Kweneng DC, the chief of Kweneng Council, two RAD [Remote Areas Development] officers. They told me as headman that I must leave this place because it is for the animals only. But I refused to leave. They were very angry when I refused to leave. They told me I must leave this place because it is only for the development of wild animals, and not for human beings. . . . They said if we refused to leave they would stop helping us with water.'

I asked him if any threats were made against him or his people. 'Masire himself when he was President threatened to bring in the army,' he claimed. 'Even now soldiers are always visiting, telling us to leave. They were last here in December [1998, a month before our visit]. Those who agreed to move were offered money, others only had their names taken to check against the list of people, in case they had been paid before and had returned. Frances's [his son's fiancée's] parents were given money, so much for each house, but they're still waiting to be given cattle.

'When the army came they asked, "When are you leaving this place?" I asked them: "Where do you want me to go, to leave this place where I was born?" They said I must leave because this place is only for wild animals. Then I said these animals are also mine, I can't leave them behind. . . . They said, you're going to leave this place by force. They said they would shoot me if I refused to leave. They were armed.'

I asked if the threat was made by an officer or by ordinary soldiers?

'They were all soldiers, in a vehicle. I was standing in the middle of the village just here [pointing to the centre of the village, shaded by some big trees]. Some of the soldiers had jumped out, the others stayed in the vehicle. I can't say who in particular said it. They were all in uniform, and several said it. They took our old guns, which they said we were using to shoot animals, and our spears so we could not continue to kill [hunt] animals and get meat. But I have a licence to hunt [he produced a licence which had recently expired] which allows me one gemsbok, one steenbok, one duiker, one of each.' In fact, the licence, printed in English, authorised much more – 2 gemsbok, 1 kudu, 20 steenbok and 4 springbok. When I pointed this out to him, Mooketsi laughed, and offered me some gemsbok meat.

He then went back to the subject of the army. He was convinced, he said, that next time the army would force him to leave, because the same thing had happened to his father. His father was told to leave Khutse, now part of the Reserve, when it was designated a game park. His father and a number of other Bushmen had refused to leave, and the army was sent in. 'My father died. They took all his belongings and forced him to carry them all on his back for a long way, and he died on the way from Khutse to Kungwane,' a village a few miles to the south. 'He had to carry all his belongings from the house – iron pots, blankets, dishes – they wouldn't take him in a lorry.'

He knew another man who had also been forced to leave

Khutse in the same way, carrying all his possessions, but he had survived. I asked him what would he do if the army came back and threatened him? 'I would rather die here and be buried near the skeleton of my father. I brought my father's body back to bury him here. . . . My ancestors lived here and are buried here. It is more important to remain with my ancestors, even if I'm killed, than to leave the place of my ancestors. But if I'm killed, I don't know what I've done that's wrong.'

Mooketsi extolled the virtues of Kikau. 'We're on an underground river, there are lots of roots here and berries. But . . . if I go into the Reserve [from Kauduane] to get bush goods, I get arrested.' He was highly critical of the Botswana education system, like every other Bushman I interviewed. 'I have four children. I tried to send them to school in Ghanzi, but I was told they had failed. I was told only that my children insulted the cook and the matron.'

When I asked him if the government was discriminating against the Bushmen, he gave an extraordinary answer, half blasphemous and megalomaniacal, although I am sure he was neither, and in turn deeply pessimistic and wildly optimistic. 'We're in a democratic country and have a democratic government,' he said by way of introduction. 'Jesus was killed for his people although he did nothing wrong. I will also be killed only because of my animals and bush foods. I am not a Christian but I have seen in religious books Jesus on the Cross and people mocking him and killing him. Jesus was telling the truth and he was killed. I'm also telling the truth about the animals and this place. I will also be killed. Jesus made the fishes multiply and the bread to multiply. I live with the animals, I don't eat meat every day so they multiply, and the bush foods under the ground also multiply.'

Mooketsi spoke warmly of John Hardbattle. 'Since he died First People are not doing anything for us. We've elected Roy Sesana to be First People's leader, Moeti as councillor, Tuelo and Nare to stand up for us, but there is no progress.' I asked why he did not do something himself. 'It's very tough for me to do it alone,' he said. 'No one comes here, because we're very remote.' He paused. 'We're struggling, but I think we will win in the end.'

This surprised me, so I asked if he was an optimist? 'Yes,' he replied. 'I'm going to win because I'm fighting for my things, my rights.'

At this point, he could not resist having a dig at the former president, Masire. 'Masire, I don't like that man. He took my gun, my spears and my horses, and made my children leave their original place. I met him once at Xade, and I said, "Are you the person that ruined this country?" and he said, "No, it's not me."' Everyone sitting on the sand beneath the big acacia laughed. Mooketsi himself grinned furiously, his face creasing into a thousand wrinkles. Bushmen enjoy a joke, especially against those in authority, and the bawdier the better.

The last village we visited, Kukama, was small and isolated. The headman, Masigitho, turned out to be uncharacteristically tongue-tied, but I established that only two families remained, the rest having left in the great exodus of 1997. There were 20 people in the family I interviewed, much the most vocal being a middle-aged woman with one eye half-closed, Maxhowa. She was voluble, dramatic and highly critical of the government. 'The government officials said we were reducing the amount of bush foods which animals depend on. A council officer said he'd send six soldiers to kill us if we continued to refuse to leave. We thought they were just joking, but we realise they're being serious. . . . We can't allow any government officers to load up our things, to pull down our huts. We will fight that, even if we are arrested . . . we will never agree to pull down our huts ourselves; we'll never do it for them. We can't leave this place, which they're trying to force us to do, because of our ancestors. If the army comes, there's nothing we can do, they'll just do whatever they want to with us. I can't even have a steenbok skin, like this, in Kauduane.' She held up the cured skin of a small antelope. 'So we asked them [the council], "why don't you instead take all these wild animals away and leaves us to live in our place?"'

When I asked Maxhowa if she was sure it was the army which had threatened them, she replied: 'The people who fire the tear gas,' which suggested she may have been referring to the police. On the other hand, the Botswana army used to carry out anti-poaching patrols in the Reserve, and there were several reports of Bushmen being arrested and beaten or tortured for alleged poaching. Maxhowa appealed for outside help. 'We want the British government to help us in our struggle to regain our own land.'

We camped in Kukama, after watching a young Bushman, Mongwegele, mime how he had hunted and killed his first gemsbok, alone, with a spear. Despite his Western clothes and baseball cap, with *Cool Dude* stencilled on it in gold letters, he re-enacted the hunt step by step; seeing the gemsbok in the distance, stalking it with dogs, taking cover, gliding from tree to tree, crawling flat until in range, then the final rush and throwing of the spear. Immediately he had done so, he jumped back out of range of the horns – which are long and extremely sharp – turned and dashed for cover, while the dogs encircled the gemsbok. Then, as the gemsbok ran, he recovered his spear, chased it, caught up with the wounded animal, and hurled the spear a second time, killing it with a thrust to the heart.

Leaving Kukama next morning for Khutse, we met three Gana horsemen from Mothomelo who had just been to Kauduane to buy tobacco, a journey of about 60 miles (100 kilometres) each way. They were disparaging about Kauduane, saying there was no 'life' there, no bush food and no hunting. They dismounted to feed off the *grewia* berries, which were plentiful, letting their horses graze, and chatting to the two Karnels. They looked free spirits, roaming at will as their ancestors had done for centuries, at home in the wilderness. Later, we passed a small herd of hartebeest, and watched from the road as two males fought with locked horns, kneeling on the ground, the dust flying up around them like some primeval halo.

Khutse is drier and more open than the central part of the Reserve, with pans where we saw our first giraffe, a sizeable number of gemsbok in small groups, and some wildebeest, which regarded us with mild curiosity. In little more than an hour, we had crossed Khutse, and in another half hour or so reached

Kauduane, which was established in 1995. We stopped at the entrance, beside a new, corrugated-iron shed – the local shop – belonging to the man who came to meet us, Mathhula, the representative of First People. He had a tale of woe to impart. He had been hunting in the Reserve with his two brothers, and had killed two gemsbok. He said he had a valid hunting licence, which entitled him to hunt two gemsbok, and since there were no gemsbok outside the Reserve, he was entitled to hunt them in the Reserve. Later, however, six wildlife officials accompanied by three police officers arrived, accused him of poaching, and searched his shop, forcing the door and scattering the goods he had just bought for 1000 pula (£143) over the floor.*

They found no meat in his shop, but they did find the remains of the gemsbok in his brothers' huts, and arrested them. He was to be questioned the next day, and was worried that he would be sent to prison – he expected his brothers to receive three to five years, the usual sentence for poaching, he said. He complained that Kweneng wildlife officials were 'more difficult' about hunting licences than officials in Ghanzi, adding: 'The only thing I see concerning wildlife licences is jail. I know one man who is in prison right now who has a licence to hunt. He killed a gemsbok on his licence in the Reserve. He was arrested last June [1998].' I asked what sentence he had received. 'The sentence is always between three and five years. He is in Molepolole [prison]. My brothers are in Takatokwane police station.'

When I told Mathhula we had heard stories about the army threatening to shoot people, he said it was true. 'I once saw some soldiers forcing a resident of Mothomelo to dig a grave for himself. They forced him into it and when he was half buried, with only his head sticking out, they told him: "If you agree to leave [the Reserve] you can get out. If you refuse we'll bury you." He refused so they just left him. They were just torturing him.' This episode sounded remarkably similar to one recounted by John Hardbattle to a reporter from the *Okavango Observer*.

* When we inspected the shop we found the door had been forced, and damaged, and the shop itself looked as if it had been roughly searched, with bottles, tins and other goods scattered about.

One day in the 1990s an army patrol arrested two Bushmen in the Reserve on suspicion of poaching. After questioning them, they made the Bushmen dig two 'graves' in the sand. Eventually, after they had dug two holes, they were released unharmed, but warned not to hunt again and told to stay in their huts.

Although some of these incidents belong to the past, the threat of the army, constantly repeated, suggests a policy of intimidation which, even if tacitly, is officially sanctioned.

CHAPTER FOURTEEN

Genocide by Stealth?

'This is your land. Take it. Care for it. Thrive on it.'

Thabo Mbeki, deputy president of South Africa, 1999

After centuries of genocide, dispossession, disease and exploitation what is the future for the 100,000 or so Bushmen who have
survived into the 21st century against all the odds? Is there real
hope that they, the aboriginal inhabitants of the continent, who
have been on earth for so many millennia, may find the next
millennium less terrible than the last?

There are, indeed, some hopeful signs. Perhaps the most
hopeful of all was what happened in South Africa in March
1999. The second most powerful man in the country, Thabo
Mbeki, Nelson Mandela's deputy president,* flew to a dusty
squatter village on the edge of the Kalahari Gemsbok Park, on
the border with Namibia and Botswana, and ceremonially
handed over to two Bushman leaders the rights to their ancestral
lands, from which they had been evicted half a century before.
One of the two men who received from Mbeki's hands the legal
title to their land was a direct descendant of virtually the last clan
of South African Bushmen whose forefathers once roamed over
the southern half of the continent. His name was Dawid Kruiper,
and his story is in itself a microcosm of the Bushmen's long
struggle for survival.

But to understand Dawid's story we have to go back to the
days of the Nama-Herero war of 1904–7 in South-West Africa.
One day, about 20 Bushmen were captured by a German patrol.
The commander gave orders for the Bushmen to be tied hand to
hand and 'wound', daisy-chain fashion, round the bole of a big
tree, probably a baobab, before being shot. This elaborate and

---

* Now President of South Africa.

macabre ritual was a piece of sadism on the part of the German commander, according to John Marshall, who was told the story years later by the son of the sole survivor. As the soldiers were tying up the Bushmen, the commander overheard one of them, who had been educated at a mission school, telling the soldiers in German to hurry up and shoot, and get the whole gruesome business over and done with. The officer immediately ordered him to be untied and spared, since he needed an interpreter. The rest of the party, including the Bushman's wife, were shot.

When the opportunity arose, the Bushman escaped, taking with him his young son who had been hiding nearby, and fled into the Kalahari far to the south-east, to the Nossob valley, on the South African border. There, at least for the time being, they were safe. The boy, who was given the name Regopstaan, which means 'standing upright' in Afrikaans, grew up to be a good hunter and the leader of the little band of Khomani Bushmen whose home this now was.

Then in 1931 the South African government declared the whole area bounded by the Nossob and Auob Rivers to be the Kalahari Gemsbok National Park. Seven years later, in 1938, the then British Protectorate of Bechuanaland government declared the area east of the Nossob to be the Gemsbok National Park. There is no physical barrier between the two, allowing game to move freely, and since 1992 they have been administered as a single, transfrontier, or 'peace' park.

As a result of the creation of the Kalahari Gemsbok National Park, Regopstaan and his band of 40 or 50 men, women and children were ordered to move out. Some died, some moved away, others squatted on the outskirts of the park, in the no man's land between the game park and the poor, parched farms belonging mainly to the Baster community. For Regopstaan and his people, the familiar cycle of dispossession and poverty continued. In 1941 temporary relief came from an unexpected quarter, in the shape of Colonel Deneys Reitz, the Minister of Native Affairs, who told the South African parliament that Regopstaan and his family should be allowed to remain in the park, since they were 'part of the fauna of the country ... We think that with their bows and arrows they will kill less gemsbok than the lions. It will be a crime to let them die out, and we have to make provision for them in some way or another.'

In 1948, however, South African politics underwent a major change. The extremists who engineered apartheid refused to accept that Bushmen were part of the 'fauna' of the country. Regopstaan and his relatives were once again evicted from the Kalahari Gemsbok. As John Marshall, who visited the park and met Regopstaan, remarked later, their poverty was considered unsightly. 'They were settled on a neighbouring abandoned farm,' he wrote. 'They acquired a small herd of goats and apparently planted mealies in years of rain.' In the 1970s the park bought the farm. Once again, the Bushmen were evicted and sent to Welkom, a small settlement in the desert near the park which, in John Marshall's caustic words, looked 'like spare parts on a beach'. They had no rights there, however, because under apartheid legislation Welkom was officially classified as a Baster 'location', and the Basters would not allow them to keep goats or plant maize. They wanted the Bushmen removed from Welkom, but the South African government had nowhere to put them.

Only 14 of the original band were still left, according to Marshall, living 'on a dune by a fence' and dependent on Regopstaan's pension, which he had earned by cleaning tourist cabins in the game park. 'Two of the Bushmen women try to sell their favours to the Basters. The old man [Regopstaan] explained that when he died, which would be soon, the others in the group would also die because they had no relatives and would have no money.' John Marshall visited Welkom in 1986 and though it was run-down and poverty-stricken was struck by the difference it made if you at least had a place to come home to ... You knew at least some of your family would still be there if you came back in a year, and touched base. The difference between that and what was happening to people like the Juwa all over Southern Namibia, was that they had no place to come home to ... that was the proposal I tried to get through to the [Nyae Nyae] Foundation.'

Regopstaan and his small family were, however, on the verge of disintegration when, in the early 1990s, Cait Andrews appeared. She had met Dawid Kruiper at Kagga Kamma and not long afterwards, she went to Welkom, and met Regopstaan, his father. With her extraordinary affinity for things Bushman, Cait was enormously impressed by him, and he by her. She says that she felt she had a mandate from Regopstaan to protect 'the tradition and, in particular, to see that the trance dance continues'. Cait had already formed a close friendship with Dawid at Kagga Kamma, and in long evenings of talk, sitting on the soft sand at Welkom, watching the great red disc of the sun drop suddenly behind the southernmost dunes of the Kalahari, they planned with Cait's friend, the lawyer Roger Chennells, how they could get the land back for the Bushmen.

The key piece of legislation was the Restitution of Land Rights Act, passed by Nelson Mandela's new government in 1994. This cornerstone of land reform, as Roger Chennells described it, had as its fundamental purpose 'the undoing of past injustices, reparations where appropriate, and the restoration or restitution of equitable rights to land'. On 18 June 1995, the 180th anniversary of the Battle of Waterloo, the Khomani clan, led by Regopstaan and Dawid, held an 'unprecedented gathering' to discuss the land claim. Sixty-three members of the clan attended and pledged themselves to fight for the restoration of their land; and subsequent research suggests that there may be as many as 300 members of the Khomani clan alive, including a dozen or so who still speak the old language, which had been declared officially extinct by no less an authority than Professor Traill of Witwatersrand University.

Less than four years later, on 21 March 1999, Thabo Mbeki stood beside Dawid Kruiper at the edge of the Kalahari, not far from Welkom, and signed a document giving back their land to the Khomani. Dawid, a diminutive figure in a springbok skin, reached up and kissed his benefactor on the cheek.

To enthusiastic cheers from members of the Khomani clan, Mbeki said, 'This is a step towards the rebirth of a people that nearly perished because of oppression. This is your land. Take it. Care for it. Thrive on it.' Bushman language, culture and wisdom would make South Africa a better place 'for all of us', he added.

In reply, on this, the proudest day of his life, Dawid, moved almost to tears, said: 'A key has been turned. A thick chain has been clasped fast together.'

The settlement of the land claim gave the Khomani Bushmen four farms totalling almost 100,000 acres, bought from white farmers after two years of negotiation for 15 million rand (£1.5 million). Mbeki summed up eloquently: 'No longer outcasts; no longer servants; no longer slaves; no longer dispossessed; but citizens and landowners.'*

The ceremony at Welkom was a triumph for many people: for Cait Andrews, who had the original vision; for Roger Chennells who brought the vision to fruition; but above all for Dawid Kruiper and his father, Regopstaan, who between them kept the sacred flame of clan survival alive, despite almost overwhelming odds.

As darkness fell, and the trance dance started, Cait Andrews recalled one of her last conversations with the old Bushman, who had died three years before so did not live to see his triumph. 'Regopstaan was lying in the shade, in a spot where the most could be made of the small stirring of dry air that passed for a breeze in the Kalahari desert. Nobody knew quite how old he was. Unofficially his age went with the calendar year, so we called it 96. I didn't ever know when I'd be able to return to the Kalahari, or how long I'd be away, and his body was failing and he was no longer able to walk. We assumed that this might be the last time we would meet. He gave me a "plig", a duty or mandate to perform. "*Jy moet daai manne laat dans*," he said in Afrikaans. "You must have those men dance." He went on to say that the trance dance needed a place to be performed properly, so I must see to it that the Bushmen had land. And that land must have a well of sweet water, not the salty water that some Kalahari wells yield. But above all the men must do the trance dance because the trance dance brings the rain, the rain brings the plants for grazing, and the grazing brings the animals which can then be hunted for food. So from the trance dance will follow all that is needed, in abundance. He stressed that the

---

* One demand remained to be met; the Khomani Bushmen want user rights over 62,500 acres in the park, to forage for bush food, and to run eco-tourism projects by taking clients on game walks, and by teaching them to track.

dance must be performed not only for the Bushmen, but for everybody in the region, and in the whole country. We discussed how the long country-wide drought would break, how the rains would come, when land was restored to the Bushmen.

'In March 1999 I went to the dry Kalahari for the hand-over of the land to the Bushmen by the deputy president of South Africa, Thabo Mbeki. He arrived by helicopter, and after due ceremony the papers were signed. I had been the butt of quite a bit of friendly sarcasm because I had brought my umbrella, and carried it around under a clear blue sky in a dusty landscape all morning. Before the ink was dry on the paper, a dense cloud solidified above us all and the heavens opened. I couldn't resist it. As everyone dashed for cover, I opened my gaudy brolly and called out: "Anyone want to share my umbrella?" It was a lovely sight, all of us happy and wet, clothes clinging to dusty skin. And now as I write in January 2000, half the country is awash with rains on a scale that we haven't known for decades. The drought in South Africa has broken.'

How long will it be until the drought breaks for the Bushmen in the rest of Africa?

It may, alas, be a long time in Botswana and Namibia, for the signs are far from encouraging. Neither country, since independence, has had a leader of the calibre of a Nelson Mandela; and neither country has introduced legislation to compare with South Africa's Restitution of Land Rights Act. The Botswana government, in particular, has so far shown no sign of agreeing to any kind of land rights claim for the Bushmen; in fact it has done everything it can to block such a claim. In September 1999, for example, the Minister of Local Government, Lands and Housing, Daniel Kwelagobe, made this clear when he told Bushman representatives that the government 'would not recognise rights to land in a game reserve but would only grant ownership of land to Basarwa [Bushmen] who moved out of the Central Kalahari Game Reserve and into New Xade and Kauduane.' This sounds like the old carrot and stick policy, although the carrot is virtually non-existent, since so far no Bushman family has been given land title in either place.

Despite their tough talk about refusing the Bushmen land rights in the Central Kalahari, it would seem that the Botswana government does not have a legal leg to stand on, its case having no validity, either in international law, or in terms of its own constitution, legislation or policy, as a number of experts have amply demonstrated. Take, for example, the government's contention that Bushmen must move out of the Reserve in order to promote tourism. Professor Robert Hitchcock, the American anthropologist, points out that Section 14[3] [c] of the Botswana Constitution permits 'the imposition of restrictions on entry into or residence within defined areas of Botswana of persons who are not Bushmen to the extent that such restrictions are reasonably required for the protection or well-being of Bushmen.' This statement, Hitchcock argues, could be interpreted to mean that the Constitution 'recognises exclusive rights of Bushmen communities to land and also underscores their right to determine who enter their areas, including tourists.' He goes on to say: 'The people of the Central Kalahari are within their constitutional and customary rights to maintain their occupation, land use, and resource rights in the Central Kalahari. These rights are underscored in the Constitution of Botswana, the government of Botswana's 7th National Development Plan, and the various government white papers on government land and natural resource management policy. These documents hold that all peoples, regardless of their ethnic background, have the right to land and resources.'

He also makes the point that 'the response of the vast majority of Central Kalahari Game Reserve residents to government requests that they resettle is that they have no desire whatsoever to move out of the Reserve,' adding: 'The Central Kalahari Game Reserve should remain in the hands of those who live in it. The government of Botswana could best serve the interests of the people in the Central Kalahari by allowing them to maintain their land and resource rights *inside* the Central Kalahari Game Reserve.' One way to do this would be to grant rights to various communities in the Reserve by establishing Community-Controlled Hunting Areas (CCHAs), as has been done in other areas of Botswana. Another way would be to hand the Central

Kalahari Game Reserve over to the residents of the Reserve, making it, in effect, a kind of cultural park or biosphere reserve. From a human rights perspective, many experts think, the Botswana government's best strategy would be to provide development assistance to those people who wish to stay in the Reserve. Those who wish to leave, however, should be fully consulted, their claims to land, resources, and assets properly assessed, and met with fair and just compensation, both in land and cash; and finally they should be guaranteed a livelihood at least equal to or better than before, in keeping with internationally accepted practice.

The Botswana government, however, has chosen to ignore such liberal – and expert – advice. In March 2000, it published new hunting regulations. These stated that residents of the Central Kalahari Game Reserve with legal hunting rights 'may be permitted in writing by the Director [of Wildlife] to hunt specified animal species and collect veld products in the game reserve, subject to any terms and conditions and in such areas as the Director may determine.' This may sound innocuous enough, but closer examination suggests otherwise. What it means in effect, as Professor Hitchcock points out, is that Special Game Licences – the normal hunting licences held by most Bushmen families in the Reserve – will no longer be issued. Instead, Bushmen will have to apply in writing to the Department of Wildlife and National Parks in order to obtain hunting rights in the form of a Director's Licence. The idea that Bushmen should apply in writing for a hunting licence is surely bureaucracy bordering on lunacy. Most Bushmen are illiterate, and all are poor. That is not all: permission for wives and daughters to collect the bush foods of the Kalahari will have to be co-ordinated, in Hitchcock's view, not with the Department of Wildlife and National Parks, but with the Ministry of Agriculture, which oversees such matters. That sounds as daft as the instruction issued by the British governor to the trekboers of the Cape forbidding hunting beyond the frontier, in Bushmanland, unless permission was first obtained from Cape Town, several days' journey away. The trekboers were able to scoff at such red tape, but the Bushmen will not be allowed to.

The introduction of new hunting regulations was particularly significant because in 2000 the Central Kalahari Game Reserve was the only place in Botswana where Bushmen still had hunting rights. Everywhere else in Botswana they had been suspended. Yet, ironically, most human rights organisations, including Ditshwanelo and Kuru, run by the Dutch Reformed Church, seemed unconvinced that the issue of hunting rights ought to be pursued, an attitude seen as incomprehensible by Bushmen, who consider hunting rights as crucial. Meanwhile, Bushmen continued to be arrested, jailed, fined and deprived of their horses, donkeys, weapons, bridles and saddles for alleged illegal hunting – a form of harassment John Hardbattle frequently complained about. On 14 July 1999, for example, 13 Bushmen from New Xade – Kelatlhegile Karame and 12 others – were detained for hunting illegally. Seven were arrested inside the Central Kalahari Game Reserve, and six were charged with killing a gemsbok in GH10, a controlled hunting area in Ghanzi District. Those arrested however, were carrying hunting licences and the case, originally due to be held a year later, in July 2000, was eventually dismissed.

Another much more serious incident took place in August 2000, when several members of the Department of Wildlife's anti-poaching unit and two tribal policemen drove into Molapo village and arrested 13 Bushmen for alleged poaching. First reports from Department of Wildlife sources said the 'poachers', under contract to 'a Motswana' [non-Bushman] from Rakops, a small town just outside the Reserve, had killed 8 giraffe, 8 eland and 26 gemsbok. Subsequent reports from Bushman sources, however, suggested these figures were grossly inflated and spoke of only 1 giraffe and 1 eland. Roy Sesana, head of First People of the Kalahari (FPK), and two other FPK members visited Molapo in September and October and drew up a report which said the police and wildlife officials did not initially seek to establish whether the Bushmen had valid hunting licences – which in fact they had – but 'forced' the suspects to open their own huts and other people's huts as well, and once inside handcuffed them and beat them, knocking one old woman to the ground, and confiscating any game meat they found.

Afterwards the 13 suspects were taken to a camp in the bush some distance away – one of the FPK representatives recorded its position by GPS (Global Positioning System) – held without food or water for three days and tortured, while their captors 'enjoyed' the meat they had confiscated. This is how the report described the interrogation: 'The 13 men were tortured in different ways, one by one. Some were beaten, while tied by their feet to the bull bars of the [Wildlife and police] vehicles, and supporting themselves with their handcuffed hands. In some cases, fires were lit underneath them while in this position. Others were severely kicked, punched and had ropes [lanyards] put round their necks. The ropes used were those the guards and police use for their whistles and have tied round their shoulder. One person was mistreated to the point that he was almost castrated. On the fourth day, they were finally taken to Rakops [police station] for fingerprints. They were denied the right to go to the hospital, but one succeeded in getting away and went . . . [for] some medical attention. His medical card was later given to FPK. Another one was taken to the hospital in Ghanzi some days later.'

The report then dealt with the death of Roy Sesana's brother, Mathambo, the Molapo headman whom I first met in 1998, when he so movingly described how the Bushmen would never voluntarily leave the Reserve, because they were 'made the same as the sand'.

'It is believed,' the report said, 'that Mathambo Sesana . . . died as a consequence of this assault. He had for some time suffered [from] a heart condition and is said to have been so upset by seeing what was happening, that he collapsed. It is also said that he was himself beaten but this cannot be certified. He was taken to the hospital in Ghanzi where he eventually passed away, without coming to himself and being able to tell what really had happened.'

Public reaction to allegations of torture and the death of Mathambo was virtually non-existent in Botswana. Neither the local press nor the local human rights organisations, such as Ditshwanelo, the Botswana Christian Council and Kuru, said

anything. It was left to international human rights organisations
to demand action.

In London, Survival International's director general, Stephen
Corry, wrote to the Wildlife Department on 28 September
explaining that Survival was 'extremely disturbed' by reports of
Bushmen from Molapo being 'arrested and beaten up by Wildlife
officers'. In a similar letter to Roy Blackbeard, the Botswana
High Commissioner in London, Corry demanded that the
allegations of 'arrest and torture' by Wildlife officials be
investigated, and the persons responsible brought to justice.
'Such abuse of their authority by employees of the Wildlife
Service shows an attitude of racist contempt towards the
"Basarwa" [Bushmen],' he added. As citizens of Botswana they
were entitled to a proper trial, 'not lynch law'. Corry did not
receive a reply to either letter.

Early in the New Year, Survival International sent a
researcher, Fiona Watson, to Botswana to investigate. Her
report, based on interviews conducted separately with 11 men
and one woman on 20 January 2001, supported the torture
allegations in detail. Its main finding was that on August 29
2000, four Wildlife officials and two policemen arrived in
Molapo in three Land Rovers and arrested and beat up twenty
Bushmen and four women. A number of the men, including one
who was too old to hunt, were taken into the bush nearby and
'tortured over a three to six day period until they said they had
killed eland and/or giraffe' – which Bushmen are forbidden to
hunt. The report also confirmed the death of Mathambo Sesana,
who 'was allegedly beaten up and died a week later. People say
he had a bad heart and believe the stress and shock of the
incident triggered a heart attack from which he never recovered.
They also said that Kebatseisa Thekiso was beaten on the head
and went crazy afterwards.'

When interviewed by Fiona Watson, however, Kebatseisa gave
a lucid and detailed account of his arrest and torture. 'They
made me open my older sister's hut,' he began. 'They found
gemsbok meat and said it was giraffe meat. They cancelled two
gemsbok from my [hunting] licence and I had to say it was
giraffe meat. They beat and handcuffed me in the hut and took

me and my father to a camp in the bush . . . In the camp they told us to clear the bush and we spent the night there. That night they said that we would be dead by 5 [a.m.]. I was tied to the bush bars of the vehicle and beaten all over my body . . . with fists and kicked . . . "If you don't say you killed a giraffe you will die," they said. This went on the whole day and part of the night with no food. We were not able to sleep because we were tied up until the following day . . . I was beaten until I thought I was dying so that I would say I had killed a giraffe. "You are Khwe [Bushman], we can kill you and nothing will happen to us," they said. They took us into the bush to show us where we killed the animals. When we got there I fainted. We went on until they found some giraffe bones and they forced me to say I killed it. This was at a distance down south from Molapo. I just agreed with them because I was so beaten. They pointed at me with a gun and said "If you don't agree we will kill you."

'It was very painful over my whole body. Since then I feel pain in my veins because the handcuffs were so tight. This lasted a whole six days . . .' Kebatseisa said he wondered who gave the orders for 'the Wildlife guys to do this to us?' and answered his own question by blaming the Botswana government '. . . it tells the Wildlife people to beat us because we are resisting relocation. They are still trying to relocate us. They say we are finishing the game so we have to move.'

Like many of the other torture victims, Kebatseisa Thekiso said he was now afraid to hunt. 'They might shoot me to death if they find me hunting . . . whether I have killed a gemsbok or not, they will kill me because I am Khwe [Bushman], because nobody will take them to court, because they are being sent by the government. We are starving because I can't hunt . . .'

Molatlhwe Mokalake, referred to in the report as community leader, and whom I had interviewed in 1999, said of the officials: 'They searched and went into huts and beat people up. . . . They pushed me around . . . They forcibly photographed me with the skull of an eland [which] they got . . . from the bush.' Another elder, Gakeitsiwe Gaorapelwe, said he was knocked down for refusing to open a hut, tied up, and thrown in the back of a Land Rover. 'While I was lying down, they jumped on my back wearing their boots. My daughter was crying . . . she had a 10-month old baby, and the Wildlife people threw them both onto the ground . . . My wife was crying too . . . She was pushed and dragged by the feet. . . . One of the Wildlife people got into the vehicle, got a rifle and pointed it at me. My mother was crying so they pushed her and slapped her when she stood up and pushed her down again.'

Gakeitsiwe said he and the rest of the arrested men were taken to the bush camp, 'handcuffed to the Land Rovers with our feet tied to the bush bars until 10 p.m. For the first two days we slept tied up to the bush bars. On the third day we were released and slept in a tent. I felt very bad . . . the government was showing me the end of my life . . . what the government does show very well [is] that she is killing me. I was very ill that day. My arms were swollen and my whole body seriously ill. I was unable to eat. They gave meat to people but my throat was damaged so I could only drink water.'

One of his relatives, Kgwathiswa Gaorapelwe, was told by officials: 'Today you Bushmen are in for it. Today is your day because you've been an eland [hunter] for a long time . . . Today you will never have sex with your wife like you used to . . .' They were taken into the bush, and he was tied up to a tree, with a fire burning close by. 'The fire was by me and burning me. I don't know for how long I was left like that. . . .'

Several of the interviewees, including Sesoto Sesana, the senior wife of Roy Sesana, the chairman of First People, and Mathambo's sister-in-law, said they believed their treatment was partly racist. The officials forced their way into her hut, she told Fiona Watson, and searched it for game meat, but did not find anything. 'They beat me with handcuffs and the butt of a rifle. I was feeling pain. I don't know why they did this because I can't hunt . . . I thought they would kill me for nothing. After that they went to the [bush] camp and they came back for Mathambo. . . . They treat us like this because of our race . . .'

Mbonego Gaorapelwe had a similar view. 'They did this because they got orders from the government. We don't know why but maybe it's because we are resisting resettlement out of the Reserve. Maybe because we are Bushmen.' He said he had been arrested because he had 'a rope' made of kudu skin in his hut which the Wildlife officials claimed was eland. 'They tied me upside down and handcuffed me and started to beat me. It was very painful because I was kicked and eventually collapsed. Then they beat you until you woke up again. They were kicking and kept on asking me where the rope was. I told them they had taken it . . . I was assaulted for doing nothing. I didn't kill anything . . . Early in the morning they got us to take off our clothes and we were tied to the vehicles.'

Moipolai Moyawaphuti had much the same story: 'They handcuffed me and beat me. They said I had hunted eland. They beat and kicked me and . . . I had to say I'd killed an eland. As I was tied to the vehicle they reversed it and I felt something in my backbone. They reversed and stopped and this lasted five days . . . Hunting is important because we hunt to eat. We get no food from the government . . . I haven't hunted since because I don't want to . . .' Practically all the witnesses spoke of the overriding importance of hunting to them and their families. One man, Kebadirela, said: 'Hunting is my everyday life. I will suffer and starve if they stop it. I haven't hunted since the incident because I am afraid and I'm not fit enough because I have pains in my chest.'

Botshelo Gaorapelwe also said he had not hunted since the arrests 'because I'm afraid of being killed. There's no way I can feed and help my family. There are three of us and we live from hunting because we are not working. We are very poor people and for us to survive we have to hunt. This is my land. It's important to broadcast this because people will help me when they hear my problems.' The majority of those questioned were in favour of Survival publishing their statements. Sesoto Sesana said 'maybe the government will feel ashamed and let me lead the life I lead.' Thekiso Thaadintshao agreed: 'It's good for the outside world to know about this. It's better they hear about it even if they can't do anything.'

The Wildlife officials had with them 'a list of names, and knowledge of who owned certain huts, and their location'. The Molapo Bushmen did not know who had given them this information but suspected it came from former residents now living on Rakops cattle ranches who still visited relatives in the Reserve. After their last visit they had taken home presents of gemsbok. 'Either these people reported their relatives or someone else tipped off the authorities,' the report concluded.

Running through the Survival interviews is the complaint that even valid hunting licences were deliberately ignored by Wildlife officials. Molatlhwe Mokalake said 'though we recently got government hunting licences we were beaten up. We tried to show the Wildlife people our licences but they didn't take any notice ... the licences are like traps.' Kebadirela agreed: 'I thought because I had a licence they wouldn't beat me ... The licence is no use to us nowadays because they just beat you when you show it to them.'

Government officials, and even ministers, often allege that Bushmen must leave the Reserve because they are killing off the game. In fact, nothing could be farther from the truth, as no less an authority than the Department of Wildlife and National Parks itself has attested.

In its second draft management plan for the Central Kalahari Game Reserve – the first having been rejected by the government as being too generous towards the Bushmen – it states categorically: 'Wildlife numbers have been increasing steadily.' The plan, which has the declared purpose of greatly increasing the Reserve's tourist capacity – and earning power – looks however more and more like a Trojan Horse. Instead of enabling the Bushmen to continue to live in the Reserve and make a living from ecotourism, it looks increasingly as if it will at best relegate them to menial work for some safari company, paid a pittance, or, worst of all, banish them from their ancestral territories, and deprive them of their old freedom and independent way of life.

Faced by what appear to be overwhelming odds, what are the Bushmen and their supporters doing to fight for their rights? So far, very little, compared to what has been achieved by and for Australian Aborigines and North American Indians. After the long hiatus caused by the death of John Hardbattle, however, things are at last beginning to move.

The most important single initiative is the mapping of the

Central Kalahari Game Reserve, originally started in the mid-1990s by John Hardbattle and Paul Sheller, a former Bushman Survey Officer, with the goal of producing a detailed record of traditional Bushman hunting and gathering territories, passed down from generation to generation, and including food and water sources, underground rivers, and even trees and other physical features. Much of this impressive work has been done by Bushmen themselves, employed by First People, who successfully mastered the intricacies of mapping by GPS, using satellite technology to record exact locations. Secondly, more than 200 adults, representing a total population of between 400 and 500, have been registered as *residents* of the Reserve to 'prove' the mandate of the Negotiating Team, a representative body of Bushman activists and advisers which the Botswana government has consistently refused to recognise. The third prong of attack is the preparation of a land claim, in the sense of recognition by the government of the Bushmen's right to live in the Reserve, backed up by oral testimony from residents, past and present. Glyn Williams, a partner of Roger Chennells who orchestrated the successful Khomani land claim in South Africa, and who is adviser to First People of the Kalahari, says his strategy is 'ideally to resolve it [the land claim] through negotiations – that's always the best solution.'

It is too early to know, however, if the Botswana government will finally recognise the Negotiating Team's mandate and agree to negotiations. Meanwhile, the whole situation surrounding the Central Kalahari Game Reserve has become, in the view of some observers, 'highly precarious', with many contradictory signals emanating from both the government and local authorities. Even in this volatile and unpredictable state of affairs, one is bound to ask what the real reasons are for the change in the hunting laws, and the use of storm trooper tactics – savagely beating up anyone who hunts, irrespective of whether he has a valid licence or not? It is hard if not impossible to escape the conclusion that they are part of a deliberate policy to force the remaining Bushmen finally to abandon their ancestral lands, and enter the resettlement 'places of death'.

*

The latest news from Botswana would seem to confirm the worst suspicions. On 30 March, 2001, Ghanzi District Council passed a resolution to cut off all services – water, food and health – to the six Bushman villages of the Central Kalahari Game Reserve. As Survival International was quick to point out, this could 'destroy' the Bushman communities in the Reserve. Stephen Corry, its director general, in a strongly worded letter to President Mogae, said it was hard to interpret the Ghanzi Council vote as 'anything other than yet another attempt . . . to evict the last remaining people from the CKGR'. Referring to the alleged torture of Bushmen at Molapo and the death of the headman, Mathambo Sesana, he wrote: 'This brutality towards the Bushmen is both abhorrent and totally unwarranted.'

Mr Corry also said that 'Botswana's outrageous and illegal treatment of its Bushmen today makes a mockery of its claim that its diamonds are clean.' President Mogae had recently met members of the British government and had appeared on British television portraying Botswana as a democratic and free nation, in order to encourage people to buy Botswana's diamonds. 'However your government's treatment of the Bushmen falls far short of accepted ethical standards and international law [ILO Conventions 107 and 169] which recognises indigenous peoples' right to own their land collectively and to live according to their customs.'

In another letter to Robin Cook, the British Foreign Secretary, Corry wrote that he understood Mr Cook had met President Mogae during his recent visit to discuss among other things the question of diamonds. Survival International was deeply concerned about the situation of the Bushmen. 'Bushmen are regarded as inferior and suffer immense discrimination . . . It is also clear that the [Botswana] government wishes at some stage to exploit the diamonds which lie in the Central Kalahari and view the Bushmen as an "obstacle" to this . . . Clearly the government wants the Bushmen out before going ahead with the [Gope] mine.'

On the hunting issue, Mr Corry wrote: 'We believe that ultimately the Bushmen will be banned from hunting altogether. Hunting is extremely important both in terms of the vital proteins which it supplies and because it is a fundamental part of Bushman culture. Ironically by banning hunting and evicting people from the CKGR the government is destroying the Bushmen's self sufficiency and pride, and increasing their dependence on government handouts. To the Bushmen, and to us, this is the very reverse of "development".' Finally, Corry said both Britain and the European Union were supporting Bushman projects in Botswana. Both were 'important trading partners for Botswana; beef, diamonds and tourism are all major money earners there'. In view of this relationship he urged Mr Cook to raise the issue with the Botswana government since its treatment of the Bushmen was 'totally unacceptable and violates some of their most fundamental rights, particularly their right to collective ownership of their land'.

In my own view, failing a change of heart on the part of the Botswana government, only international opinion and pressure will avert the tragedy of the final eviction. I hope that Mooketsi, the Odyssean headman of Kikau, will be proved wrong when he said that 'like Jesus' he would be killed because he was telling the truth, and proved right when he said: 'We're struggling, but I think we will win in the end . . . because I'm fighting for my rights.' Let us hope that the story of Regopstaan and his son, Dawid Kruiper, of John Hardbattle, Mooketsi, and all the other Bushmen of southern Africa may yet, in the words of Laurens van der Post, 'help the redeeming moon in us all on the way to a renewal of life that will make now forever'. As Kabbo, one of the last of the now extinct Xam, told Wilhelm Bleek in 1873, as he prepared to go home after completing his sentence at the Breakwater Prison in Cape Town:

> He [Kabbo] only awaits the return of the moon;
> that the moon may go round, that he may
> examine the water pits, those at which he drank . . .
> For he did go away, leaving the
> place, while strangers were those who walked
> at the place. Their place it is not; for
> Kabbo's father's father's place it was.

Index

Figures in italics indicate captions.

INDEX

pass laws 95
Penn, Nigel 63, 69; *The Northern Cape Frontier Zone, 1700–c.1815* 54–5, 57, 59, 61, 64, 68, 70, 76, 81, 87, 90, 96, 102
Penny, Joshua 70
Pentecostal Church 157
Philip, Dr John 95
Phodiso 215
Phuduhudu, Thogoya 228
Piketberg 61
Pisamboro (a god) 6
plants, edible 7–8, 14, 27, 86, 227, 231, 243
Platje, Captain 84
Plettenberg (formerly Seekoei) River 76
Plumtree, Zimbabwe 178
porcupines 16, 40–41
Portuguese 149; exploration 49–50
pottery 26–7
Pretoria 123, 124
Pringle, Thomas 97–8, 165

quagga 94

Rabaoikanyo, Moepi 229
Rabaoikanyo, Mooketsi 229–32, 252
rain-making 9
Rakops, Botswana 244, 245, 246, 250
Ramotswa, near Gaborone 173
Raytheon Corporation 141
Regelen (a farmer) 120
Regopstaan 237–40, 252
Reitz, Colonel Deneys 237–8
Remote Areas Development (RAD) officers 229, 232
Restitution of Land Rights Act (1994) 239, 241
Rex v. Becker 125
Rex v. Brand and two others 131
Rex v. Majerero and twenty-three others 134
rhinoceros 22, 24
Rhodes, Cecil 105, 170
Riebeeck, Jan van 51, 52, 54
Ritchie, Claire 148–52, 158
Robben Island 93
Roberts, Anne 191
Robinson, Mary 203
rock art 9, 18–25, 27, 29, 30, 37, 67n
rock gongs 36–9, 41
Rockefeller, Nelson 191
Roggeveld 62–6, 68, 75, 80, 81, 83, 85, 88, 98, 100, 101
Rousseau, Jean-Jacques 17, 165
Ruijter, Captain 83
Ruppel, Mr (of the Mandates Commission) 132
Ruruaiku, Chief 153
Ryneveld, F.J. van 128–9, 130

Saal, Corporal 129
Sahara 15

St Lucia Bay 105–6
Sak River 66, 67, 76, 80, 82, 85, 88, 89, 91, 93, 94
Sakanabe, Mr (of the Mandates Commission) 132
Samutchoso (van der Post's guide) 19, 20–21, 30
San 71; *see also* Bushmen
Sandenbergh, Peter 208n
Sandface 16, 172, 175
Sandveld 58, 59, 117, 125, 133
SAS 27–8
scherms (Bushman huts) 10, 20, 145
Schietfontein 98
Schoeman, Professor P.J. 136–7, 142
Schoeman commission (Commission for the Preservation of the Bushmen) 136–8, 147
Schultz, Sergeant 126
Seagars, Morton 129
Setswana, Botswana 13
Seekoei (later Plettenberg) River 72
Sefo (policeman) 249
Seganaphofu, Thabo 227
Seiner, Franz 115
Seitz, Theodor 113, 115
Sekalabue, Tuelo 207–8, 209
Serogola (a Bamangwato) 187
Serowe 188
Sesana, Mathambo 5, 11, 217–20, 226, 245, 246, 248, 252
Sesana, Monyaku 214–15
Sesana, Roy 11, 183, 191, 194, 196–9, 207, 212, 214, 218, 225, 231, 244, 245, 248
Sesana, Sesoto 248
Sesi (a Bushman) 10
Setswana language 184, 185, 188, 228n
Shakawe, Botswana 26
shamans 9, 22, 218
Shark Island 109
Sheller, Paul 251
Silberbauer, George 8n, 9–10, 17, 163, 166–8, 176n, 197
Sixpence (husband of John Hardbattle's half-sister) 216
Skoonheid farm, near Gobabis 154, 155, 156
Slow (Wildlife official) 249
Smuts, Jan 122–5, 132, 133
snakes 15, 29, 217
Sneeuberg 65, 67, 68, 72, 73, 78, 79, 96, 97
Soaqua (Sonqua) 53–4
Sonneblom farm, near Tallismanus 156, 157
South Africa 15; extermination of Bushmen in 35–6, 38; invasion of South-West Africa 122–4; justice 125–7, 130–31; 'poor whites' 127–8; South-West Africa part of its apartheid system 132–3; withdraws from South-West Africa 133, 153; withdraws from Angola 153; and the Central Kalahari Game Reserve 196; creation of the Kalahari Gemsbok National